"The transformation of Christianity into a predominantly non-Western faith is one of the great facts of our time. In this compelling assessment, historian Scott Sunquist analyzes the complex roots and historical significance of this epochal development. The treatment is fully attentive to the interaction between worldwide trends and local peculiarities, and the global perspective brings pressing missiological issues of the day into sharp focus. Written in accessible language but with penetrating insight, *The Unexpected Christian Century* sheds considerable light on Christianity's prospects in this century by reviewing the last. A valuable addition to a vital discourse."

—**Jehu J. Hanciles**, Candler School of Theology, Emory University

"This volume could be Sunquist's best offering yet. He remarkably bridges the self-aggrandizing, imperialistic Christian world of a century ago, which he represents as an English-literate, hypereducated, resource-wielding, Caucasian, middle-aged male, and today's unencumbered, multilingual, migrating, dispossessed, suffering, and multitudinous throng of Jesus's Spirit-led followers, in which he enthusiastically participates. Sunquist's insightful interpretations of world Christianity's transformations over the last one hundred years provide empowering gateways through which those who hear this book's message can stride forward with renewed vision, hope, and courage."

—**J. Nelson Jennings**, Overseas Ministries Study Center

THE UNEXPECTED CHRISTIAN CENTURY

The Reversal and Transformation
of Global Christianity, 1900–2000

SCOTT W. SUNQUIST

Foreword by Mark A. Noll

Baker Academic
a division of Baker Publishing Group
www.BakerAcademic.com

Published by Baker Academic
a division of Baker Publishing Group
P.O. Box 6287, Grand Rapids, MI 49516-6287
www.bakeracademic.com

Printed in the United States of America

Library of Congress Cataloging-in-Publication Data
Sunquist, Scott, 1953–
    The unexpected Christian century : the reversal and transformation of global Christianity, 1900–2000 / Scott W. Sunquist ; foreword by Mark A. Noll.
        pages cm
    Includes bibliographical references and index.
    ISBN 978-0-8010-9746-1 (pbk.)
    1. Church history—20th century. I. Title.
BR479.S86 2015
270.8′2—dc23   2015014039

15   16   17   18   19   20   21   7   6   5   4   3   2   1

Dedicated to the memory of Dr. Samuel Hugh Moffett (1917–2015), pastor, missionary, professor, scholar, mentor, and friend. Sam lived through most of the twentieth century and with his wife, Eileen, made it a better century through their lives of grace and love of the church of Jesus Christ.

Contents

Figures

Foreword

MARK A. NOLL

The great merit of Scott Sunquist's book is to narrate the recent history of Christianity as a genuinely and thoroughly *world history*. It is no longer fresh news that over the course of the last century the Christian faith has expanded into world regions where it was previously unknown, and that it has also receded significantly from areas that it once dominated. A distinguished array of learned experts—Andrew Walls, Dana Robert, Philip Jenkins, Lamin Sanneh, David Martin, among others—has provided landmark academic and popular publications announcing these facts. Such scholars have been joined by editors, denominational officials, mission executives, interested laypeople, and sometimes governmental leaders in analyzing, interpreting, projecting, strategizing, and reconceptualizing in the face of these new realities. Nevertheless, accessible histories that feature the broad general developments of the recent past, and yet that remain connected to particular stories of particular places, remain rare. *The Unexpected Christian Century* is a notable addition to such efforts.

Scott Sunquist features five themes that serve him well for charting a complex history. These themes are his way of keeping faith with both forest and trees—both the large-scale patterns in recent history and the individual people, movements, denominations, conflicts, circumstances, tragedies, and triumphs that make up the nitty-gritty of historical development. Others might come

Mark Noll is the author of *From Every Tribe and Nation: A Historian's Discovery of the World Christian Story* (Baker Academic, 2014).

up with different interpretive categories, but it is hard to imagine a better set for summarizing a history that sprawls in every possible direction.

One theme describes twenty-five notable Christians as illustrating the most important world Christian developments. They include figures like Mother Teresa, Billy Graham, Dietrich Bonhoeffer, Martin Luther King Jr., and Popes John XXIII and John Paul II, who are widely recognized in North America and Europe. But to follow Sunquist as he explains why Simon Kimbangu, Mercy Amba Oduyoye, John Sung, and Georges Florovsky belong on such a list begins to reveal the broader dimensions of a *world* history.

It is similar with the interinfluencing of modern Christianity and modern warfare. The blow to the traditional European churches from World War I and World War II is well known, but not the very significant fallout of these conflicts for Christian faith throughout the whole world. How these large wars, as well as a never-ending series of smaller conflicts, have both promoted and retarded Christian expansion shows how thoroughly the "sacred" and the "secular" have marched together in the recent past.

The apparently most conventional chapter of the book sketches the story of Christianity's major denominational families: Orthodoxy, Roman Catholicism, Protestantism, and the newer spiritual and Pentecostal movements. Yet as Sunquist traces the unfolding trajectory of these families throughout the globe, they come alive with telling interpretive impact. How Orthodoxy survived under Communist rule, how the Catholic church balances decline in Europe with dramatic expansion in the global South, how formal and informal instances of Protestant ecumenicity affected vast numbers, and how the universe of nonaligned Christian movements has burgeoned spectacularly—these individual stories, when woven together, demonstrate the relevance of traditional denominational history to the new global Christianity. As only one of many examples, Sunquist shows that, in their particular local engagements, similar traits can nonetheless be observed in many of the world's Pentecostal and independent spiritual movements. Just this kind of approach is needed to realize how much, despite also real differences, has been shared by John Sung in China, Aimee Semple McPherson in Los Angeles, Pandita Ramabai in India, the Methodist Pentecostal Church in Chile, and the Church of God in Christ led by Charles Mason.

Sunquist's fourth theme is migration. Bible readers should not be surprised at the revelations of this chapter. For believers, the scriptural accounts of the exodus, the Hebrew experiences of exile, the itinerant teaching of Jesus, and the journeys of the apostle Paul have always defined the character of living Christian faith. The settled history of Western Christianity, however, had made it easy to forget the unsettled character of this biblical record. A welcome corrective comes in seeing how important migration has become in the contemporary Christian world: non-Christians pouring into Europe from Africa and the Middle East, Christians from Asia, Africa, Latin America, and the South Seas pouring into the United States, urbanization and economic opportunity drawing millions of believers into the world's great cities, warfare destroying Christian communities in some regions and planting the seeds for new churches in others, political change and disease sending still others to new places. More clearly than ever, it has become obvious that "the church on the move" is simply *the* church.

The book's last major theme considers Christian interactions with other religions. For an era like ours, violent clashes inspired by religion are a fixture of the daily news cycle. In Europe, India, Burma, Nigeria, Egypt, and other regions, the intermingling of religious communities has sparked well-reported acts of violence. As the pages below indicate, however, more peaceful encounters have been just as important for the global Christian picture. With nearly infinite variety, the world has witnessed a growing number of venues with Christian-Hindu, Christian-Buddhist, Christian-Muslim, and Christian-nativist interaction. How such interactions will develop in the future is not foreordained by how they have come to exist in recent decades. But observers and those who must make decisions will explore future possibilities with much greater wisdom if they pay attention to how that development took place.

The book ends with a series of conclusions explaining the significance of a genuine world history of Christianity. Those conclusions are, of course, historical. But for those with eyes to see, they also open the door to compelling theological and spiritual insights as well.

Professor Sunquist would be the first to acknowledge that his book cannot be the last word on realities of a Christian movement that now is at home in almost every corner of the globe. Readers who pay attention to what he has written will, nonetheless, find the book a godsend for opening up a vitally important history and pointing the way toward responsible Christian life in the future.

Preface

One of the most influential classes in my seminary education was on the book of Acts taught by a great New Testament textual scholar (and full-blooded Pentecostal). Acts has many textual questions, and it also has classic expressions of Pentecostal Christian life. It was a great experience as well as a great course. What was most memorable, however, was the first week. The professor asked us to read through the whole of the book of Acts in one sitting and come to class prepared to talk about it. At the beginning of the next class he simply asked, "Well, what did you notice?" Everyone sat in silence hoping that someone else would state the obvious, because the obvious would implicate all of us. No one wanted to be the person to make the corporate accusation that we were all guilty; actually, we are all guilty today.

"Dr. Fee, the obvious thing we all noticed is that Christianity—or being a Christian—as told in the book of Acts, is nothing like Christianity today. What was going on in the lives of the apostles and those early Christians is like . . . well, it's like a whole different religion." I do not know who said this, but I wish I had been honest enough to state the obvious. Christianity as it has been practiced in the West for the past, well, at least for the past millennium, bears only slight resemblance to the life of the early Christians. The good professor drove home this point merely by asking us to read through the Acts of the Apostles.

The Unexpected Christian Century

The twentieth century redrew the lines on the religious globe. However, most of the rewriting was done through a great and surprising transformation of

xvi   Preface

Christianity; in fact, it was a great reversal. When Christianity entered the
twentieth century, it was a confident, strong, imperial religion of the West.
Many of the leaders accepted the scholarly dictum that the twentieth century
would be the "Christian century." No scholar—or as far as that goes, not even
a madman—predicted that at the end of the twentieth century Christianity
would not be recognized even as a cultural factor in Europe by the nations
that today compose the European Union. No prognosticator predicted that
more Christians would be worshiping each Sunday in China than in Europe or
North America. And, what might be surprising to us today, even the greatest
mission leaders at the Edinburgh Missionary Conference in 1910 had pretty
much given up on Christianity in Africa. Most of the missionary leaders,
even in their most optimistic moments, thought Islam had the upper hand
and believed Africa would become a Muslim continent. Fast-forward and we
find that the opposite is true, for there are more Christians than Muslims in
Africa today.

Yes, the twentieth century surprised the religionists, the historians, and the
politicians. It was one of the three great transformations in Christianity in
its two thousand years. The first took place early in the fourth century, when
Christianity began to get imperial recognition in three small nations and one
empire: Osrhoene, Armenia, Ethiopia, and the Roman Empire. Royal conversions not only ensured that the religion would not be wiped out by belligerent rulers spreading other religions but also that Christianity would begin to
develop differently with the support of kings and queens. Christian buildings
began to look very nice. Christian life was no longer threatened. It was possible to fit into the larger culture very comfortably with little need for sacrifice
or compromise. Christianity in these kingdoms and empires had moved from
being a persecuted minority to being a favored faith. This changed everything.

The second great transformation occurred in the fifteenth and sixteenth
centuries. This was the period of the European Reformation, but that was not
the supremely important transformation that I am thinking of. From about
the 1450s to the 1550s Christianity broke out of its small enclaves of Western
Europe, South India, and Ethiopia and became a truly worldwide religion.
It didn't have to happen that way, but it did. Muslim rulers, or certainly the
Chinese, could have dominated the world. Instead, and very much for theological reasons, it was the Christians from Iberia who spread the Christian
faith to places as far away as the Moluccas, the Kongo (Congo), Peru, and even
Japan and China. As late as 1492 it was still not clear whether Christianity
would devolve into a tribal faith of Western Europe.

The third great transformation took place in the twentieth century, a great
reversal that I have written about before. It was certainly a reversal in that

the majority of Christians—or the global center—moved from the North Atlantic to the Southern Hemisphere and Asia. But it was also a reversal in that Christianity moved from being centered in Christian nations to being centered in non-Christian nations. Christendom, that remarkable condition of churches supporting states and states supporting Christianity, died. The idea of Christian privilege in society was all but killed. And yet the religion seemed stronger than ever at the end of the twentieth century. No one saw this coming.

An important dimension to that transformation was what might be called the globalization of the faith. Christianity was already spread to almost every region throughout the globe before 1900. However, Christianity was developing very distinctively by region and continent and ethnic group. For example, Latin America was Catholic. Vietnam was also Catholic. The East Coast of the United States was almost completely English-speaking and either Euro-American or African American. All of this changed in the twentieth century. Christianity participated in (we might even say was one of the pioneer movements in) globalization. By the end of the twentieth century we find African Independent Churches in Ukraine, New York, and London, not just in southern or western Africa. Independency and Spiritual churches (where the authority is found in the Holy Spirit) now span the globe, whereas they were almost nonexistent in 1900. Here are a few global statistics that reveal the dramatic change that took place in Christianity and what this book will describe.

1. In 1910 Europe was 90 percent Christian; in 2010 Europe was less than 84 percent Christian.
2. In 1910 Asia was 2.4 percent Christian; in 2010 Asia was about 9 percent Christian.
3. In 1910 Africa was 9.4 percent Christian; in 2010 Africa was 48 percent Christian.[1]

A thick description of this great change would reveal much more than these statistics tell. For example, less than 5 percent of the Christians in France are active, meaning they attend Mass regularly. Close to 9 percent of France is Muslim, which means that there are more active Muslims in France than active Christians. Another way of looking at the great transformation in global Christianity is to reflect on this fact: a larger percentage of people attend church in China, Malaysia, Singapore, Indonesia, and South Korea than in

1. Johnson and Ross, eds., *Atlas of Global Christianity*.

Peter Becker

Figure 1. One visible sign of the decline of Christianity in the West is the number of churches and monasteries that have been sold and used as restaurants, night clubs, dance halls, or even Hindu temples. Here St. Peter's Episcopal Church, built between 1873 and 1883 and vacant from 2005 to 2014, is under construction to become the new home of the Waldorf School of Philadelphia, in the Germantown neighborhood of Philadelphia, Pennsylvania.

almost any country in Europe today. It is amazing to think of South Korea, the land of Buddhism and Shamanism, as being more Christian than England or Poland or France, but it is true.

The causes of this globalization include the spread of Pentecostalism, but other causes include forced migrations of people, ongoing missionary work, and the advances in communication and transportation. As a result, it is not really possible to talk about Christianity by region or continent because so many of the themes are global. In the past it was necessary to talk about Christian development by country and region since Christian development was very national. We would study Lutherans in Germany and Denmark, and Catholics in France and Italy. Today the important themes that help to explain the nature and identity of Christianity are not geographically determined. We understand more clearly what Christianity is today by looking at major movements and themes of the twentieth century. Thus this volume will help to explain the religion that is Christianity by looking at major themes rather than going from country to country or continent to continent.

The Unexpected Century from Five Vantage Points

Our study of the great transformation—at times we will call it a reversal—that took place in twentieth-century Christianity will unfold almost as five separate stories. Others have told and will tell the story of modern Christianity as a single story or as geographic stories.[2] I have written this type of history for a few decades. However, sometimes we learn more if we focus on only certain parts of the drama rather than on the whole story. I have this bad habit when I go to a play (seldom) or opera (even more seldom) of watching just one performer. I imagine what he or she must be thinking and how it must be to be in the performance as that person. What we do in this volume is like looking at an opera from the vantage point of five participant observers. We could describe an opera from a seat midway in the opera house. That would be one perspective. But let's imagine for a moment that we are a flutist in the orchestra pit. That would be a whole different experience, having to look up at only part of the acting and sitting with low lights on our sheet music. Again, we could describe the opera from the view of the stage crew. They would view the opera very differently, seeing what goes into the entrances and exits of the singers. Again, what would it be like to observe the opera as the prima donna, from a place where the spotlight is on us as we stand on the stage and sing our leading solos? Finally, we can describe the opera from the position of the conductor, who has an enviable place of observation, but has to look in so many directions to monitor singers, actors, choirs, and orchestra players. Each perspective would be unique, but by looking from all these perspectives together we would have a much better understanding of the complex art form called opera.

In this volume we will look at Christianity in the twentieth century from five different perspectives—or through five different lenses. First, however, we need to know something of how Christianity became the religion it was in 1900. How did Christianity, a West Asian religion whose genesis is told in the book of Acts, become a Western religion with foreign outposts? What did global Christianity look like in 1900? We answer the first sweeping question in the introduction. The second question is the story of chapter 1. After the first chapter—describing what worldwide Christianity looked like on the edge of the great reversal—we pick up the first lens. The first lens (chap. 2) is actually twenty-five lenses, like the compound eye of a honeybee. We look in this chapter at what might be considered the twenty-five most influential

---

2. See Irvin and Sunquist, *History of the World Christian Movement* (hereafter *HWCM*), in two, soon to be three, volumes.

Christians of the twentieth century. In other words, who were the people around the globe who were having the greatest impact on shaping Christianity, the faith we have inherited? These twenty-five represent most continents, both genders, and all four confessional families. This is the personal, or biographical, lens. The second lens (chap. 3) is the political lens; we look at the impact that political changes had on the Christian movement. Movements of secularization (including Communism), colonization, and decolonization are major themes in this chapter. But closely related to these political movements is persecution. We have heard it said many times that the twentieth century was the century of greatest persecution and martyrdom for Christianity. I am not sure how we would measure or test such a claim, but it is no exaggeration that the twentieth century was a century of much martyrdom and persecution.

The third lens (chap. 4) is church families, or confessional families. We look at how the four major church families (Roman Catholic, Orthodox, Protestant, and Spiritual) fared during the century. Their stories were very different, as we will see. This lens helps us to see that theology, identity in society, and religious practices do make a difference. The fourth lens (chap. 5) may not have been predicted, but it has always been important in understanding Christianity from the day of Pentecost in Acts 2 until today. This lens is migration. We look at how migration has shaped Christianity as people are enticed and pulled to other lands and (mostly) how they are pushed out of their land or country. The fifth and final lens (chap. 6) we look through is the lens of the world's religions. Christianity has been shaped by its encounter, relationship, and at times conflict with other religions. The twentieth century was noteworthy in that Western and Asian theologians developed a robust series of theologies of religions, trying to make sense of the ongoing vitality of other religions. The reigning assumption had been that the other religions would eventually capitulate to Christian missionary activity. The twentieth century proved otherwise. Many religions were revived by their encounters with Christians and Christian beliefs.

We conclude this volume with a word of hope and a word for history. As a historian I am quite aware that history is always with us. Certain traditions and habits, both good and bad, are woven into our present practices and beliefs. Unaware of this history, we often react against something we do not like (pews, liturgy, hymns, Sunday school, etc.), and lose both the meaning and the form. Thus in the concluding chapter you will hear a plea for a healthy, if not robust, appreciation of Christian history with all of its variegated blessings and curses. But as dark as this history may look, and as persistent as the persecution may continue to be today, the Christian faith is still one of hope and promise. Eschatology, where the future lies, is pulling us forward, and it is important to be able, with the wisdom of the future hope, to trace the lines of grace today. Christians should be able to see grace and hope where it may seem to be almost extinguished by deceit, violence, and seduction. Still the light shines. The church is still the signpost and hope for a cynical and lonely world.

Acknowledgments

The idea for this book came out of a decision made by contributors to the book *History of the World Christian Movement* (*HWCM*) to write a different kind of history for the twentieth century. The idea was simple: in looking at the twentieth century we can no longer talk about the development of Christianity in South Asia as separate from the development of Christianity in North America or in West Africa. With globalization coming to flower in the twentieth century, Christian movements like Pentecostalism occurred almost simultaneously in China, South Korea, northeast India, Chile, California, and Scandinavia. It is more honest to talk about global themes than about geographic regions. Yet, to keep the form of the *HWCM*, this radical departure from the first nineteen centuries was dropped. And so I had twentieth-century chapters written, but they were left to languish on my hard drive for two years.

Chapters written but unused are the sad tale of many an author. At the suggestion of church history colleagues at Fuller Theological Seminary, James Bradley and John Thompson ("It sounds like you have a book already."), I began to look over the material I had written. In fact, with some rewriting (much more than I had thought), I did have a book. The book took on a thesis with the suggestion of the title by my editor, James Ernest. Thus I am indebted to James, John, and James that these chapters were resurrected, reshaped, and given purpose.

I sent out a note to some friends around the world asking for pictures that illustrate something of the vitality as well as the decline of Christianity. Thanks go to Fred Foy Strang for his excellent photos from East Africa. Thank you also to Kristin Horner of Pittsburgh for the photos from Brazil; to Lipsong Chen of Kota Kinabalu for the photos from China; to Christopher Humphrey, also of Pittsburgh, for the photo of an Orthodox baptism; and to Cetta Kenney for the photos of Paul Knitter, Samdech Preah Maha Ghosanand, and Irfan Ahmad Khan. The cover concept was first developed by our daughter, Bethany Lomelino, for which I am grateful.

My greatest note of appreciation, however, goes to another daughter, Caroline Noel Becker, who has been my student and my coeditor, and is now my first line editor and encourager by use of a Google "task sheet" ("Dad, are you going to look up those footnotes? What pictures do you want in that chapter?"). She has done a tremendous job sharpening my outline, keeping me going, and making suggestions that have greatly improved the quality of the work. I am thankful to God for a daughter who turned out so much like her mother, with the interests of her father.

Once again, books are written when there is time and some solitude, and both time and solitude are precious commodities for a dean who is also a teacher, husband, father, and grandfather. I wish to thank my assistant, Wendy Walker, for strong-arming my calendar with grace and persistence. Most of all, I wish to thank my wife, Nancy, for her encouragement, patience, and support. She has been an incredibly insightful, understanding, and helpful mate, giving me the time to write, but reminding me of who I am when I get carried away. Together we "write" these books and together we negotiate schedules and travel across the States to love our children and grandchildren. This book would not have been completed without this partnership.

Fuller Theological Seminary has been my place of scholarship since 2012, and it has been a delightful place for the exchange of ideas, learning from Christian leaders from around the world, with a good library to support scholarship. As the School of Intercultural Studies celebrates fifty years of leadership in missiological thinking, it is appropriate that this book would come at a time of our anniversary, as a way to look back and to assess. The School of World Mission (now School of Intercultural Studies) has always been looking forward. It is my hope that this volume will help to provide the context for our ongoing scholarship and innovation, which Fuller has been known for, in service of God's global mission.

Introduction

From Jesus to the End of Christendom

In this introduction we will, with broad brushstrokes, tell the story of how following Jesus changed from stories like Acts 2—or for that matter, Acts 3 and Acts 4 and every other chapter of Acts—to the imperial forms of Christianity that dominated the world in 1900, the year our volume begins. So let's look at this story spanning nineteen centuries, noting the major shifts and turns that took place until we end up with Christianity of the imperial age, or the Gilded Age, when almost all Christians lived in the West. In fact, in 1900 82 percent of Christians lived in the North. The center of Christianity was also still in Europe. This *introduction* is about how Christianity, an Asian religion, became a European and Euro-American religion. This *book* is about how the twentieth century, actually just the latter half of the twentieth century, changed all of that.

The Earliest Jesus Followers: The First Two Centuries

Jesus was a real person who lived in West Asia at the corner of three continents and at the edge of two mighty empires. He was not a generic or theoretical human being, but a specific, culturally embedded peasant and a wandering Jewish teacher who lived, taught, acted, was killed, and was buried. He ate grilled fish and wore sandals. He was remarkable to a small crowd of mostly Jewish followers, but he would not be the subject of this book if he had merely been a wonder-worker and then stayed in the ground. His closest followers, many of them women, claimed to have seen him after his death, when he

1

changed all their lives by giving them an impossible assignment, which they accepted. Simply put, they all understood that the formerly dead Jesus told them to tell people from every culture in the world to follow him; "to make disciples" was his expression. And so they did.

The early Jesus followers, as far as we can tell, talked about Jesus wherever they traveled and performed miracles in his name. The beginning of Christianity was a movement, the Jesus Movement. By the end of the first century there were Jesus followers, loosely connected by the teachings of Jesus, from Spain to Persia, and possibly all the way to India. Spread without political will or military might, this movement was the most remarkable eruption of a religion ever on the globe. Immediately the teachings were being gathered and translated into Greek, Syriac, and Armenian. Other languages soon followed. A few centuries later and Christian communities could be found, headed up by regional leaders (bishops), from Afghanistan to South India to present-day Yemen and Ethiopia and Sudan, all across North Africa, and in Europe and the British Isles. It was a diverse movement becoming a major transcontinental institution, still with no political support. There was much persecution. Some of the earliest writings, besides the biographies of Jesus, were written to encourage Christians to be strong and faithful to Jesus even when being persecuted. Generations after the death of Jesus, these followers had remarkable resolve. Other early writings were defenses of the new religion as it was being attacked by philosophers, by other religious leaders, and even by the military. It was a precarious existence until a few rulers accepted the faith as their own.

In rapid succession the king of the small kingdom of Armenia, Tiradates III; the Roman emperor, Constantine; and the emperor of Ethiopia, Ezana, all turned to Jesus.[1] The results transformed the new religion. In regions where there was no political support and little tolerance, such as Persia after 225, the followers of Jesus remained few. In the ancient world, and, up through most of the world even in modern times, a "people," or a nation, had a religion, a single religion. Celts worshiped Lug and Athenians worshiped Athena. Hebrews worshiped YHWH. A people were identified with their God. Thus the early spread of Christianity depended to a great extent upon the conversion of rulers. When Constantine converted to become a follower of Jesus, he quickly made Christianity the religion of the Roman Empire, an empire that included many nations. That was really the only option: a single religion for a people.

---

1. There was another small client kingdom, Osrhoene, with its capital, Edessa, that turned to Christianity much earlier, but this was not an independent kingdom, and it was soon taken over by the Roman Empire (216).

The ruler determined the religion. Our modern concept of toleration did not develop until the eighteenth century.

Christianity Becomes the Great Church

From the beginning, Christianity had a missionary impulse. Believers understood that being a follower of Jesus meant taking the faith to others. These believers also understood that the faith could be translated into different languages and different cultures. In each location where the teachings were taken, Scriptures were translated and liturgies became part of local customs. One of the important themes of Christianity from the fourth through the tenth centuries was the struggle for cultural appropriateness and ecumenical (all-the-world) unity. Is it still the same religion if worship is done in different ways? Most religions require prescribed methods of worship or of ritual. Can we really say that this new group is following the same religion if they celebrate Easter on a different day? In some regions a particular language became the trade language and then it slowly became enshrined as the Christian language. In Persia the trade language of Syriac became the Christian language, and in Western Europe Latin became the worship language. In Eastern Europe Greek was the language of worship. Having a single language for worship in a region helped with unity, but this unity slowly developed into a type of religious hegemony of one culture or one language over others. In South India, Christians were worshiping in Syriac, a language that was all but dead, but the Christians spoke Telugu or Tamil in their daily comings and goings.

Something essential to the DNA of the gospel—the importance of the nations—was lost in this type of unity. Empires are concerned about unity, and so emperors called for and supported councils that would bring things into a common order. Councils were called to help bishops enforce common beliefs and practices in the diverse lands. Diversity in Christianity from the very beginning was a matter of how Christian belief was to be expressed in local cultures. Local beliefs and practices, as well as great philosophies of the age, were part of the cultural context that Christian teachings spoke to and spoke into. Thus most of the early councils reveal the struggle of Christian leaders to express the meaning of Christ in ancient philosophic concepts. Some of these expressions that were agreed upon in the fourth or fifth century made perfect sense to ancient Christians steeped in Greek philosophy; they make less sense to us today. For example, we seldom talk about the substance or essence of Jesus today in our devotions or our evangelism, but it was very important as Christianity was beginning to speak into Greek philosophy. The church must be one, but it must also be as diverse as the nations of the world. Local contextual expressions must not overshadow the concern for unity. Unity was a very important concern for bishops and emperors. Actually, it was also very important for Jesus (John 17).

The impulse for unity often became a need for uniformity. One way Christians resisted this social and political control, as well as the newfound wealth in the church, was in the formation of monastic orders. Monasticism developed first in North Africa and Syria, and soon spread to Italy and France and among the Celts in the British Isles. Ascetics sought to preserve the life and teachings of Jesus by leaving family, home, and village. Fleeing to the desert, they sought closer communion and identity with Jesus, in the pattern of John the Baptist. Many monks, such as Saint Anthony in Egypt, became models for Christians living in the cities. Their lives of self-denial and poverty pointed away from the wealth and pomp of imperial Christianity and toward the suffering Messiah. Thus in the early Middle Ages the church struggled to maintain unity (often imposed by rulers) and purity (often in the model of desert monks).

Monastic Christianity and the Conversion of Tribal Europe

Monastic Christianity developed as a structure parallel to local parish Christianity. In this separate structure monks preserved the missionary character of Christianity as they set up houses throughout Europe and scattered in regions of western Asia and North Africa. When a few monks (often twelve, in the pattern of Jesus and his disciples) set up a monastery, they would soon start copying the Scriptures and constructing a church building. Much of the conversion of the tribes of Europe occurred in this fashion. Benedict of Nursia (480–543?) is considered the father of monastic (also called *coenobitic*, or common life) communities, whereby monks took vows of obedience and lived together in daily patterns of prayer and work: *ora et labora*. Other patterns, or rules, were established in the West, with greater or lesser times given for work and worship. With the many invasions of tribes from central Asia (Ostrogoth, Visigoth, Hun, Vandal, etc.) from the second through the eighth centuries, it was monastic communities that preserved the "memory" of Europe and of Christian teachings. Most of the literate people in Europe lived in monasteries or in palaces. Culture was preserved, teachings spread, and slowly the illiterate tribes were converted and learned the basic practices of Christians. It was a long and slow process that took about one thousand years. Rulers like Clovis and Charlemagne of the Franks and Ethelbert of the English came to faith and enforced the faith. Many were compelled to "come in" to the church, and so the peaceful and gentle Messiah became identified with military conquest and enforced belief. In was a long and slow European devolution from Jesus as the Good Shepherd to Jesus the conquering King.

Outside of Europe monastic forms of Christianity were also the main missionary form of the faith. In Syria monks lived in caves or alone in the wilderness among the wild beasts. They became voices in the wilderness, calling the people to be faithful and not trust in worldly goods or positions of power. In Asia Minor monastic communities (practicing coenobitic forms of asceticism) were more common. It was in this region where monks began to locate their communities closer to the urban centers to serve the people in the cities. The earliest hospitals, such as they were, were developed by monks. Food distribution for the poor and care for the sick in times of famine and plague were monastic endeavors by the early fifth century. Monastic forms of Christianity responded in diverse ways to popular and political culture, but everywhere they both preserved the Christian tradition and served as a signpost of Christian responsibility.

In Persia monks were identified as "Sons of the Covenant" or "Daughters of the Covenant," and they often built their places of refuge farther and farther out, slowly evangelizing frontier regions in Persia and to the east. By the seventh century (635) some of these Persians had wandered all the way to China, to the capital of the Tang Dynasty in Xian. In China they began to translate and paraphrase many Christian teachings, and they started other monastic houses throughout the country. Some Chinese nationals were coming to faith in Jesus in the seventh century, whereas in Scandinavia and Ukraine it would be three centuries later before missionaries were able to establish an ongoing presence.

Monastic forms of Christianity preserved and spread the teachings of Christ, but the results were not the same in all regions. Western Europe was slowly evangelized, and more and more lands became church lands. Monasteries (and cathedral schools), as places of learning, became the earliest forms of universities. Monks, and later friars, moved away from a prophetic stance—resisting the domination of the church by political leaders—to become institutional leaders. Outside of Europe, monastic forms of Christianity had different histories. In Persia, where Christianity was persecuted by Zoroastrian leaders from the middle of the third to the middle of the seventh century, monasteries were places of Christian refuge; persecution limited the ability of monasteries to develop either as missionary bases or as great centers of learning. Christianity atrophied under the Persian, and later Arab, rulers. Asia was unique in that Christians encountered multicultural and ancient religions (Hinduism and Buddhism), as well as a newer multicultural religion, Islam.

Resistance to Jesus: Hinduism, Buddhism, and Islam

Asian and North African Christianity had a troubled history when compared to Christianity in Europe. The conversion of emperors and kings in Europe made it possible for Christian liturgy, theology, and practice to develop in a protected environment. Except for Armenia and Osrhoene in far west Asia, Asians never had this benefit. Christianity was tolerated under the pluralistic Parthians, but from 225 on, under a fundamentalist reform of Zoroastrianism in Persia, Christianity has constantly been under pressure or persecution for about eighteen centuries. It is a wonder Christianity survived at all.

Only in Asia did Christianity encounter large transcultural (often called "world") religions. In Persia it was Zoroastrianism; in India it was Hinduism and its reform movement, Buddhism. By the middle of the seventh century it was Islam. All of these religions had an inner strength and coherence because of their transcultural nature: they were not tribal faiths. Christianity's success in its encounter with transcultural faiths is always more limited than in its encounters with tribal faiths. In India, Christianity survived, but it began to be shaped by the caste structure of this culture: Christians formed their own social group, mostly involved in trade. In Persia Christians were not allowed to propagate their faith, and soon they were not allowed to repair their existing buildings or to build new ones. Christianity that is cut off from its missionary expression atrophies, and so it happened in Persia.

With the arrival of Arab Muslim invaders in the middle of the seventh century, Christians saw some relief. Whereas Zoroastrians believed in two gods and seemed to worship fire, the Muslims, like Christians, believed in one God and called him Allah (Persian Christians used the Syriac term *Al-o-ha*). For a time Christian life seemed to improve; Christians were among the most literate and well educated, so they helped with accounting and running prisons for the Arabs. But slowly, restrictions were imposed on the Christians, and they found that once again they were living as a *melet* (ghetto) community. All evangelistic outreach was outlawed, and soon Christianity, as it were, was turned in on itself in Persia as well as the Middle East and North Africa.

The rise of Islam hemmed Christianity in to Western Europe. Christians who lived in West Asia and North Africa were cut off from the larger ecumenical community, were restricted in public witness, and had to pay excessive taxes. Conversion to Islam was encouraged by many means. Not all were violent, but restrictions were enforced by the sword. Christian piety required, or at least strongly encouraged, pilgrimage to Jerusalem, to walk where Jesus walked, but Muslim rule restricted such travel. Many pilgrims were killed, and so Christians developed a narrative of militant support of innocent pilgrims.

Military monastic orders were founded (Knights of the Templar) to protect pilgrims, and then crusades were planned to reclaim "Christian lands." How did this all happen?

Today it is hard to imagine Christian military conquest, but it made perfect sense in 1095, when Pope Urban II called for a military conquest of the Holy Land. Christendom, a union of empire and religion, viewed land and territory as a nation-state views it today. For Christendom, the empire or nation is Christian, and therefore the land and people must be protected. The Christian idea of the kingdom of God was conflated with the Holy Roman Empire or the Kingdom of Russia. The idea of sacred land and holy sites helps to explain Europeans' preoccupation with the Holy Land. A secondary concern, one that became much more important in the fourteenth and fifteenth centuries, was trade: how can Europeans get the delicious spices from the Far East when Muslims are blocking the way? Christianity was hemmed in, and in 1491 it looked like Christianity would remain only as a tribal religion of Western Europe with some small outposts in Ethiopia, India, and the Middle East.

Sixteenth Century: Two Great Transformations of Christianity

In some ways Christianity had lost its missionary dimension during the Middle Ages. As a result it was hard for Christianity to have a critical, and therefore prophetic and missional, distance from its own context. When this happens, Christianity becomes seduced to local power and privilege. Theological controversies were inward looking, and the nations were not even in view. Christians who challenged the Christendom culture were labeled heretical. Jan Hus and John Wyclif in the fourteenth century, and Pierre Valdès (also known as Peter Waldo) much earlier, in the late twelfth and early thirteenth centuries, called for changes that looked very much like those demanded by the later Reformation leaders. All were calling for a faith that was closer to the Bible, which meant all people would need to read the Bible in the vernacular. Churches in the West had added numerous practices such as pilgrimages and forms of penance that Reformers wanted to remove to draw closer to Jesus as described in the Bible.

All of this changed in the fifteenth and sixteenth centuries. Once Christendom broke out of its Western European isolation, Christianity entered a new phase. It is one of the three great transformations that have taken place in Christianity in two thousand years. Christianity developed four major families from two, and Christianity became a world religion.

From Two to Four Families: Reformation and Division

For most Protestants the sixteenth century was a great century; it was the period when a more pure and biblical form of Christianity was rediscovered. Christian Europe was *reformed*. The mystery and magic of Roman Catholic practices were made reasonable. In some ways, the Renaissance call of *ad fontes* (Back to the sources!) was expressed in the church as a call back to Greek reason and rational thought. Pilgrimages were critiqued, and reading and preaching in the common language were required. The Reformers, however, had different ideas of what the original sources of Christianity were, and this was part of the problem. Was the original "source" of Christianity the Holy Spirit–directed church we see in Acts? For those who answered yes, a new form of Christianity developed that we might call the "Spiritual" family of Christianity. They formed churches that were called out to be faithful to how the Holy Spirit guided them. Other churches protested certain practices such as vestments, Latin liturgy, the papacy, and so on. These began another family of Christianity known as "Protestants." Most Protestants developed churches in their own languages and thus in their own nations. National churches developed. Scotland, after a long struggle, followed the teachings of John Calvin and formed a Reformed Church. England followed a "middle way" and formed a national church called the Anglican Church (Church of England). Southern Europe, closest to and including Rome, stayed Roman Catholic. A number of countries followed Luther, and so their national churches were called Lutheran or "Evangelical" for their focus on the gospel (Germany, Norway, Sweden, Denmark).

Christianity became divisive in Western Europe in the first decades of the 1500s. Things didn't really settle down until many were killed (mainly over definitions of the Eucharist and the role of bishops), and many friends were at odds with one another. It was a bloody mess of disagreement over what the church was and what it was to do. The final gasp of violence was the Thirty Years' War, which ended with the Peace of Westphalia in 1648. Again, for many Protestants it is a noble period because the Reformed (Calvin) or Lutheran (Luther) or Anglican (Cranmer et al.) or Mennonite (Menno Simons) church began around noble concerns for a more pure church. However, for Roman Catholics and Orthodox it is a terrible blot on the church's history to see how division marred the witness of Christ in the world. It was an age when all Europeans were Christians, all kings and queens were responsible to help lead the church, and all matters religious were life-or-death issues. The Crusades were still a vivid memory, and the Muslims (considered heretics by most Catholics) had only recently been removed from Roman Catholic Spain (1492). Great theological and biblical writings were produced during the period. It is a bittersweet irony that such violent conflict can often also bring out some of the best in us.

Two of the major outcomes of the period were that Christianity divided, using much of its energy against itself, and that most of the newer churches developed a theology of the church that was static. The definitions of church that most Protestants developed defined the church in opposition to the Roman Catholic tradition. Thus one of the classic definitions of the church that came out of the Reformation was "Where the Word of God is rightly preached and heard and the sacraments are rightly administered."[2] Some added the carrying out of church discipline, but the definitions had no reference to mission or outreach because the definitions were being made in a divided and Christian Europe. It was assumed all people were Christian, so the "true church" must have the true marks proving that it is not a "false church." Protestants, both because of their theology (three marks of the church) and their lack of ability (behind in naval technology), did not participate in the great missionary work of the sixteenth and seventeenth centuries.

Christianity Breaks Out of the Small Corner, Europe

The Portuguese and Spanish were more advanced in all things nautical, and so they were the ones who moved out from Iberia down the coast of West Africa and across to the Caribbean and Brazil in the fifteenth and sixteenth centuries. Roman Catholics maintained a fragile royal-religious cooperation. It was assumed that the national rulers were in service to the pope (or at least popes were very clear on this). Thus the popes, through various papal bulls, established royal patronage for papal missions. In brief, all lands that were claimed by the kings and queens of Portugal and Spain were to be claimed in the name of the pope. The church made it clear that the Portuguese rulers were to finance the various missions to evangelize lands they claimed. To rule meant to evangelize the local people. All were to be brought under the rule of the pope, as well as of the secular rulers. And so immediately friars and monks were on ships heading for newly discovered lands. The methods of evangelization in this early period were often medieval (convert or else!), and yet Latin America was slowly evangelized. Christian outposts were established in Portuguese colonies: Goa, Brazil, Mozambique, Timor, Malacca, Kongo (Congo), Luanda (Angola), Guinea, Macao. The Spanish conquered large areas and sent in monks and friars to bring Christian civilization to their regions: the Americas and Philippines.

2. Leith, *The Church: A Believing Fellowship*, 21.

Less than a century after breaking out of the peninsula of Western Europe, Roman Catholic missions were establishing churches with local people in all of the Americas, the Caribbean, West Africa, East Africa, India, the East Indies, Japan, Vietnam (Annam and Cochin China), and even China. It is really a remarkable moment in global history. Christianity, which had been blocked in a small corner of the world by the surrounding Islam, broke out by going out the back door (to the unexplored west) and ended up circling the globe and encircling Islam. Even in areas where they did not have colonies or an empire, Roman Catholic missions established churches, farther out and farther in than the sailors and soldiers dared go. In this great movement of humanity and the remarkable spread of Christianity, Protestants were left behind.

Christian Mission Recovered: Seventeenth through Nineteenth Centuries

After the period of reformation and Iberian colonization, Christianity became more missionary throughout. More money was spent on missionary work. Kings and popes spent more time establishing churches in newly discovered lands. Much of the evangelization was simply enforcing the same basic theology and structures (even the Latin language) that were in Europe, but some missionary orders were more concerned to present Jesus in Asian or American or African clothes. The Society of Jesus (Jesuits), founded by Ignatius of Loyola at the time of the Protestant Reformation, developed a new approach for monastic order, an approach that asked questions about local cultures and formed missionaries in newer, individualistic ways. Today it is called Ignatian spirituality.

Catholic Missionary Work

The Jesuits became the new pioneer missionary order outside of Europe and the police enforcers of the Catholic Reformation in Europe. They were the first to reach Malacca (now Malaysia), the Spice Islands (Moluccas) of the East Indies, Japan, China, and Vietnam. They were the first Christian martyrs in what would become the United States (in present-day Georgia and Florida). The Jesuits, in a sense, were Renaissance scholars who studied well and took that zeal for learning to study local cultures. Many of their pioneers developed the first glossaries, translations of the liturgy, and even books on local flora and fauna. In Asia they sought to present the gospel in local forms as they sought to take on the role of a local holy man (*sannyasi* in South India, *bonze* in Japan, and Confucian literati in China). In short, the Jesuits were the first modern missionaries as they sought to present Christian faith in local forms and language. Before this time (and for centuries later) missionaries for the most part were transplanting the faith and the forms as one unit.

The Jesuits were not the only missionaries seeking to extend the Spanish and Portuguese empires' rule in all areas of life. Augustinians, Dominicans, Franciscans, Capuchins, and others traveled on royal ships, establishing monasteries, churches, and relocation communities (*reducciones*). Until the nineteenth century all Catholic missionaries were men, and most were "religious," that is, members of a religious order. By the middle of the sixteenth century most of the Americas south of the Rio Grande were moderately Christian. However, the rulers in church, missions, and government were Iberians. This would set in motion a racist hierarchical reality for all of the Spanish Americas. The Kongo in Africa, evangelized by southern European missionaries, was for a time a third Christian kingdom (Ethiopia and Nubia were the other two). Coastal areas of East Africa and South India were also evangelized. In the seventeenth century the Jesuits started an important Jesus movement in Japan. All of these movements were initiated by royal missions of Spain and Portugal until the Vatican established its own missionary initiative, the Sacred Congregation for the Propagation of the Faith (Propaganda Fide) in 1622. Tension existed for centuries in Catholic missionary labors over who really controlled, directed, and therefore had to financially support these important missions. It was inconceivable to Catholic royalty and to the papacy that new lands would not be Christianized, for Christendom by definition required it. The papacy soon realized that friars and monks sent by the pope had less-divided loyalty in such an important task, and so they sought to more directly guide the work of the newly globalized Catholic Church.

Protestants Awaken to the World

Looking from the advantage of the twenty-first century and the rapidly growing churches of the global South, it is hard to believe that Protestantism started in the sixteenth century but did not become a global force until the nineteenth century. This was three hundred years after the Roman Catholics entered the global missionary movement. Of the reasons for the late arrival of the Protestants, two are the most significant and important. First, Protestants were not dominant naval powers. Some of the strongest regions for the Reformation (Germany and Switzerland) had no navies and relied on overland trade or trade with Roman Catholic countries. Missionary work required transportation to far-off regions, and such transportation was not readily available to most Protestant nations. Second, Protestants were not safe and secure until late in the seventeenth century. Mission for Protestants in their infancy years really meant survival and fighting off or converting Roman Catholics. With the signing of the Peace of Westphalia in 1648, the religious lines of Europe were set, but there was still much to be done in Protestant Europe before there was enough security and confidence to begin to think about the rest of the world. Contact, or some basic knowledge of non-Christians, is a prerequisite for the missionary call. Early Protestants lacked that reality.

Protestant mission was also hampered by an underdeveloped theology of the church. Reformation churches were concerned to recover (as they understood it) not only a more robust theology of Christ and the Eucharist but also a theology of the church that lifted up the importance of the verbal proclamation of the Word. Preaching and proper practice of the sacraments were central to the definition of the church for most churches that were protesting against Roman Catholic eucharistic theology. What Protestants lacked was a recovery of the basic missionary nature of the church given by Jesus to the apostles before his ascension. Missing this missionary understanding of the church, Protestants were more focused on purifying Christian churches than on converting non-Christians. In fact, a theology had developed that taught that the disciples had obeyed and fulfilled Jesus's command to preach to all the nations, and so, in a sense, non-Christians had already had their chance.

When Protestant missions did finally commence, it was in a pattern similar to that followed by the Catholics: a Christian king seeking to convert his lands. The first king was Fredrick IV of Denmark, who, feeling the competition of Catholic kings, decided he should also send missionaries to his small holding in India. Thus in 1706 the first real overseas Protestant mission was founded. It was not really until the end of that century, with the arrival of English Baptists in India (1793), that nonroyal Protestant missions began. In the early nineteenth century Protestant missions were still more eccentric than integral to Protestantism. One of the struggles of early Protestant missions was a simple question of transportation. Most of the means of transport were from ships owned by private companies whose sole concern was profit from trade: the British East India Company (EIC), the Dutch West Indies Company, and so on. These companies had little to no concern for evangelization. For example, Robert Morrison, first Protestant missionary to China, had to sail from London to New York and then sail on a US boat to East Asia, since no EIC ship would take him to Hong Kong. Later, Protestant missions and both companies and countries negotiated common callings in the growing empires. Many times governments would subsidize mission schools so more civil servants could be trained. At other times governments signed treaties with local rulers protecting the latter from the "invasion" of missionaries. It was impossible for missionaries from the West not to be identified in some way with Western imperial powers, whether they wanted to be or not.

Protestants developed patterns of missionary work much like the Jesuits, with concern for local cultures, especially learning languages. Because of the strong Protestant principle of having the Bible in the language of the people, Protestants everywhere began by learning the local languages and translating the Bible and publishing glossaries. As medical understanding grew, Protestants pioneered in surgery, vaccinations, and other innovations throughout the world. Education and medicine became the two great and powerful tools in the toolbox of Protestant missions. Translation enhanced the spread of the teachings of Jesus, whether there was greater or lesser cooperation with colonial powers.

Christianity, Modernity, and Missions in the Nineteenth Century

Christianity in the nineteenth century was closely wedded to the advancing Christian kingdoms in the world. Throughout the nineteenth century, when Chinese saw British boats unload kegs of opium followed by missionary families, it was difficult not to see that this was all part of the same foreign invasion. Chinese culture was being attacked through the body and the soul. When missionaries in East and West Africa brought in pianos and organs and taught against polygamy, dancing, and the use of drums, it was hard not to assume that this was all an attempt to erase African cultures. Protestants in the late nineteenth century, unlike those of the early nineteenth century, were more sophisticated and had the modern ideology of progressivism and social Darwinism. Missionaries often saw themselves as helping lower civilizations rise to become more civilized like them. The missionary calling was confused with the civilizing effort of Western nations. Jesus's mission was to make people like Jesus; civilizing meant to make people like us. The two became confused in the late nineteenth century.

Modernity is in part a movement led by rational application of the mind to understand and even quantify the natural world. The modern or Enlightenment world studied the universe in all its great expanse and all its microscopic detail. This movement did not find God. God became an unnecessary presupposition for the modern person. Christianity dwelled in an uneasy alliance in this new world. As a result Christians struggled to make sense of how to appropriate this new knowledge. All Christians had to deal with the new reality. Some adapted the new teachings and saw that in the Bible and Jesus's teachings there is also development and progress. However, in the original teachings of Jesus, as these Christians read them, the real Jesus was not the miraculous atoning savior; he was a model and example of what it means to be fully human. Jesus was more like a perfect human than a God-man. These teachings emphasized the humanity of Jesus and the goodness of humanity. People and societies would be nurtured and slowly evolve or develop to greater peace and harmony. The era was an optimistic and progressive one, and this version of Christianity became known as liberal or modern Christianity.

Other Christians responded by confronting the new teachings, holding on to the past and affirming a scientifically verifiable Bible. They used the word "inerrant" to describe the Bible and began to defend literal (can we say scientific?) interpretations of the Bible. In an effort to fend off newer theologies that treated the Bible as any other history book and Jesus as any other man, these Christians circled the wagons and established fundamental teachings about Jesus and the Bible that must be believed. Some of this group remained evangelical (focused on the evangelistic message and the need for conversion); others turned fundamentalist (more concerned with hard scientific facts to prove the Bible and creation). Christianity, especially Protestant Christianity, was being divided from within. Without any outside persecution, Western Christianity began subdividing and rapidly declining. Missionaries in the early twentieth century carried these tensions and convictions with them throughout the world.

We have concluded our very cursory overview of nineteen centuries of Christianity. We have left out many important themes, and almost all names and places, but we have tried to explain some of the major trends and movements so that our coming tour through the twentieth century will make sense in context. Before looking through our five lenses we need to stop and describe Christianity from the end of the Gilded Age through the Great War. It was a transition period, so looking at these two or three decades will help us to better understand what a miracle the great reversal was for Christianity in the twentieth century.

1

World Christianity

The Gilded Age through the Great War

[Governments] are thinking of the world chiefly as a market house, and of men chiefly as producers and consumers. We now seldom have wars of succession or for mere political dominion. Places are strategic primarily from the commercial standpoint. . . . If the product tarries too long in the warehouse, the mill must shut down and discontent will walk the streets . . . the battle for markets is at its fiercest. The great quest for governments is for markets.

> Benjamin Harrison, speaking at the Ecumenical Missionary Conference
> in New York City (Ecumenical Conference on Foreign Missions, 27)

We are face to face with the great question of the evangelization of Africa. We need to send the natives to evangelize their fellow-men, natives of the country and trained on the spot.

> Rev. Robert Laws of the Free Church of Scotland, giving his report
> on Africa for the same conference (ibid., 461)

The year 1900 was not 2000, and yet it seems so little has changed. In the two quotations above we see some of these themes that are so similar and yet are at the same time worlds apart. Global consumerism, mentioned by a former president in 1900, is even more of an issue for the church and the nations of the world today. However, the concern for evangelization of Africa is not the same at all. A century after this comment was made, much of Africa has been evangelized and Africans are planting some of the largest churches in Europe.

In this chapter we want to look carefully at what global Christianity looked like at the moment when the very confident and very Christian West, without blushing or winking, could say to the world, "This will be the Christian Century."[1] On the basis of the spread of Christian empires most church leaders agreed that this miracle would clearly lead to global Christianization. It was a very small logical step, although a large theological leap, to imagine that if Christian nations ruled the world, then the world would become Christian. The theological leap that is required would mean that Jesus's kingdom, a kingdom of peace and gentleness, would be ushered in by the multinational corporations and armies of Christian nations. It has always been a problem to identify Christian rulers with the King of kings or Christian nations with the kingdom of God.

Rather than just looking at one year (What was global Christianity like in 1900?), we will look at the dynamics at play in Christianity around the turn of the century. Broadly speaking, we will look at Christian presence globally during the transition from the Gilded Age[2] (1870s to 1900) through the Great War (World War I). This will give us a more accurate feel for Christianity as a movement through time and space, rather than as a static institution at the beginning of the "Christian Century."

Entering the Twentieth Century: Globalization, War, Flu

At the time of the Great War, Christianity's center was shifting, but it was a very brief shift across the Atlantic. It was not so much the spiritual and theological weight of North American Christianity that caused the shift as it was the political dominance of the latest imperial power. In earlier centuries we have seen how global powers have dominated the Christian religion, and yet we now know that this is seldom the main story. Even as American "big business"

---

1. The Disciples of Christ published a periodical called the *Christian Oracle* (founded 1884), which was moved to Chicago in 1892 and renamed the *Christian Century* in January 1900. C. A. Young, managing editor at the time of the first renamed issue, wrote, "The nineteenth century has witnessed an extraordinary growth in the extent of Christianity. Sixty percent, or nearly nine hundred million of the world's population are governed by the Christian races. Christianity grew more in the past century than in all the preceding centuries since 'Christ died for our sins, according to the Scriptures.' May not the coming century be known as the Christian Century?"

2. The term was coined by Mark Twain in his novel *The Gilded Age: A Tale of Today* (1873).

Christianity was influencing the direction of the ecumenical and missionary movement, the real center was (almost imperceptibly) moving away from the North Atlantic region to Latin America, Africa, and Asia. But early in the century there were only hints that the North Atlantic Christian dominance was more a veneer painted by worldly mammon than a spiritual furnace for the global church. Despite the theological divisions over evolution, science, higher criticism, and the Holy Spirit, North Atlantic Christianity was still flooding the world with missionaries and building institutional Christianity in far-off cities and villages. Big American and European money built YMCA buildings in Shanghai, Singapore, Tokyo, Cape Town, Mexico City, Madurai—everywhere missionaries and international businesspeople traveled.

The Great Century for Missions is generally assumed to have ended with the 1910 World Missionary Conference held in Edinburgh. Periodization is seldom an exact science, and the end of the Great Century is a prime example of this difficulty. Christianity was firmly enmeshed in empires, movements of civilization, and ideas of social uplift. Many missionaries who traveled to the East and the South in the early decades of the twentieth century brought with them ideas of teaching democracy, economic theory, and modern science, along with the Christian religion. The Great War changed all of that. The early decades of the twentieth century were a period of global transition; the great influenza pandemic of 1918–19 is a type of marker. It was a period of Christian transition globally. Western Christianity was suffering a crisis of credibility after such a bloody war, in which Christians were killing other Christians. The revelation that European Christians were warlike Christians was not lost on Christians in Asia and Africa who witnessed the conflict between German and British missionaries. Western Christendom suffered one tragedy upon another. The great flu was a global pandemic, killing more than fifty million people in the first year. Soon after, the world suffered from a major economic collapse, which was followed by the rearmament of Germany and increased global tensions in Europe and Africa. Ironically, Western Christian missions remained confident and progressive thinking. Plans went ahead for ecumenical conferences to bring together Christians to work for unity on issues of faith and order and for cooperative work in society. The movement for missionary unity continued also, though delayed by the Great War. Non-Western church leaders were quite aware that Western Christianity was struggling to rise above its own materialism and nationalisms.

Will there be any good prospect for the native after the end of the war? Shall we be recognized as anybody in the best interests of civilisation and Christianity after the great struggle is ended? . . . In time of peace the Government failed

to help the underdog. In time of peace, everything for the European only. . . .
But in time of war it has been found that we are needed to share hardships and
shed our blood in equality.[3]

The first decades of the twentieth century were truly a period of transition
for Christianity as a world religion, but it was not the transition that most
theologians, clerics, or missionaries in Christendom had expected. The main
story would not be the rise of a powerful ecumenical movement based on a
modern Western business model. The war, flu, and economic collapse slowly
revealed the vulnerability of Western Christendom. The main story would
be the spreading decay of this Christianity in the West (a continuation of
the decay wrought by the Enlightenment and *Philosophe* scholars) and the
remarkable vitality of Christianity from the margins, a Christianity that was
planted by that same waning Christianity in the West. Even the amalgamation
of Christianity and commerce, along with the loss of Christian confidence
in faith, did not prevent Christianity from becoming a modern faith for the
non-Western world.

Colonialism and Christianization

One of the greatest themes of this period of transition in the early twentieth
century was the relationship between Christian missions and colonialism.
While Western Christendom's decline was accelerating, Christian missions
and Western colonialism were still showing signs of vitality. It was this
delicate and complex relationship between mission and empire that took
center stage.

Historians have tried to make clear statements about the relationship
between Christian missions, Christian growth, and colonialism, but it has
proved very difficult to do so. Colonialisms were not of a single type, and
missionary lives in various global contexts were as diverse as the agencies
and individuals who were involved. Here we give a few examples of the
diversity involved, showing that any consensus understanding of the relationship between colonialism and Christian missions must be very general
and heavily footnoted.

Colonialism and Christian mission in East Asia in the nineteenth century was
a very diverse experience. The Philippines were heavily colonized over a period

3. John Chilembwe (1870–1915) of Nyasaland, present-day Malawi, who had studied in
Scotland. Quoted in Koschorke, Frieder, and Delgado, *History of Christianity*, 222, which in
turn quotes from *Nyasaland Times*, no. 48, November 26, 1914.

of four hundred years by a country whose king was obligated to spread religion and rule as one interwoven fabric. It is hard to refute the observation that as a result the Philippines, named after a Spanish king, became mostly Christian. Vietnam was colonized for only a century by France, and Christianity is much less prominent in that country. The Dutch slowly increased their colonial rule in the East Indies for more than three and a half centuries, and yet the Christian population remained very small. In actuality, Christianity grew much more after the Dutch were removed. Siam (Thailand) was not colonized, missionaries were intermittently free to work there, and yet it is one of the least Christian nations in Asia. China was colonized only along the coasts; it had a very long history of missionary work, and also decades of intense religious persecution and Communist secularization, yet today Christianity is growing very rapidly. In China, Communism proved more of a stimulus to growth than imperialism did. Japan also had a long history of missionary involvement; it was

Library of Congress

Figure 2. This photo is a great example of the complex relationship between mission and empire at the turn of the century. President McKinley (who had particular Protestant interests in the Catholic Philippines) and Admiral George Dewey bow in prayer as Cardinal Gibbons gives the opening benediction for a celebration in Washington, DC, to honor Dewey's successful defeat of the Spanish during the Battle of Manila Bay, October 1899.

never colonized, and Christianity is a very small minority community. Then we have Korea, colonized not by a Western Christian nation but by China and Japan. Its terrible history with foreign nations and its very brief period of evangelization have helped to produce a very strong Christian presence by Asian standards. We pause to underscore that there was no Christian imperialism to support the missionary work in Korea, and yet it became one of the most Christianized of nations in Asia.

And so we might ask, did colonial experiences help the growth of Christianity or hinder it? The answer is both. Oppression, more than colonialism or imperialism, seems to be the most important factor. Suffering imposed by local or foreign powers is an important variable, more important than the support of a colonial government. However, other variables are involved. Japan, an oppressive imperial power in East Asia, had a "Christian century" (1550–1650) during which it seemed that Christianity was going to win the hearts and minds of the Japanese, but then the change in rule crushed the young Christian movement. Later Christian influence, with minimal Western colonial influence, had little impact on the rising imperial nation.

But Christian impact is only one of the questions. The larger historical question that needs to be asked to understand this complex history is about the intent of the colonial powers and the intent of the missionary societies. Were the colonial powers intent on dominating other nations to the extent that the local peoples would become "European" in life, language, and religion? Not at all. This could be applied to earlier Portuguese and Spanish expansion, since the pope had given the kings the responsibility to spread the faith wherever the Portuguese or Spanish flag was unfurled. These Iberian missions were taken up from a position of power, from which Spain or Portugal enforced their rule. Spain proved to be the enforcers and soldiers, while the Portuguese were the traders and sailors. The Dutch and British had no such dream of evangelizing their overseas lands, nor did they have papal obligation to do so. When their religion got in the way of trade, they made treaties that would exclude missionaries and missionary meddling in local cultures. We have seen this in both Africa and Asia. However, when missionary schools would help to train civil servants, the colonial rulers would provide financial support for the mission schools. Many of these mission schools became the best schools in Asia and Africa. Most European imperialists were powerful businessmen: pragmatists when it came to rule and religion.

Belgian colonialism was unique. The Belgian Congo was basically a private holding of the Belgian king, Leopold II. After attempting to buy the Philippines from Spain, he turned to Africa and procured his own private empire by force. Nineteenth-century imperialism was never a pretty thing, but the severed hands of children and adults make Leopold's empire one of the worst. Finally, after decades of investigations, followed by imprisonments and violent responses, the combined efforts of missionaries and reporters forced the king's violent empire to be turned over to his government. In an interesting twist of events, it was an early Presbyterian African American missionary, Rev. William H. Sheppard, who led an international campaign to end the Belgian king's rule in the Congo. After the private kingdom was nationalized, missionaries slowly trickled in, but not before an estimated ten million Congolese suffered premature deaths caused by Belgian imperialism. In the first decade of the twentieth century not only Belgium but also France was trying to step away from its own history of genocide in the Congo.[4]

German expansionism, a very late form of colonialism, was much more clearly a matter of cultural domination and not just economic exploitation. Otto von Bismarck, who helped to unite Prussia and Germany, sought a new *Weltpolitik* (world policy) to extend German influence. It was not his early desire to become a colonial power, but imperialism became the German design, and so Germany extended its cultural influence into Africa, Asia, and the Pacific.

Missionaries, much more concerned with making Christians than making Germans, often resisted German cultural hegemony. One example will illustrate the tension. Franz Michael Zahn was a German Pietist mission statesman who headed up the Bremen Mission working in Togo, a British land that was taken over by the Germans in 1890. Germany refused to let the missionaries teach English to the indigenes because it would promote African independency and ideas of emancipation. Zahn fired back, "I feel we should make use of any means at our disposal to win the privilege of the freedom of mission. Therefore, I suggest we complain again, first to the Reichskanzler . . . then, to the Kaiser, to the Parliament, and to the press." He was very clear that the German idea of *Kulturvolk* ("civilized people") was the enemy of Christian ministry in Africa. As director of the Bremen Mission, he wrote to one of his missionaries in 1888, "I am against colonies anyway, and naturally, that is enough today for one to be branded a traitor to the Fatherland. But if a missionary enters into politics, and through his influence supports the German colonial acquisitions and motives—then, whatever he may think otherwise, I regard this as a grave mistake, not to say a crime."[5]

Such attitudes became prevalent especially in the last decades of colonial expansion. Colonial powers were wary of the rise of well-educated local people, the very thing that missionaries, at their best, were working to effect. Christian leadership demanded literacy, education, and independence. Much of the independence was granted later than hoped for, and yet work with indigenes was the very warp and woof of missionary work. It was only tolerated by colonial powers, which were more intent to maintain their hegemony over vast lands and cultures from the Caribbean to the Indian Ocean to the Pacific.

---

4. An excellent exposé of King Leopold II's rule in Congo can be found in Hochschild, *King Leopold's Ghost*.

5. Quoted in Ustorf, "Franz Michael Zahn," 124.

Lamin Sanneh has remarked that in the missionary priority to translate the Bible and then develop literacy in each culture, missionary work resisted colonial goals and empowered indigenes.

> Christian missions are better seen as a translation movement, with consequences for vernacular revitalization, religious change and social transformation, than as a vehicle for Western cultural domination. . . . Even the nationalist point of view that came to dominate much historical writing about the new Africa was to a large extent molded by the missionary exploration of indigenous societies.[6]

To this we must add that local people often could not distinguish the purpose, motives, or concerns of German missionaries from those of the German colonialists. In East China, violence against foreigners, which eventually spilled out in the form of the Boxer Rebellion, began with violence against a German missionary who reflected more of his sense of German cultural superiority than the spirit of a missionary educator. We see that in many rebellions in which missionaries were attacked, the anger was directed at all foreignness. Earlier rebellions tended to be more grassroots, from those who were less educated and from those less exposed to the West. It is ironic that by the 1920s, resistance to the West was led by Indians, Kenyans, Chinese, and others who had the benefits of Western education, usually from mission schools.

A further complicating issue in our study of Western colonialism and mission is the arrival of secular Western ideologies as new forms of political liberation and (at times) of cultural imperialism. In the 1920s Soviet Russia began to export its form of liberation to Asia. In Indonesia, China, Vietnam, and India it won a hearing as a form of nationalism. Communism provided a vocabulary and ideology for resistance to foreign domination. Russia sent advisers (political and military) as well as money to encourage particular people and movements for independence in Asia. As early as 1918, Chinese revolutionary leader Sun Yat-sen was in communication with Russian Communists, who portrayed China's resistance to colonial powers as the same as Russia's proletarian revolution. Writing to Sun in 1918, Soviet foreign minister Georgi Chicherin implored:

> At a time of so great trial, when the imperialist Governments are stretching out greedy hands from the west and the east, the north and the south, to strangle the Russian revolution and to take away from the Russian peasants and workers

6. Sanneh, "Christian Missions," 334.

what they won for themselves by a revolution such as the world has never seen before, when the Peking Government, the creature of foreign bankers, is prepared to join these robbers—the Russian working classes turn to their Chinese brothers and call them on to the common fight.[7]

During the decade of antiforeignism in China (1920s), a movement that was strong among university students, a new foreign influence was already penetrating the local Chinese cultural context. This form of foreign influence had much more of a cultural agenda to it. Communist ideology, a new form of Western influence, barred Asian religions from participation in society, something that did not occur under the colonialism of Protestant countries.

If we stand back to see a four-century global picture, we can see that the global age that was pioneered during the age of discovery became a globalized age of worldwide ideologies, technologies, and trade. Christianity was part of that four-century-long period of globalization. It had its role to play, but its role was not unqualified support for the colonial agenda. At times Christianity benefited from global movements, at times missionaries were the pioneers of global movements, and at times global powers resisted missionaries. But the overall story is that the history of Christianity was woven into the new global context. Rather than seeing Christianity as the spiritual component of colonialism, it may be more accurate to say that Christian mission planted the seeds for the survival and revival of Christianity in non-Western lands, and at the same time planted the seeds of future movements of liberation in Asia and Africa. Missionaries were often unwittingly preparing leaders for the soon-to-be-liberated modern nations of Africa and Asia.

And yet little of this was seen in the triumphal Western Christian period before the Great War. The twentieth century was dubbed the "Christian Century," and most people meant by that that it would be the Christian century for the Western Christian Church and its foreign offices (much like the British Empire). The confidence of Western civilization was headed toward disaster, yet at the same time Western Protestants were planning for the conclusion of the imperial and missionary task. The World Missionary Conference in 1910, led by European and American church leaders and laypeople, should be seen as the zenith or capstone of the great century of Protestant missions. It also marked the end of an era. This one conference functions as a large picture window into Western Christian self-understanding at the end of an age.

---

7. "Letter from Chicherin to Sun Yat-Sen," March 9, 1918. For further discussion on these early relationships between Moscow and Beijing, see Saich, *Origins*, 38–48.

Edinburgh Missionary Conference

Headed up by the American Methodist layman John R. Mott (1865–1955), Edinburgh 1910, as it has come to be called, was a massive, carefully planned, nine-day meeting that reflected a major stockholder's business meeting more than a church council. Marked by optimism, zeal, industry, and exacting planning, it took its watchword from the World Student Christian Federation (WSCF): "The evangelization of the world in this generation." Eight commissions were established with about twenty-eight members in each, the representation being determined by the amount of money spent on missionary work. Thus there were ninety-two British members; fifty-one from the United States; and only twenty-two from France, Germany, Holland, Switzerland, and Scandinavia combined. Of the British representatives, about half were Anglicans. A number of missionary conferences had been held both internationally (beginning in 1854) and locally in the non-Western world, but this conference was a working conference for which the planners prepared for more than two years, for which thousands of surveys were sent to Africa and Asia, and that was supported and led by major political figures. It is a major watershed for Protestant Christianity, world Christianity, and the ecumenical movement. A few themes and highlights will help us to understand the situation of Christianity at the time.

First, the conference can be seen as the transition of Western Christianity from spiritual movement to modern business affair. Bible study and prayer were still important elements as at earlier missionary conferences, but the tone of the conference, even as it is described in the official literature, highlights how well organized—even businesslike—the conference was. Speakers could respond for only seven minutes, and they had to give their names to the chairman, John R. Mott, a day in advance. Efficiency, clear communication, order, statistics, and unity were major common concerns. This businesslike efficiency in 1910 is ironically developing at the same time as modern Pentecostalism and revival movements in East Asia and Africa.

Second, the conference reminds us how divided Christianity had become since the sixteenth century. Edinburgh 1910 was seen as a great "ecumenical" event, and yet in order to include the High Church Anglicans (the largest delegation was from the Church Missionary Society), the conference had to exclude the whole Western Hemisphere from their discussions. Anglicans would not allow mission among Roman Catholics to be discussed, and so although the conference was able to include Anglicans, it became a conference on the Asia-Pacific and African mission worlds. Roman Catholics were not part of this conference, nor were any Orthodox communions. There was much unity to be celebrated, for High Church Anglicans, Southern Baptists, Moravians,

Figure 3. The assembly at the World Missionary Conference at New College, University of Edinburgh, 1910

and the China Inland Mission were meeting and praying together. However, they could not celebrate communion together as one body.

Third, the conference marks how central the missionary movement had become to Western cultures. All of the meetings were packed with thousands attending. Three reporters from the *Times* of London covered the event, and government officials (former parliamentarians, a former secretary of state, etc.) provided much of the leadership. This was a major political as well as religious event. Heads of churches and heads of state now fully embraced the missionary movement, whereas scarcely a century earlier it was an eccentric, fringe affair. Protestant missionary work had become the main story in Western Christianity, if only for a brief time. As Scottish theologian James Denney commented, "The Work of missions has attained to such dimensions, and has entered so largely into the general movement of human things, that it is impossible for intelligent people not to have some kind of interest."[8] Even some major theologians became part of the missionary movement.

8. Denney, "Demands Made," 322.

Fourth, the event marks the internal struggle that Western missionaries and their missions had to give up leadership of their overseas institutions. In the hundreds of various meetings in and around the conference (women's meetings, medical missions meetings, public meetings, etc.), very few non-Westerners spoke at all, although some very distinguished Africans and Asians were present. The president of Meiji Gakuin College, K. Ibuka, and the ex-minister of education for Korea, Yan Chi Ho, made brief addresses. The most telling and prophetic speech was that made by the future bishop of the Anglican Church in South India, Vendanayagam Samuel Azariah (1874–1945). Azariah swam against the tide of optimism and happy feelings of cooperation and said very directly that as much as he respected missionaries, they did not treat Indians as friends or as equals: "The relationship between the European missionaries and the Indian workers is far from what it ought to be, and . . . a certain aloofness, a lack of mutual understanding and openness, a great lack of frank intercourse and friendliness exists throughout the country." His concluding comments to his speech were winsome, uncompromising, and memorable: "Through all the ages to come the Indian Church will rise up in gratitude to attest the heroism and self-denying labors of the missionary body. You have given your goods to feed the poor. You have given your bodies to be burned. We also ask for *love*. Give us FRIENDS."[9] While a few Asians were present and were given some time to talk, no Africans were heard from at all.

Fifth, at this twentieth-century conference, there was still a consensus theologically that Christian mission was rooted in the atoning death and resurrection of Jesus Christ for all peoples. In the discussions about other religions, there was sympathy for truth found in other religions, but there was unanimity that "this is a decisive hour for Christian missions . . . to undertake without delay the task of carrying the gospel to all the non-Christian world. . . . The gospel is all-inclusive in its scope." All people must have an opportunity to hear the gospel, and those in the conference sensed it was a *kairos* moment—a time for action. "The threatening advance of Islam in Equatorial Africa presents to the Church of Christ the decisive question whether the Dark Continent shall become Mohammadan or Christian." And speaking of the "disintegration of the animistic and fetishistic beliefs," the final report said, "The responsibility of the Church is grave to bring the gospel to them quickly, as the only sufficient substitute for their decaying faiths."[10] From this point on, Western Protestant Christianity would not have such a clear voice about Christianity and other

9. Azariah, "Problem of Co-operation," emphasis original.
10. World Missionary Conference, *Report of Commission I*, 363, 364, 365.

world religions. Modern higher-critical studies, global politics, and two world wars eroded the confidence in Christendom's message and purpose.

Finally, the conference does mark the beginning of one of the major themes of Christianity in the twentieth century: the ecumenical movement for global Christian unity. The conference ended with a unanimous decision to establish a continuation committee. This committee, well funded and with active, well-connected leaders who had come up through the Student Volunteer Movement (SVM), marked a turning point. Missionary involvement in the student work globally laid the foundation for the first meeting to discuss issues of faith and church order, to try to bring the churches together. At Edinburgh this call for unity was affirmed, and four months later at the General Convention of the American Episcopal Church it was given as a call: "We believe that the time has now arrived when representatives of the whole family of Christ, led by the Holy Spirit, may be willing to come together for the consideration of questions of Faith and Order. We believe further, that all Christian Communions are in accord with us in our desire to lay aside self-will, and to put on the mind which is in Christ Jesus our Lord."[11] The call was made, in light of Jesus's high priestly prayer (John 17:21 NIV), that "all of them may be one . . . that the world may believe." It is significant that it was American Episcopal Bishop Charles Brent who initiated the call and who led the first conference, much delayed because of war, at Lausanne in 1927. It is also quite significant that the Orthodox were included. This happened, again, because of important relationship-building that took place with the World Student Christian Federation (SCM international). John R. Mott, Nathan Söderblom, and Strenopoulos Germanos all met at a WSCF conference in Constantinople in 1911. Strenopoulos was later Archbishop Germanos of Thyatira, and in that position, in 1920, he was instrumental in the ecumenical patriarch's *Encyclical unto All the Churches of Christ*, a call to Christian unity. The Lausanne meeting was remarkable in bringing together 127 Orthodox leaders among the more than 400 participants.

A year later a follow-up ecumenical meeting devoted to mission was held in Jerusalem. At this meeting it became evident that the common assumptions of Edinburgh 1910 were breaking down. Major attention was now given to secularization and Communism, along with other world religions, as "non-Christian systems of thought and life." Russia, the largest Christian nation in the world, had turned secular, and even in "Christian" Europe the universities were developing secular systems of thought. Another theological turn took place, concerning the relative value of other religions and how Christians

---

11. Manning, *Call to Unity*, 124–25.

were to relate to them. Edinburgh gave a lucid vision of all nations hearing and responding to the Christian message. Jerusalem was much more nuanced and allowed a much larger place for the social sciences. Western Christians were divided on salvation and truth in other religions. Harvard professor William Ernest Hocking, no orthodox Christian himself, gave an address, titled "Psychological Conditions for the Growth of Faith," in which he argued for an understanding of human psychology to bring about a new world civilization. "If by any means such unity can be promoted, surely this silent growing together of faiths will further it; and we should realize the saying, 'I am the vine, ye are the branches.'"[12] Modern social sciences were becoming part of the language of theology, and the 1920s marks this new development along with its attendant divisions.

Whither Western Christianity?

In the age of these missionary and ecumenical conferences, global events were influencing much of the theology and experience of the global church. At the very time of these conferences, Western Christianity was also involved in major discussions about peace. Ecumenical unity required peace, and the irony is that in the midst of these discussions of church unity, Christian nations in Europe were tearing one another apart. Centuries of Christianization in Europe had not erased all traces of tribalism. In the "War to End All Wars" (1914–18), more than fifteen million people died and 15 percent of the active male population of Germany was killed. As European Christians struggled to make sense of what they had just done to one another, Christianity in the West was also being transformed from within.

North America was not the battlefield of the Great War, so American Christianity maintained greater optimism and vigor into the 1920s. American Christianity, however, was beginning a century-long divide between modernism (progressivism) and fundamentalism (and later evangelicalism). The question that thrust itself upon Western Christians was "How does Christianity relate to the modern sciences, both social sciences and the 'hard' sciences?" Whereas in the late Renaissance the sciences of physics, mathematics, and astronomy seemed to reduce the place of God in the great scheme of things, the modern studies of economics, sociology, and psychology seemed to make God almost meaningless. Some well-educated Christians uncritically embraced most of the modern sciences as God's truth, but such an embrace excluded Christians

12. Hocking, "Psychological Conditions," 8:104–5.

of a more simple belief. Other Christians, equally well educated, insisted on staking out the Christian territory before it was overrun by modern ideas. They reasoned that basic beliefs, or fundamentals, must be established first, and then Christians could begin to talk about modern ideas. They were not as enamored of modern ideas of positivism, evolution, or determinism. They had greater respect and regard for what was ancient and tried. Older questions of miracles and the resurrection persisted, but newer questions of human evolution and a very old evolving earth were added. To these questions, the social sciences added questions of human determinism. Human behavior, they said, is not free to respond to God, and is certainly not controlled by God, but it is a matter of environment and conditioning. Modern behavior modification techniques were used extensively in World War I. Where is God in all of this if we can merely create the right conditions to make people good? Sin became more of an environmental issue than a personal inclination of the human heart.

In tandem with such a materialist view of the world, civil authorities began to step in to take over many of the previous functions of the church. The big battleground in the early twentieth century was education. It is helpful to see this as the ongoing influence of the French Revolution. States in Europe began to provide the funding for comprehensive elementary education throughout the countries, and these schools were still run by religious orders (Roman Catholic) or by churches (Protestant). But in the late nineteenth century civil governments began to make restrictions on religious education in publicly funded schools, and later they would not allow any religious education. The Netherlands was one of the few places where Protestants and Catholics created a political coalition to prevent the de-Christianization of the schools. In most countries of Europe and North America education became a secular endeavor. The churches were trapped, since any opposition was seen as being "anti-intellectual" or "antimodern." Education became a battlefield for Western Christendom, and in this reshaping of the intellectual realm, Christian education and Christian belief were decentered from the public square. Europeans experienced this differently than North Americans, but in both continents the long-established pattern of Christian education for and in society was gone. Christians divided over whether the old pattern should be defended (and accommodated) or a new pattern should be developed.

We can look at these theological and ethical discussions in the 1920s as new and confusing discussions around the church's missional identity in a less and less Christian world. In trying to answer questions of social evolution and the public nature of Christian faith, Christians were really asking about the nature of the Christian gospel. Was the gospel to be rooted in and expressed through the secular state? This had been the norm in Christendom in Europe.

Or was the gospel to be enfleshed in countercultural communities that were signposts to a fallen world? This had been the understanding of the Spiritual reformers (Mennonites, Anabaptists, etc.). Was the sacred text that bore the gospel a divine document shaped by human cultures and personalities and therefore requiring modern critical analysis? Or was the sacred text timeless and above modern critique? Although the debate was seldom spoken of as a missiological one, it is best to frame it as such. This encounter with a "new culture" was different only in degree from the Jesuit encounters in Japan or China, or the Capuchin encounters in the Kongo. How was the Christian message and life to enter into this new modern context? Churches split over these contextualization questions, and up to the present day Christian divisions continue. What in the new culture is to be embraced and what is to be critiqued by the gospel? This missional encounter was different from those in the past, however, because the very culture Christians were trying to reach was a culture that defined itself against orthodox Christianity. Western culture had, in a sense, been inoculated against orthodox Christian belief, making contextual approaches very complex.

Struggles over modern science and conflict over the modern secular state stressed and divided Christians, but at the same time there were global movements that seemed to point to Christianity having greater vitality, if not greater social impact. We have already noted that the rise of modern Pentecostalism and independency in Africa (also in Asia) began in the first decades of the twentieth century. In some ways these issues were related to the reshaping of Christianity in the West. Western colonialism and Western forms of Christianity were often inappropriate for African communities. Africans received the message in their own languages, saw the lives of the missionaries, and then reconstituted or retranslated the message and life for their own communities. In this way Christianity became a truly African religion. In China the missionary community brought with them some of the divisions over theology and modernity. Many of the Chinese Christians received the modern American or British Christianity, along with the English language and modern political and educational theory. Others rejected the modern sciences and reappropriated Christianity for their own communities. In Shandong Chinese Christians resisted the more liberal approach of many of the seminary professors from the West, so they set up their own seminary, which soon became the largest seminary in China (North China Theological Seminary). Western missionaries established modern seminaries that taught all the modern social sciences along with the Bible. Many of the seminaries, patterned after Western seminaries, were part of larger universities. Chinese independency resisted Western imperialism along with modern Western theological teachings. Other Chinese

Christians set up their own Christian communal churches ("Jesus Family") or their own independent evangelistic associations. On the one hand, we can see this type of independency as divisive; on the other hand, these were signs of inner vitality in Christianity as it was developing around the world.

Related to these signs of indigenous vitality is another major movement coming to flower in the 1920s: Pentecostalism. Holiness and, later, Pentecostal movements are generally movements that come from the grass roots. We have seen this with the type of Christianity that thrived among slave and freed black communities in the Americas. Hierarchical churches seldom promote Pentecostal or revival movements. We have seen how these movements of revival spread in the first decades of the twentieth century. By the 1920s they had become a global force of Christianity, spreading in one generation to places that it took Protestantism three centuries to reach. With a very strong impetus for missionary outreach, Pentecostals were linking up in all corners of the earth. Direct links can be found between California, South Africa, Australia, Norway and Sweden, Sri Lanka, Northeast India, Korea, Chicago, Italy, and Brazil. These movements, in the early generations, could afford to ignore the pressing academic questions. They were impelled to spread the gospel message and await the evidence of the Holy Spirit. Such evidence was every bit as scientific and observable as that which modern science and sociology had to offer. Revivals brought stories of healings and experiences of the Holy Spirit. Pentecostalism had its own empirical proofs. Such experiences united diverse peoples and propelled the initiated to tell others. Pentecostalism was the book of Acts revisited. The repeated trajectory of the Pentecostal movement was from preaching to experience of the Holy Spirit, to community, and then to mission.

Whereas Pentecostals seemed propelled by the Spirit of God to move out, other Christians were moving because of economic or political turmoil. The Russian Revolution quickly developed into an anti-Christian revolution, and, therefore, many of the better-trained leaders of the Russian Orthodox Church began to move west. France, and then the United States, became the major receivers of a growing Orthodoxy. Orthodoxy became part of the cultural mosaic in the West. Other Orthodox, both Byzantine and Catholic, came to the United States during the economic boom related to coal mining and then steel production in the early twentieth century. Orthodox came across the Atlantic from the Balkans, Russia, Poland, and Ukraine. These new immigrants changed the makeup of Christianity in North America, and as a result people in the United States began to fear the change in the overall makeup of the country. Two acts were passed by the US Congress in the 1920s to restrict immigration from Eastern and Southern Europe. It was not until 1938 that the first Orthodox churches joined the Federal Council of Churches in the United States. Immigration was making the North American church as well as the Western European churches much less homogeneous.

Non-Western Transformations of Christianity

Europeans and North Americans assumed that if the missionary task was going to be completed, it would depend on their resolve and initiative. That is what the Edinburgh Missionary Conference was committed to work for. Viewed from the perspective of specific African, Latin American, and Asian contexts, such a view of things was far too imperialistic, far too Western. Major movements, almost prophetic foretastes of what was going to happen, were afoot on all continents. We look here briefly at some of these movements, movements that became the main story of Christianity by the end of the twentieth century, but that were often seen as "problems" at the time. First we will look briefly at movements in Africa and Asia, and then we will turn to the transformations and struggles of the churches in Latin America.

As we noted above, Western Christianity's own internal struggles along with its variegated relationship with colonialism created tensions in its relationships with indigenes in the non-Western, "younger" churches. In China, in the context of antiforeign movements of the early decades, Chinese Christians began their own movements. Inspired by American Wesleyan evangelists, two Chinese Christians, Andrew Gih (Ji Zhiwen, 1901–85) and John Sung (Song Shangjie, 1901–44), formed their own Bethel Worldwide Evangelistic Band. Sung, in reaction to Western liberal scholarship he had experienced in the United States, refused to read any book but the Bible. His preaching reflected this commitment. This movement started in South China but spread throughout all of East Asia as the evangelists traveled to all locations where diasporic Chinese could be found.

In Shandong, to the north, former Taoist and Confucianist Jing Dianying (1890–1957) began a different type of indigenous Christian movement in the 1920s. Although he attended a Methodist middle school in Tai An, Jing was not converted until eight years later, in 1920, when he was struggling with a failed marriage. He then formed the Saints Cooperative Society (Shengtu She) to call together other Christians to live a more Christian life in contrast to the corrupt lives around them. His second conversion, we might call it, came from a Pentecostal revival in 1925 in Tai An, and as a result he began praying for a full manifestation of the Holy Spirit. Soon Christian communes were springing up in the countryside.

Other independent churches, evangelistic associations, and communities developed in China in the 1920s and 1930s, almost as if a new revival was breaking out: "This period saw the rise of Watchman Nee, John Sung, David Yang and Marcus Cheng—all of whom along with Wang [Mingdao] stressed repentance, conversion, holiness, doctrine, and discipleship. They were the vanguard of a revival that swept through the Chinese churches of the late 1920s and 1930s. Evangelical and antiliberal, they decried the leadership of modernists and liberals in the churches."[13]

In the Philippines another type of independency developed. This was also rooted in the need for the Christian faith to be fully expressed in local contexts, but this was a very unusual, Roman Catholic independency. The Roman Catholic Church had been so identified with Spanish rule (colonial church) that throwing off Spanish rule, for some, required throwing off foreign church authority at the same time. In 1902 the Iglesia Filipina Independiente (Philippine Independent Church) was formed with Gregorio Aglipay as the *obispo maximo* (supreme bishop). This type of non–Roman Catholic church was very influential and later joined with the Episcopal Church in the Philippines.

In Africa independency was expressed as a major continental movement with few direct connections between the various groups. Such movements had begun before the twentieth century, but in its early decades some of these movements advanced from the fringes to the center of the African Christian story. Later they would become known as African Indigenous Churches (AICs),[14] but in the earlier decades of the twentieth century, they were seen by colonialists simply as problems and possible revolutionaries. Africans generally saw these prophetic movements as fresh and vital African religious movements. Prophetic leaders like William Wade Harris, Simon Kimbangu, and Moses Orimolade were founders of specific indigenous Christian movements. Other movements did not originate from a particular prophet, but appeared as wide-ranging spiritual movements, covering a large geographic area. Independency was not unrelated to political independence. Mission schools and indigenous Christian movements were the training ground for African leaders. By the first decades of the twentieth century Africans were ready to lead the newly formed nation-states, even though Europeans were not ready to relinquish their power or their profits. When African leaders finally did lead their nations to independence, after World War II, that independence took effect simultaneously with Christian revival.

13. Harvey, *Acquainted with Grief*, 24.
14. Also African Independent Churches, or African Initiated Churches.

In Latin America the situation of Christianity approximated the situation in Western Europe and North America more than in Africa and Asia. After centuries of colonial rule and the exclusion of indigenous leadership in government and church, societies continued to exist under the social conditions that excluded most of the non-Iberian classes. Landownership patterns that favored rulers and ecclesiastical leaders continued. Yet ideas of liberty that had fueled much of the independence energy in the nineteenth century continued to be attractive in the early decades of the twentieth century, including in Latin America. Added to older ideas of liberty and freedom were the newer ideas stemming from Marxist analysis and the Russian Revolution. The Mexican Revolution (1910–20) was fought to bring about social reforms, including land redistribution and (for many) the reduction of church power and church lands. Mexico's 1917 Constitution, which came out of the war period, was clearly anti–Roman Catholic and even anti-Christian. The new constitution included requirements that all schools be secular, outlawed religious orders (and vows), and removed all civil rights and responsibilities for church officials. Although these provisions were not rigorously enforced, they reveal the secularization of Latin American societies and the severe marginalization of the church.

In July 1926 things turned much worse for the Catholic Church when President Plutarco Elías Calles had thirty-nine articles directed against the church nailed to the doors of churches. Under these articles, Catholic lay organizations were suppressed, foreign priests were expelled, and those who questioned the law were imprisoned. The laws and their strict enforcement triggered resistance and the development of an almost underground church. Since religious vestments were not allowed, priests would often secretly celebrate Mass in homes. Often homes and businesses were raided as secret police looked for secret priests. Mexican resistance fighters took up the name *Cristiada*, representing Christ's cause in their fighting. The church was so sorely oppressed that Pope Pius XI excoriated the anti-Christian laws of Mexico and spoke out in support of the freedom fighters. It was a volatile period for Christianity in Latin America, at a time when the Roman Catholic Church was suffering setbacks in Europe as well.

At this same time, again as in North America, newer immigrants were arriving in Latin America bringing newer forms of Christianity. German immigrants, including many middle- and upper-middle-class Lutherans and Catholics, migrated after the Great War and settled in the cities of Brazil. An agrarian revolution was taking place early in the century, and this attracted Europeans who saw all of the Americas as a place of hope and opportunity.

Global movements of people increased dramatically in the twentieth century. This is one of the major themes of the period, and so we devote a whole chapter to this movement (chap. 5). Standing in the early decades of the twentieth century, one had reason to see that Christianity was at a period of both great hope and great fragility. New ideas and ideologies challenged the place of the church, as well as the very existence of God. The Christian church had never faced such a formidable and influential global idea in nineteen centuries. States were beginning to take over and exclude the church from basic areas of social life that the church had enjoyed for centuries. With indigenous movements for independence arising, the astute observer could see that the days of "favored religion status" that existed in many non-Western contexts were soon to be over.

However, at the same time, especially for the optimistic Americans, it was a time of great opportunity and hope. Christian empires were extending their influence, and churches, schools, and even Christian colleges were being built in the heartland of Hindu, Muslim, and Buddhist territories. On the horizon were early voices of independence and resistance (we might note the Boxer Rebellion in China as an example), but these were faint and weak voices when one was sitting in a cathedral in London or at a missionary society conference in New York. It seemed like the best of times for the possible "evangelization of the world in our generation," but also the worst of times for growing a Christian empire. Overall, the assessment was that the greatest opportunities for Western Christianity were ahead and that the Great Century that was coming to a close was opening the door for an even greater century. What actually happened, no one predicted. Western Christian hope was hope misplaced.

2

Christian Lives

Practices and Piety

What is really at stake is the fashioning of an authentic Christianity in Nigeria which will also be authentically African. . . . The question some have been asking now is "does the transformed Methodist Church Nigeria still operate on [Western] symbols of Methodism?"

Mercy Amba Oduyoye,
The Wesleyan Presence in Nigeria, 1842–1962

Christianity from the beginning has been the story of individuals in communities living out the life of Christ in and for particular contexts. It is the story of everyday people placing their lives, hopes, and decisions in the light of Jesus Christ and the church. And so we now turn to examine some twentieth-century followers of Jesus, particularly those who have had a great impact on the shaping of Christianity across the globe. As we look at these influential leaders of the twentieth century, we realize that, as with the church through the ages, it is generally the life of a Saint Francis or the preaching of a Jerome or the passion of a Wilberforce for fighting evil that gives the icon-like quality of these Christians. Some will be influenced by carefully nuanced theological statements, but these statements and treatises must be incarnated in the lives of priests, missionaries, and lay leaders or they will stay on the shelves.

Our selection is fairly clear. First, we want to expose the reader to the diversity of Christian leaders who have been the major players. There have been men, women, Anglicans, Orthodox, Pentecostals, and, of course, Catholics and Presbyterians. At the same time, we have selected some of the most influential people *globally*. These women and men, both in their lives and in their writings, have had an influence beyond their particular church family or particular country. Some of the following people we find to be exemplary followers of Jesus Christ; others, less so. Thus we will narrate the lives and discuss how they have helped to shape Christianity across the continents and among the four families of Christianity in the twentieth century. The twentieth century produced an amazing array of Christian leaders, writers, missionaries, and martyrs. Here we will skim over the top to gather some of the richness of the period, continent by continent.

Africa

We start with one of the most important figures in the spiritual stream of Christianity, an African Christian prophet who has become emblematic of twentieth-century African Christianity, **Simon Kimbangu** (1889–1951). In the introduction we noted that one of the strongest characteristics of African Christianity from the late nineteenth century on has been the genesis and development of hundreds, even thousands, of Spiritual movements, led by local prophets and evangelists. There are more than eight thousand African Independent Churches (AICs) today, comprising more than thirty million Christians. There have been a number of important African prophets in the twentieth century, including Mojola Agbebi (1860?–1917), Moses Orimolade (1879–1933), and William Wade Harris (1865–1929). Kimbangu stands out among these and many other prophets for many reasons, which we will look at here.

Simon Kimbangu was born in the Congo Free State, in the same region where the first West African Christian king ruled (Alfonso I) and where other prophetic movements had begun centuries earlier (e.g., that begun by Kimpa Vita, or Dona Beatriz (Beatrice), in the eighteenth century).[1] Kimbangu was raised according to traditional religious customs and beliefs, but at the age of twenty-six he and his wife were converted and baptized as Baptists (1915). Three years later, in the midst of the terrible devastation of the flu pandemic,

---

1. See Irvin and Sunquist, *HWCM*, 2:215–17.

Kimbangu received a word from the Lord: "I am Christ. My servants are unfaithful. I have chosen you to bear witness before your brethren and to convert them."[2] Further, he was told to preach and to heal in the name of Jesus Christ.

Kimbangu fled from such responsibility and landed in the city of Léopoldville, where he tried to put the experience behind him. However, in April 1921, while visiting his home village of N'Kamba, he prayed for a sick woman, and she was immediately healed. Other healings followed, and soon N'Kamba became a place of pilgrimage as people came from far off to be healed by the Christian *ngunze* (healing prophet) and to respond to his preaching. Kimbangu preached a message of repentance from sins, the sacrifice of Jesus Christ, and removal of all fetishes, but unlike most other prophets, he spoke against both dancing and polygamy. He had been known also to speak in tongues and to have other ecstatic experiences expressed through shaking and receiving prophetic words.

Within only five months a mass movement started, N'Kamba was being called the New Jerusalem, and missionaries (especially Roman Catholic) were calling for the prophet's arrest. And so he was arrested. With only five months of public ministry, Kimbangu turned himself in to authorities, was given 120 lashes, and was taken off to a prison a thousand miles away for the rest of his life. Never has such a brief ministry had such a lasting impact. Kimbangu's church was the first independent church to start its own seminary and to join the World Council of Churches (WCC). Today the Kimbanguist church, Eglise de Jésus-Christ sur la Terre par le Prophete Simon Kimbangu (EJCSK: Church of Jesus Christ on Earth through the Prophet Simon Kimbangu) is the largest AIC and one of only four recognized churches in the Democratic Republic of Congo (the others being the Roman Catholic, Orthodox, and Church of Christ). Five months of ministry and thirty years of quiet, imprisoned holiness laid the foundation for this important church.

Another African, a white South African, raised the voice and place of Pentecostalism in the global church. **David du Plessis** (1905–87), known as "Mr. Pentecost," was born about the time of the Azusa Street Revival. His family was removed from the Dutch Reformed Church because of their acceptance of a type of Pentecostal theology: the "Latter Rain" of outpouring of the Holy Spirit in preparation for Jesus's return. Healing and speaking in tongues, according to this theology, came as signs of God's Spirit at work in the lives of individuals. Du Plessis's father came to the Pentecostal faith through preachers from John Alexander Dowie's church in Zion, Illinois. Dowie's missionaries established the churches that call themselves Zion Churches in South Africa.

2. Martin, *Kimbangu*, 44.

While a teenager, du Plessis had a Pentecostal conversion and was filled with the Holy Spirit. He was moved to seek such an experience by his observation that the black Africans had a vital and transformative faith, but the faith of many Westerners seemed lifeless. After the experience he was soon preaching, and then, in 1936, while serving as general secretary of the Apostolic Faith Mission, he met the famous English Pentecostal preacher Smith Wigglesworth. Wigglesworth prophesied that du Plessis would be an important leader in a coming worldwide ecumenical revival. This came true. In fact, du Plessis became one of the most traveled Christian leaders of the century, building bridges between Pentecostals and Roman Catholics as well as with non-Pentecostal Protestants.

Early in his ministry, du Plessis's attitude toward mainline Protestants and Roman Catholics typified the attitude of most Pentecostals: these other Christians, in his view, were incomplete at best and heretical at worst. Wigglesworth's prophecy opened his mind to consider building bridges, and then later his own Pentecostal experience confirmed this ministry. He records his debate with God about relating to non-Pentecostals:

> Lord, they're enemies.
>   Then love them.
> How can I love people that I don't agree with?
>   Forgive them.
> I can't justify them.
>   I never gave any child of mine authority to justify anyone. I gave you
>   full authority to forgive them. That's all you have.[3]

From the time of his ordination in 1930 until a chance meeting with President John Mackay of Princeton Theological Seminary in the early 1950s, du Plessis was a key leader, bringing greater unity to global Pentecostalism. He was one of the main organizers of the first Pentecostal World Conference, held in Zurich, Switzerland, in 1947. He also helped to organize the second meeting in Paris, in 1949. Du Plessis noted that in between those two meetings, Protestants gathered in Amsterdam to form the WCC. Pentecostals said the WCC was an instrument of the devil. This was the ecumenical climate that du Plessis stepped into. At their first meeting in Princeton, Mr. Pentecost and Mr. Ecumenical (as du Plessis called Mackay) quickly became close friends. This partnership and trust, along with a mutual concern for Christian unity, made it possible for du Plessis to attend every WCC assembly from the 1952 meeting of the International Missionary Council (IMC) in Willingen, Germany, until

---

3. Du Plessis, *Simple and Profound*, 120.

the Vancouver Assembly in 1983. His influence at ecumenical gatherings was winsome and trust building. At the 1952 meetings, he claims, he spoke to 110 of the 210 delegates. He shared with many of them, "I had a drink of water in 1916; I was baptized with fire in 1918; and I have been boiling over ever since."[4]

Soon afterward du Plessis began to build bridges with Roman Catholics. In 1961 he met Father Bernard Leeming at the New Delhi Assembly of the WCC. Leeming, a close friend of Pope John XXIII, opened the door for further dialogue within the Roman Catholic Church. Such discussions were costly. While he was developing greater trust and understanding with Protestants and Roman Catholics, du Plessis was losing that same trust with his Pentecostal friends. From 1962 to 1979 his ordination was revoked. Still, he pioneered in the Roman Catholic–Pentecostal dialogues from 1972 to 1982. Pentecostal churches and the related AICs owe their reception in the ecumenical church in large part to the ministry of David du Plessis.

African Christianity has very much been involved in political movements and social concerns in the twentieth century. In South Africa the policy of segregation known as apartheid provided the context for the most famous African Christian leader at the end of the twentieth century. **Archbishop Desmond Mpilo Tutu** (b. 1931) was raised in and remained devout in and committed to the church of his birth: Anglican. From within the colonial church Bishop Tutu's voice clearly opposed discrimination against and oppression of black Africans by Euro-Africans. Tutu was born in Klerksdorp, in the province of Transvaal, and became the first black African to be dean of a cathedral (St. Mary's, Johannesburg), first to become general secretary of the South African Council of Churches, and first to become a South African bishop, in 1976. Tutu consistently and clearly advocated peace with justice for his deeply divided land, and for all countries. In 1984 he was awarded the Nobel Peace Prize for his work for peace. Tutu, as Anglican bishop, challenged the government for its violence against blacks and at the same time decried the counterviolence of antiapartheid activists from certain factions in the African National Congress. Under international economic pressure, the South African government of F. W. de Klerk dismantled the apartheid order and paved the way for open and democratic elections, which left the country in need of much healing. The Truth and Reconciliation Commission (TRC) was formed to give the country time to deal with the violent and unjust past without falling into patterns of revenge and other new forms of violence. Archbishop Tutu was selected to head up the commission, and, in a very gutsy move, he chose a white clergyman, Piet Miering, to assist on the TRC. The commission listened to truth telling regarding

4. Quoted in Menzies and Ma, *Spirit and Spirituality*, 4:279.

events that occurred as early as 1960, the year when sixty-nine black Africans were shot in the black township of Sharpeville; most were shot in the back by South African police. By 1998, when Tutu stepped down as chair of the TRC, the commission had heard about twenty thousand testimonials and received four thousand applications for amnesty. It was an explicitly Christian process of forgiveness and justice but was carried out in an interreligious context. As Tutu said at the beginning of the process,

> I hope that the work of the commission, by opening wounds to cleanse them, will thereby stop them from festering. . . . We cannot be facile and say bygones will be bygones, because they will not be bygones and will return to haunt us. True reconciliation is never cheap, for it is based on forgiveness, which is costly. Forgiveness in turn depends on repentance, which has to be based on an acknowledgement of what was done wrong, and therefore on disclosure of the truth. You cannot forgive what you do not know.[5]

When his part was over, he wrote in the introduction to the TRC report,

> We have been privileged to help to heal a wounded people, though we ourselves have been, in Henri Nouwen's profound and felicitous phrase, 'wounded healers.' When we look around us at some of the conflict areas of the world, it becomes increasingly clear that there is not much of a future for them without forgiveness, without reconciliation. God has blessed us richly so that we might be a blessing to others.[6]

It is a great irony that one of the greatest peace activists of the twentieth century should have grown up in an environment of such great violence and oppression.

Africa has produced great Christian leaders in the twentieth century, both men and women. Some of the earliest women leaders in Africa have been prophetesses who have founded church movements outside of missionary Christianity. In addition to Dona Beatriz, other women prophets have arisen from the Roman Catholic Church. The Legion of Mary, or Maria Legio, was founded in Kenya in 1963, and one of the first leaders was Gaudensia Aoko. Aoko's first two children died on the same day, and so she renounced all sorcery, joined the Maria Legio, and in two years founded her own movement because

5. This was a response given by Bishop Tutu when he was appointed chairperson of the Truth and Reconciliation Commission, Nov. 30, 1995. Quoted here from Lewis, *A Church for the Future*, 72.

6. Truth and Reconciliation Commission of South Africa Report (March 2003). Available at http://www.justice.gov.za/trc/report/finalreport/vol6.pdf.

Figure 4. Archbishop Desmond Tutu at a December 2009 press conference following the Ecumenical Celebration for Creation Service at Copenhagen Cathedral

she found that the role of women was becoming too restricted. About the same time another woman, Mama Maria, believed to be a black reincarnation of the Virgin Mary, started a movement among the Luos of Kenya, a movement that spread quickly and became multiethnic and international.

Women prophets and spiritual leaders of the twentieth century arose from outside Roman Catholicism as well. Coming out of the Harrist movement in West Africa, Mary Lalou, a childless woman, founded the Deima Church after she experienced dreams and visions instructing her to preach. Grace Tani founded the Church of the Twelve Apostles in 1918, sharing the leadership with a man, Kwesi John Nackabah. Throughout Africa there have been many women leaders, but only in the latter half of the twentieth century did the first women rise up who would have a global impact on Christianity. One of the first was the Methodist **Mercy Amba Oduyoye** (b. 1934). Oduyoye has contributed to Christianity in several ways. First, as a scholar she has contributed to books that have both explored traditional Christian themes and applied theological issues to the African and broader women's contexts. One of her main themes is the dialogue between Christian theology and cultural hermeneutics. Her books—such as *Hearing and Knowing: Theological Reflections on Africa*, *Daughters of Anowa: African Women and Patriarchy*, and *Introducing African Women's Theology*—show how she constructs these issues.

Second, she has been both a leader and a pioneer in the ecumenical movement beyond Africa. In 1978, Oduyoye and seven other African women attended the WCC-sponsored Consultation of Women Theological Students,
held in Cartigny, Switzerland. It was at this meeting that women from outside
the North Atlantic region began to come together and that at the same time
Oduyoye began to provide leadership for that movement. The women at this
important meeting noted that most theological education was not relevant
for women, and the African participants,

> pleased to discover one another, . . . determined that, once back in Africa they
> would look for the other women in Africa studying theology and bring as many
> as possible together in a consultation of African Women in Theology . . . to find
> out just what women theologians are doing in Africa, to question the meaning
> of ministry and women's part in it, to look critically at theological education
> in Africa, to encourage women to become more active in the emerging theolo-
> gies and to discover how the church can be more responsive to the issues and
> needs of women.[7]

Oduyoye did follow through on this, and as a result she became one of the
most respected leaders, representing women's issues at ecumenical gatherings.
By 1987 she moved to Switzerland and became the deputy general secretary
of the WCC, a position that brought her into contact with Christian women
leaders throughout the world. In 1989, during the WCC's Ecumenical Decade
of Churches in Solidarity with Women (1988–98), she founded the Circle of
Concerned African Women Theologians ("Circle").

This brings us to the third great contribution of Mercy Oduyoye: recruiting
and empowering women in the global church. Oduyoye's commitment from
the Cartigny meeting became a lifelong effort. She continued to seek out other
women in Africa, and in 1980 she helped to organize the first conference of
African Women Theologians in Ibadan, Nigeria. She founded the "Circle" in
Ibadan as well (the organization is now headquartered in Pietermaritzburg,
South Africa), and later she founded the Talitha Cumi[8] Centre (Institute of
African Women in Religion and Culture) at Trinity Theological Seminary in
Accra. Through these organizations many African women have been brought
together in consultations on women's issues, many women have been able to
do graduate study in theology, books and articles have been published, and
many initiatives for women have been spawned throughout Africa. As a result
of the work of Oduyoye and many other women whom she has worked with,

7. Scott and Wood, *We Listened Long*, 45.
8. A reference to Mark 5:41.

women's voices are being heard in Africa, voices that must be heard in the midst of ongoing poverty, violence against women, and the continuing crisis of infectious diseases.

Asia

Although Jesus Christ was born and lived out his life in a small section of West Asia, influential Christian leaders in Asia—leaders whose voices were heard around the world—began to develop only in the twentieth century. It was in South Asia that a number of theologians began to speak out in voices that challenged the global church. We think of the sound leadership of Bishop V. S. Azariah (1874–1945) in developing the Anglican Church in South India and in starting an indigenous missionary movement. Later in India, ecumenical leaders such as D. P. Devanandan (1901–62) brought serious study of Hinduism into the discussion of the Christian responsibility of nation building. From Ceylon (Sri Lanka) the famous ecumenist D. T. Niles (1908–70) provided leadership in the WCC and was one of the founding members of the regional ecumenical body, the East Asia Christian Conference (later the Christian Conference of Asia). Like Devanandan, Niles used local religious concepts (in his case Buddhism was more important) to develop a Christian vocabulary and theology for Asia. Niles, however, was more interested in developing a responsible apologetic and missiology for Asia and less interested in the nation building of Indian theologians.

A number of Asian theologians began to have a global impact from China, Korea, and Japan as well. We think of Zhao Zhensheng (1894–1968), the first Chinese Roman Catholic bishop in China; T. C. Chao (Zhao Zichen, 1888–1979), Chinese Protestant theologian and ecumenical leader; and Han Wenzao (1923–2006), an important church leader during the early days of the People's Republic of China and cofounder of the Amity Foundation, which had printed more than thirty million Bibles by the time of his death. Korean church leaders shepherded the Korean church through the days of oppression under the Japanese and then through the partition of the country and the exodus of people from the north.

Here we will look at a representative sample of Christian leaders from Asia: first South Asian leaders, then East Asian. The leader we start with was not a Christian, but he had a great impact globally on Christian theology, justice, and peacemaking until today: Mahatma Gandhi.

Mohandas Karamchand Gandhi (1869–1948) came from a fairly humble Vaisya (third-level caste) family. His experiences in England (where he studied law) and in South Africa (where he experienced racial discrimination) formed his theology and his concept of passive resistance. In London he faced the challenge of adhering to a vow he made in India (to eat only vegetarian meals), and he was also encouraged to study his own religious background. The exposure to Christianity began to raise religious issues in his own life. Although he would never convert to Christianity, he greatly admired Jesus Christ, and his followers often followed him to prison while reading the Sermon on the Mount. So much of his life conformed to the teachings of Jesus that he was asked on more than one occasion if he was a Christian. "The missionaries come to India thinking that they come to a land of heathen, of idolaters, of men who do not know God. My own experiences all over India have been on the contrary. An average Indian is as much a seeker after truth as the Christian missionaries are, possibly more so."[9]

For Gandhi, being a seeker after truth was more important than being a part of any one religion or religious community. After his experiences in the United Kingdom, and then later as a lawyer in South Africa, he worked to reconcile all religions.

His experiences in England were wide ranging. He encountered the Theosophists and also met Cardinal Manning and the great Baptist preacher Charles Spurgeon. He returned briefly to India, but once again did not find success in his home country, so he responded to an opportunity in South Africa. In South Africa he was confronted further with a form of Christian exclusivism, this time racism, when he was denied entrance into a white church. As a non-white Indian, he experienced much discrimination in South Africa. He began to organize the Indians in South Africa to seek the right to vote. Although they did not win that right, the Indians became organized as an important political force through his leadership. When he returned to India, British rule was tightening its grip on Indians by increasing taxes. Gandhi organized poor farmers and laborers, supported greater rights for women, began boycotts against imported goods, and raised the issue of *swardj*, or independence for all of India. One of his most famous instances of passive resistance (*satyagraha*) was his 1930 Salt March of 400 kilometers (almost 250 miles). This *satyagraha* was supported by thousands of Indians who marched to the sea to make their own salt rather than buy from the British. Approximately sixty thousand people were imprisoned, many taking their New Testaments with them on the way.

9. This quotation was first identified as coming from the great ambassador for Hinduism, Swami Vivekananda. See Bhide, *Swami Vivekananda in America* (electronic book; no page numbers). Gandhi said this in a lecture he gave to missionaries in 1925. It can be found in many places. See Ellsberg, "Address to Missionaries," in *Gandhi on Christianity*, 33–37.

Gandhi opposed violence of any kind and therefore spoke against the British for the mistreatment of Indians, but he also spoke against Indian radicals who responded to violence with violence. One of his best friends through the struggles for independence was the Anglican priest, missionary, and scholar Charles Freer Andrews (1871–1940). Andrews was a dialogue partner in most of the social work in which Gandhi participated. He was sent on behalf of the Anglican Church to help the Indians in South Africa and was also sent to investigate the treatment of Indian laborers in Fiji. He developed deep respect for Gandhi's understanding of the Hindu concept of *ahimsa* (nonviolence), a concept he viewed as very close to Jesus's teaching that the peacemakers will be blessed. Gandhi was clear that violence must be met with love. "An eye for an eye makes the whole world blind," he would say. Influenced by Buddhist, Hindu, Jain, Islamic, and Christian teachings, Gandhi brought his concepts of *ahimsa* and *satyagraha* back into Christian movements such as the struggle against apartheid in South Africa and the civil rights movement led by Rev. Martin Luther King Jr. in the United States.

Another very influential Indian who opposed much of Western civilization but embraced Jesus was the mystical Christian guru **Sadhu Sundar Singh** (1889–1929?). He was raised in the Punjab region of British India by a devout Sikh father and a Hindu mother, who prayed that her son would become a guru, a holy man. Sundar Singh was a very bright and devout young man who was reported to have memorized the *Bhagavadgita* by the time he was seven years old. In addition he read much of the Qur'an and was familiar with the *Vedas* before he was a teenager. Attendance at a Christian mission school, the death of his mother, and his own violence against the Christian holy book weighed heavily on Sundar Singh in 1904. As he described it, he was suicidal, but a bright image of Jesus Christ in his room one dark morning confronted him and changed his life: "Why do you persecute me? See I have died on the cross for you and for the whole world." The transformation was sudden and thorough. After he was baptized the next year, he would forever remain a holy man, a Christian *sadhu*. Wearing a saffron robe and a turban, but without sandals, Sundar Singh traveled around India, and especially the Himalayas, preaching the gospel in the most difficult of regions. He became known as the "apostle of the bleeding feet." It is reported that he made about twenty trips to Tibet, where it was illegal to preach about Christianity.

By the end of the first decade of the twentieth century, Sundar Singh had become world famous for his austere and radical following of the teachings of Jesus Christ. Before he mysteriously disappeared in the Himalayas in 1929, he had traveled to Britain, the United States, Burma, Ceylon, Australia, and Malaya. Both his lifestyle and his writings have contributed to Sundar Singh's ongoing influence. He lived according to the life of Jesus, with no home and no job, driven by the concern to tell all about Jesus Christ. His writings are both mystical and proverbial. His long periods of fasting, imitating Jesus's forty days of fasting in the wilderness, gave Sundar Singh greater insights but also raised the spiritual over the physical and social. He lived on the edge of death and preached resurrection of the dead. Even his death, somewhere in the mountains of Tibet, is a mystery.

The third person who shaped global Christianity from India was neither a man nor an Indian. **Agnes Gonxha Bojaxhiu** (1910–97), better known as **Mother Teresa**, was born to Albanian parents in Skopje, Macedonia. From her earliest years she had a very special calling from God to be his light in the darkest of places on earth. She besought the church to let her respond to a call from Jesus Christ, as she describes it, to start a religious order for women, "who would be [Jesus's] fire of love amongst the very poor—the sick—the dying—the little street children."[10] Her persistence paid off, and in 1950 she received permission from the Vatican to start a new order in Calcutta. She founded the Missionaries of Charity, an order dedicated to minister to the most needy and the dying. Teresa was very clear that this was not a work she chose, but it was a work that she was called to do. "The voice kept pleading, 'come, come carry me into the holes of the poor. Come, be My light.'" Her first sisters were thirteen in number, and they began their work in a former Hindu temple in Calcutta. Today what started as a small group of Indian sisters (and also the related order of brothers) has grown to a movement of more than four thousand in approximately one hundred countries. Mother Teresa's consistent prolife approach led her to intervene on behalf of the starving, the imprisoned, and the unborn. Before her death she had received the highest awards of recognition in her adopted country, India, as well as the Pacem in Terris Award from the Roman Catholic Church and, in 1979, the Nobel Peace Prize. In 2003 she was beatified.

Mother Teresa is significant because in this one very small, frail woman were held together some of the best of medieval mystical piety, Christian activism for the most needy, and political activism for the unborn and the dying. Her name and her image are among the most popular of all Christian figures in the twentieth century. In India she was awarded a state funeral, and her funeral was broadcast around the world. India has produced many holy men and a few holy women; Mother Teresa will be among the most remembered. The power of her influence will only be increased by the revelation that after she had clear words and visions from Jesus Christ, and after her

10. All quotations are taken from Kolodiejchuk, *Mother Teresa*.

Evert Odekerken/Wikimedia Commons

Figure 5. Mother Teresa

work was begun, she led a life of faithful ministry during which fellowship with Christ was gone. In fact, for forty-nine years she felt nothing anymore of God's presence, and yet she continued, driven forward by the voice and vision of 1946. She recorded at a retreat in 1959, "Before there was so much love and real tenderness for the Sisters and the people—now I feel my heart is made of stone." Much later, in 1985, she confessed to a Jesuit priest, "Father, I do realize that when I open my mouth to speak to the sisters and to people about God and God's work, it brings them light, joy, and courage. But I get nothing of it. Inside it is all dark and feeling that I am totally cut off from God." This small Albanian woman, an Indian saint, will cast a very long shadow that will reach out into the future; it will provide shade for the exposed and suffering, but it will also be a shadow of the absence of God, in the midst of obedience.

Whereas Gandhi was devoted to political action through passive means, and Sundar Singh was devoted to spiritual transformation through self-denial, and Mother Teresa was devoted to quenching the thirst of Christ through serving the poorest of the poor, the great ecumenical leader **M. M. (Madathilparampil Mammen) Thomas** (1916–96) was devoted to ecumenical Christian participation in nation building. Thomas, raised a Christian in South India, studied the teachings of Gandhi and sought also to relate Christian teachings to Marxism. Like many in the ecumenical movement, Thomas became involved in global church leadership through the student movement of the World Student Christian Federation (WSCF). His experience with the international youth movement prepared him for his participation in the preparatory discussion on "the church and the disorder of society," for the first meeting of the WCC in Amsterdam (1948).

He was the only non-Western participant in these preparatory meetings. Always a layman and a self-taught scholar, M. M. Thomas read widely in the areas of theology, Bible, social ethics, and church unity. Two of his great contributions to Indian Christianity were his cofounding (with D. P. Devanandan) of the Christian Institute for the Study of Religion and Society in Bangalore and his series of twenty Bible studies written in his native Malayalam language. As with Sundar Singh, Thomas was interested in being fully Indian as a Christian. This meant something very different for Thomas. He argued that Christians should welcome the Indian Renaissance, much of which was Hindu in belief, so that Indian Christians could have a uniquely Christian influence in society.

Figure 6. Professor Madathilparampil Mammen Thomas, World Council of Churches staff member photo, 1953

Indian Christians were not to withdraw from the world, as Sundar Singh had done, but should assume responsibility to point to the work of Christ wherever that is seen in the world. Thomas was one of the most influential theologians in the WCC during the 1960s and 1970s, even though he remained a layman.

We turn now to the Far East, to China, where a number of leaders arose whose ministry and writings continue to shape the global church. The Chinese Christian leader whose impact was felt globally, although only among Chinese speakers, was **John Sung** (Song Shangjie, 1901–44). Sung would become one of the greatest evangelists of the twentieth century, but since he ministered entirely in Chinese, and completely in China and Southeast Asia, few outside the region have heard of him.

Sung was born in a Christian home in Fujian Province, but during his remarkable period of studies in the United States, he began to stray from his purpose in studying: to train for the ministry in China. From 1920 to 1926 he completed bachelor's, master's, and PhD degrees in chemistry. He was offered jobs in Germany, but remembered his calling, and so he left for Union Theological Seminary in New York, arriving during Wu Yaozong's last year of study.[11]

11. Wu represents the Three-Self Patriotic Church as Sung represents the Chinese indigenous and revivalist church. The great irony is that these two leaders passed through the same halls of Union and became leaders in the two main streams of Chinese Christianity.

Sung wanted to complete the three years' study in one year, but he was sorely disappointed by the liberal theology of the professors. In late December 1926 he was deeply moved to repentance and tears by the preaching of a young female evangelist only fifteen years old, preaching in Harlem, calling for all the congregation to be baptized in the Holy Spirit. Sung returned to his dorm room a changed man. During the next month and a half he sought God through reading, tears, and prayers. He describes this as a period of weeping over his sins, pleading with God, and seeing visions of Jesus Christ.[12] The seminary administration, observing this dramatic conversion and evangelistic zeal, assumed he had developed a mental illness. Union president Henry Sloan Coffin had the future evangelist committed to an asylum, where he spent 197 days; Sung used this time to read through the Bible forty times, each time following a different theme. After his return to China, the Bible would be his only textbook, and he would retain a great distrust of Western theologians and missionaries.

Sung's significance, in terms of his ministry and his reputation, comes from his strong commitments to basic issues of Christian lifestyle and Christian teaching. He lived very simply, eating mostly rice, vegetables, and tea, with very little meat. He wore a simple white Chinese cotton outfit and prayed for hours every day for specific people he had met in his travels. Although he began his ministry by joining the Bethel Worldwide Evangelistic Band of Andrew Gih (Ji Zhiwen), by 1933 Sung was on his own, traveling not only in China but also to Chinese communities in the Philippines, Indonesia, Malaya, Singapore, Taiwan, and Thailand. In his travels he spoke clearly about repentance from sin and the need to reshape lives in conformity to that of Jesus Christ. His preaching was quite dramatic, more like the preaching of the evangelist Billy Sunday in the United States than like that of most preachers in China. He used props in his preaching—a coffin, a dirty robe, a clean gown—and he would walk back and forth across the front of the church or the auditorium. In each of the towns or cities where he would preach, he would form evangelistic bands, who were to study the Bible together, pray for the salvation of others, and then go out to evangelize their communities. Some of these bands continued to meet and minister for more than fifty years. Sung had no concern for denominations, and so he would accept invitations to preach at Presbyterian, Methodist, or independent churches. He briefly worked with Watchman Nee, and Sung's funeral was conducted by Wang Mingdao. Sung preached in many large denominational churches throughout Southeast Asia. It is hard to estimate the number of people converted under his ministry, but it is thought

---

12. His son, Levi, has translated a single volume of excerpts from more than thirty volumes of personal diaries. See Sung, *Journal Once Lost*.

that by 1936 more than one hundred thousand had been converted. This was before his major overseas work, which began in 1935. Sung represents a very strong stream of Chinese Christianity that has a Confucian concern for right behavior, a Chinese concern for independence from the West, and a "Bible only" approach to theology.

One of the best-known Chinese Christians in the West is probably **Watchman Nee** (Ni To-sheng, 1903–72). Nee and his mother were converted under the preaching of the famous female Chinese Methodist evangelist Dora Yu in 1920 and immediately he began to write. Nee says that his calling to Christ was a call to serve Christ. And yet in China at that time many, if not most, of the Chinese pastors were still employed by foreign missions. Nee would have none of that, for he did not want to be beholden to foreigners. Nee's early career was one of failure in preaching to his classmates and to his neighborhood. His failures, lessons he learned after that from a few single women missionaries, and then his deepening prayer for others are important themes in his life. Nee began to fashion a Chinese Christian movement that was deeply personal and that, though it would benefit from European and American Christianity (especially the Keswick movement's spirituality), would in the end look more Confucian than Anglo-Christian.[13] Nee was trained in the Chinese classics through junior high and then at an Anglican high school. He also attended Dora Yu's gospel school.

Nee began his literature ministry in 1923, at the age of twenty, editing some of the earliest Chinese Christian periodicals, first *Revival* and then later *The Christian*. His first major book, *The Spiritual Man*, was published when he was twenty-five. He would publish more than sixty books, and all would be translated into English. In 1927 in Shanghai he founded the Local Church (often called the Little Flock). This independent-thinking man soon became one of the main leaders in the Chinese indigenous church movement that took place in the late 1910s through the 1920s and 1930s.

Other indigenous churches that were founded at about this time were Wang Mingdao's Christian Tabernacle (1924) in Beijing and Jing Dianying's communal Christian movement called the Jesus Family (1927) in Shandong. Chinese Christians were reacting against European and North American Christian imperialism, and what they saw was Chinese Christian leaders who were too much a part of Western liberal theology. Nee, Sung, Wang Mingdao,

---

13. Keswick was an annual holiness convention in Keswick, England, focused on the "higher Christian life." It began in 1875 and through the decades greatly influenced evangelicalism and inspired holiness movements in the United Kingdom, the Continent, the United States and in various mission fields. See Bundy, "Keswick Higher Life Movement" in Burgess, *Dictionary of Pentecostal and Charismatic Movements*, 820–21.

and other Chinese Christians spoke against what they saw as the theological compromises of Christians such as Wu Yaozong (Y. T. Wu), graduate of Union Theological Seminary in New York and the first chairman of the Three-Self Patriotic Movement (TSPM).

For Nee, resisting Western theology and money was only part of his concern. He chose to develop a particular Chinese theology and at the same time chose a particular path toward Christian unity. The church divisions that were brought to China and propagated there by missionaries, Nee believed, were opposed to biblical teaching. There should be only one church in each geographic area: "the Local Church," he called it. His ideas were widely spread by his disciples, some of whom, like Witness Lee, traveled overseas. Nee chose to return from Hong Kong to lead his flock even after his church was threatened by the new Communist order. "If the house is crashing down, I have children inside and must support it, if need be with my head."[14] In 1952 he returned and was arrested, and he spent his last twenty years in prison. By 1949 his churches numbered more than seven hundred, and his members more than seventy thousand. His loyalty to his flock, his writings, his deep spiritual cultivation, and finally his suffering have made him a very influential Christian leader globally. Most of Watchman Nee's churches did not join the TSPM and became, and continue to be to the present day, one of the major streams of the underground church movement in China.

In contrast to these Chinese evangelists and spiritual leaders are those Chinese Christians who accepted Western theological thought and political theory and developed theology and church leadership more publicly. We have mentioned Wu Yaozong, who helped to guide the Chinese Church into a public and accepted place in the new China of Mao Zedong. Equally significant for the future of Chinese Christianity was the leadership of Bishop Ding Guangxun, better known as **K. H. Ting** (1915–2012). Ting was educated in the cosmopolitan city of Shanghai at the Anglican St. John's University, where he met many of the future leaders of the Chinese church. Ting, like many ecumenical leaders, came up through the student movement (in his case the YMCA) and then served in Canada as a mission secretary for the Student Christian Movement (SCM). He also studied at Union Theological Seminary in New York City and then worked with the WSCF in Geneva before returning to China. These international contacts and his international experience greatly influenced his later leadership. From his earliest days in Canada (1946) he was challenging students to think of the implications of the gospel for society. His country

---

14. Bob Laurent, *Watchman Nee: Sufferer for China*, 175. Originally in Angus I. Kinnear, *Against the Tide: The Story of Watchman Nee*, 145.

was going through a great upheaval in the twentieth century, and it was important to think of the place and contribution of the church. Ting and many members of the SCM in China gave a clear prophetic call to the United States: "Washington war-mongers and American finance-imperialist adventurers are still stubbornly credulous of the possibility of successful intervention on the side of the reactionary forces of China."[15] Ting personally, but not publicly, supported the Anglo-Catholic Marxists.

Ting returned to China in 1951 at the encouragement of friends, one year before Watchman Nee returned in spite of his friends. Ting would become the head of the government-recognized China Christian Council (CCC), and Nee would be imprisoned. It is not our responsibility here to make judgments, but we should briefly note that the work of the CCC made it possible for churches to reopen after the death of Mao and for Bibles to be published and seminaries to reopen. Those Christian churches that refused to register in the 1950s continued to worship underground (illegally), and it was later discovered that Christianity had exploded through their ongoing ministry. Ting became the most important interpreter of Chinese Christianity to the world during the 1970s. Even as the principal of Nanjing Union Theological Seminary, he lost his positions with the church during the Cultural Revolution. However, his disfavor with the government was brief, and he returned to represent the church to the world in the early 1970s. Until his retirement from work with the CCC and TSPM in 1996, Ting was more of a political theologian, thinking and writing about how the church can exist and participate in society. He did this during some of the most tumultuous years of modern Chinese history. He was the Chinese Christian leader who helped to reintroduce the Chinese church to the world at the WCC's 1991 Canberra meeting and who argued for greater religious freedom while a member of the National People's Congress and at the Chinese People's Political Consultative Conference.

Ting's positions were strongly criticized by many Christians overseas and by Chinese Christians who suffered during the first three decades of Communism. What cannot be argued, however, is the great impact he has had on Chinese Christianity and, globally, on how Christian theologians think about Christian life in society. As early as 1946 he prophetically realized the weakness of Western Christendom. In a 1947 report to the SCM on his time in Canada, he commented that Canadian students no longer had the confidence to go out and evangelize the world: "[This was] not a bad sign at all [because] many students feel that their efforts to evangelize the world are constantly driving them back to re-evangelize themselves because they sometimes feel

---

15. Wickeri, *Reconstructing Christianity*, 63.

Figure 7. K. H. Ting and other participants gathered together for the World Council of Churches Meeting of the Central Committee, Galyateto, Hungary, July 28–August 5, 1956.

that they have been pretty well de-evangelized."[16] The churches of Europe and North America began to confront this issue in theological writings thirty years later—in the 1980s—and continue to do so today.

In Japan, a Christian who brought together many of the spiritual concerns of a John Sung or Mother Teresa with a political engagement of a K. H. Ting was the theologian, writer, and activist **Kagawa Toyohiko** (1886–1960). Kagawa attended the newly formed Presbyterian seminary in Kobe, Japan, and while a student there moved into the slum district (Shinkawa) to minister to the poor. Later he would begin a labor movement in this same district. From 1914 to 1916 he studied at Princeton Theological Seminary, where he developed lifelong Christian friends and learned about Christian social responsibility during the height of the social gospel movement. Kagawa returned to his home country with greater conviction than ever that Christianity must convert the soul to active love.

> The religion Jesus taught is a religion of life. People who are fully alive, people who are living strongly, can understand it; but those who deny life, who do not want to live, cannot get its meaning. The God of Jesus is a God of Action. People who stay at home and read their Bibles and pray and meditate, and do

16. Ibid., 69.

nothing for the poor who beg help before their very doors—such people will find the God of Jesus unintelligible. His God is One who is naturally reflected in a man's heart when he has saved even one suffering human being, or lifted up one who has been oppressed. The loveless do not know God. Only when a man has plunged into the blindly struggling crowd and tried to save them from their sins and failures, can he know this God. Only through the active movement of love will he intuitively come to know the God of Action.[17]

Kagawa, like Mother Teresa, made no distinction between saving from sin and saving from oppression and sufferings in this world. He would not tolerate oppressive conditions and unnecessary sufferings. He helped to organize farm cooperatives and labor unions, and he struggled for women's suffrage with the same zeal that he preached Jesus to any who would listen. It is hard to imagine how this social activist had time to write, but in addition to his outspoken criticism of Japanese aggression and the oppression of labor, he wrote 150 books, many of which are still in print in English translations today. He was imprisoned for his opposition to the war effort and also appealed to the United States to refrain from war. Kagawa was a well-respected—though, like Ting, an often misunderstood—leader who took the Christian message into the political sphere. His participation in the 1938 IMC meeting in Tambaram (Madras), India, not only reintroduced him to Christians from America but also introduced him to Chinese Christians—Christians from the very country his country was invading. His life and teachings during the war leave him open to much criticism, but all of his actions need to be placed in the light of his passion for both Jesus and Japan.

Latin America

As we turn to Latin America, we note two important issues, one that shows continuity with many of the great Asian Christian leaders, and one that is a departure. As with Kagawa or Ting, political considerations loom very large in the theological writings of Latin American Christian leaders, especially in the latter half of the twentieth century. Unjust structures that developed under colonialism became important issues to this new generation of indigenous Christian leaders. Few of the great Latin American Christian leaders, those who are having a global impact, are Protestant. Almost all of the great leadership that has had an impact beyond Latin America has been from Roman Catholic theologians, most of them men. The voices of a few women leaders

---

17. From Kagawa, *Religion of Jesus*, 19–20.

have been heard beyond the region, women like Mexican-born Methodist theologian Elsa Tamez, but again, women theologians in Latin America were only beginning to be heard in the twentieth century.

One of the most significant theological voices from Latin America in the twentieth century was that of the Brazilian archbishop of Olinda and Recife, **Dom Hélder Pêssoa Câmara** (1909–99). Dom Hélder was born in Fortaleza in the northeast region of Brazil, and by age twenty-two he was ordained a priest. Bright and politically aware from his early years, he first became politically active by joining the Integralistas, a quasi-fascist group that opposed Communism. He later turned against this group and, influenced by the writings of the French Catholic philosopher Jacques Maritain, turned to a more socialist critique of politics. Maritain was one of the main theologians who influenced a whole generation of liberation theologians in Latin America. The church transferred Dom Hélder to Rio de Janeiro, the national capital, in the 1930s, and it was here that he began to develop his commitment to Catholic action on behalf of the poor and his organization of the laity in local communities. In time this work with laity would develop into grassroots groups called *communidades ecclesiais de base* (CEBs, "basic ecclesial communities").

Dom Hélder may have shifted from fascist to liberationist model in his analysis, but he was consistently concerned to provide leadership and answers for the poor. In 1952, with the encouragement of the Vatican, he founded the National Conference of Brazilian Bishops, and in 1955 he helped to found the Latin American Episcopal Council (CELAM). In each of these organizations, local leadership initiative meant that local issues would be confronted in context. His concern for the poor in all matters earned him the title "Bishop of the Favelas" (squatter settlements). Political tensions that developed with the 1964 military overthrow of President João Goulart led to the timely transfer of Dom Hélder to Olinda and Recife. He brought his commitment to the poor with him as he participated in the Second Vatican Council (1962–65). At the council he promoted the idea of the "church of the poor," not just the church for the poor, and he continued this line of thought in the 1968 CELAM meeting in Medellín, Colombia. The Medellín meeting was very important for promoting liberation theology, denouncing institutional violence (both from local governments and foreign governments), and promoting CEBs. These CEBs became an important element in applying biblical teachings to the laity, and in helping local communities organize to solve local community problems. Although Dom Hélder promoted nonviolence, he and his followers were denounced as Communists, and a number of his followers were threatened and attacked by government death squads.

Figure 8. Dom Hélder Pêssoa Câmara (1981)

Later in life he continued to be a "voice to the voiceless," even though his political activism abated. He had given away church land to the homeless and established credit unions for the poor to help them establish their own businesses. He was always aware that the gospel required both critical words against injustice and constructive work with the dispossessed. In a 1972 speech titled "Mansi Tese" (Outstretched Hands), delivered to youth who were completing a march for the poor in Italy, he identified the evils inherent in the first (capitalist), second (socialist), and third (developing) worlds. Although the speech is dated, he clearly saw that the issue for the Christian was to "demand justice as a condition for peace." His denunciation of gross consumerism and the power that multinational corporations wield over the poor was clear and enduring. Dom Hélder's ongoing influence owes much to the clear and poetic imagery in his writing. In writing about personal identity and consumerism, he wrote the poem "Do You Want to Be?," which describes the emptiness we try to fill with material excess, leaving no room for ourselves or for God.

Dom Hélder spoke out against the violence and was fortunate enough to escape that violence himself. Many Catholics who stood up to speak about the violence and the arms importation were not as fortunate as he was. In the last quarter of the twentieth century, governments in Central America identified religious workers as enemies of the state. Not only were these workers speaking out directly against killing squads and in support of relatives who were abducted and killed by the army, but they were also involved in educating the poor and the indigenous populations, giving them the power to organize and to prevent ongoing oppression. Latin America, and especially Central America, had become a point of contest in the global cold war. In the Americas there was nothing cold about this war.

One of the most notorious killings of the period was that of **Oscar Romero** (1917–80), archbishop of San Salvador. Like Dom Hélder, Romero did not start out with liberationist or even socialist ideas. In his early ministry as a priest he was critical of liberation theology as expressed by such Latin Americans as the Jesuit Jon Sobrino. However, Romero's mind was changed in 1975. Although he had been ordained in 1942, Romero had always been a trusted ally of the oligarchy or ruling elite. But in 1975, in his own diocese of Santiago de María, the national guard raided a village on the pretext of looking for concealed weapons, dragged out residents, and sliced them to pieces with machetes. Romero was in disbelief. He wrote the president of El Salvador, and then later he wrote US president Jimmy Carter to tell him to stop selling arms to El Salvador. The lack of response convinced him that it was true; his own government was slaughtering innocent and poor citizens in a supposed effort to control Communist influences.

Soon after, Romero was named archbishop in the capital city of San Salvador. Now, as an opponent of the government, having alienated the elite, he was the country's archbishop. Consistent with his identification with the poor of his country, he refused the bishop's palace and instead moved into a humble hospital for the poor. The bishop became one of the oppressed. Romero called for all churches to be places of sanctuary when the "death squads" came to villages to harass and kill people. The death squads responded by killing Jesuit priest Rutilio Grande, a good friend of Romero, and two parishioners, one a seven-year-old boy. When he had beheld the remains of his friends, Romero wept. Then he responded. Without government permission, he buried the slain, excommunicated those who committed the murders, closed all the churches in the city, and held a single service in the public square at which tens of thousands worshiped. In a context in which power was in the hands of a few, Romero gave power back to the people: "God needs the people themselves to save the world."[18] He had come to the

---

18. Romero, *A Shepherd's Diary*, 408.

conclusion that genuine liberation for the poor would not happen until the poor were their own masters. The poor must not simply wait for handouts from churches or governments, but they must be the protagonists in their own liberated future.

The theology of Vatican II was being extended to include a teaching that the church is not just the church of all the people, but is the church primarily of the poor. Romero was called to the Vatican during this time, and he returned with a simple message from the pope: "Courage." Romero knew that he was on the list of death squads, so he faced his future as a Christian. He spoke clearly: "Let my death, if it is accepted by God, be for my people's liberation and as a witness of home in the future. . . . A bishop will die, but God's church, which is the people, will never perish."[19] Between the homily and the celebration of the Eucharist on March 24, 1980, Archbishop Oscar Arnulfo Romero was assassinated by a shot through the heart. His blood was mingled with the host. The theme of his homily was Jesus's words, "Whoever would save his life will lose it, and whoever loses his life for my sake will find it."

A quarter of a million people attended his funeral, and the killing accelerated. Forty people were killed when a bomb exploded during his funeral, and during the next year nearly twelve thousand citizens were killed by the military and paramilitary forces. Many were dragged from their homes, were shot in their doorways, were decapitated, or simply disappeared.[20] Romero's death is as significant as his life. His tomb has become a place of remembrance and pilgrimage. Pope John Paul II visited his grave, honoring his life and his message. Even the Anglican Church has remembered him, erecting a statue of him among the twentieth-century martyrs in Westminster Abbey.

Romero's life and martyrdom have become a message of the gospel of liberation, but it has been **Gustavo Gutiérrez**, OP (b. 1928), who has most clearly articulated the theology of liberation. Gutiérrez was born a mestizo (mixed European and Native American) in Peru. He began his career studying medicine and psychology and later studied theology in Lyon and at the Gregorian University in Rome. As with most indigenous, or contextual, theologies, theology of liberation was expressed by people like Gutiérrez after it was the lived theology of the people in Latin America—lived, for instance, in CEBs. The important Bishops' Conference (CELAM) in Medellín in 1968 promoted CEBs in Latin America. These local communities of believers were specifically encouraged to offset the power of the "minority" (elite groups). From these ecclesial groups

19. Quoted in Brockman, *Romero: A Life*, 248.
20. As cited by the United Nations Refugee Agency website, at http://www.refworld.org /docid/3dee03944.html.

developed a theology and a practice of empowerment at the grass roots. In 1971 Gutiérrez published the first book explaining this theology of liberation that was developing throughout Latin America: *Teología de la liberación: Perspectivas*. Within two years it was published in English as *A Theology of Liberation*. One of the great contributions to all of theology is Gutiérrez's understanding of praxis as a requirement for theological reflection. Praxis is not mere practice, doing something. "In praxis, one not only does things but also does them out of a commitment to God's justice and with a critical perspective that moves naturally into reflection."[21] Therefore scholastic theology devoid of active participation in justice on behalf of the oppressed was misleading at best and was oppressive (a tool of the elite) at worst. As Gutiérrez said, "It is through encounters with the poor and the exploited that we shall encounter the Lord."[22] This type of active theology reveals God to us. Gutiérrez has become, along with Leonardo Boff (b. 1938), Jon Sobrino (b. 1938), and Juan Luis Segundo (1925–96), one of the most important proponents of liberation theology both as a theology and as a method of doing theology. We might say that liberation theology became the first major theology from outside the North Atlantic to challenge that theological establishment. This theological movement inspired other oppressed groups, both minorities (African Americans, Hispanics) and majorities (Koreans, Filipinos), to begin developing their own theologies with the same or similar assumptions: liberation is a primary

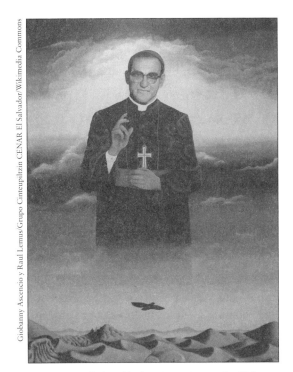

Giobanny Ascencio y Raul Lemus/Grupo Cinteupiltzin CENAR El Salvador/Wikimedia Commons

Figure 9. Mural of Archbishop Oscar Romero by Giobanny Ascencio y Raul Lemus

21. González and González, *Christianity in Latin America*, 255.
22. Gutiérrez, *Power of the Poor in History*, 33.

category of salvation, theology must begin with praxis, theology must critique not only individual sin but systems of sin that oppress, and there is a divine preferential option for the poor.

North America

North American Christians who had a global impact in the twentieth century are of two main types: those who expressed many of the concerns of liberation theology and its concern for the oppressed, and those who sought renewal of Christianity as it waned during the century. As we have seen, North Atlantic Christianity in the twentieth century confronted both violence and a rapid decline of membership. The Christian leaders we look at here express both concerns.

An American woman who took on many of the injustices of society was **Dorothy Day** (1897–1980), the founder of *The Catholic Worker*, a periodical on Catholic social teaching. Day was raised with little religious interest, but the birth of a daughter and the sense of gratitude she felt (when she thought herself sterile) led her to have the girl baptized and led her to join the church. Equally influential for her career on behalf of the poor and the homeless was her meeting Peter Maurin, who had formerly belonged to the Christian Brothers and who lived a life in the model of Saint Francis. Daniel Berrigan, SJ, commented, "Peter struck a match to her combustible heart. He offered her both a theory and a persuasive and patient example; a Christianity at once worldly, matter of fact, intensely personal; a method and a means."[23] Two earlier influences on Day's life came together in her discussions with Maurin: her earlier encounters with Roman Catholicism and her reading of Upton Sinclair's novel *The Jungle*. Day saw the Roman Catholic Church in the United States as the church of the immigrants, minorities, and the poor. She had a strong social conscience that had led her to protests and imprisonments, but now she developed a theology of advocacy, peace, and justice on behalf of the poor.

The Catholic Worker, from the very beginning of its publication in 1933, met a felt need for clear Catholic social teaching in a period of conflicting teachings and ideologies. The first issue was published on May 1, International Workers Day. By December, circulation had grown to more than one hundred thousand. Of central theological concern was that Christian hospitality knows no bounds. When asked how long we should be hospitable to the homeless

23. Introduction to Day, *Long Loneliness*, xvi.

or the indigent, Day responded, "We let them stay forever. They live with us, they die with us, and we give them a Christian burial. . . . Once they are taken in, they become a member of the family. . . . They are our brothers and sisters in Christ."[24] The movement shifted from encouraging individuals to have a Christ Room in their houses for the needy, to urban Catholic worker houses and rural farming communes.

Day and her colleague Maurin were thoroughgoing pacifists. Their pivotal text, as for many in the pacifist and civil rights movements of the twentieth century, was the Sermon on the Mount. During the Spanish Civil War, when many Catholics supported Franco as a defender of the faith, and during World War II and on through the cold war, Day lost many supporters. And yet her message increased in credibility and clarified her understanding of Catholic discipleship. "Our manifesto is the Sermon on the Mount," she said, referring to love of enemies. She then said, "We love our country. . . . We have been the only country in the world where men and women of all nations have taken refuge from oppression."[25] Near the end of her life Day's ministry was affirmed by the church when she received Communion from the hands of Pope Paul VI in 1967. Later she received a visit from Mother Teresa: Day was a lay American woman who came later in life to the Christian zeal for the poor, Teresa a religious Albanian woman with a lifelong passion of service to Christ. Both have left a lasting impression on the world Christian community.

Next we turn to the two most influential Christians from the United States in the twentieth century: two Baptist preachers from the South. When we think of an American who has left a worldwide lasting mark on the Christian community, few people would come to more minds than **Billy Graham** (b. 1918). Graham had preached to more than 210 million people in 185 countries by the mid-1990s. Through television, radio, and recordings he has preached to hundreds of millions more, more than any other person. And yet Graham's influence for Christianity is more than his personal preaching.

Graham was raised on a farm near Charlotte, North Carolina, and came from the fundamentalist stream of Southern Christianity. He studied at fundamentalist schools before transferring to Wheaton College, and then he was ordained as a Southern Baptist preacher at the age of twenty-one. His marriage to a Presbyterian missionary daughter, Ruth Bell, began to open him to the mainline denominational churches. His willingness to engage and work with non-fundamentalist churches would later cause many to pull away from

24. As quoted by Ashe, *The Feminization of the Church?*, 20.
25. From the *Catholic Worker*, January 1942, 1.4. The article can be found at the Dorothy Day Collection: http://dorothyday.catholicworker.org/articles/868.html.

his ministry. Graham briefly was a pastor before he found his calling as an evangelist, first with Youth for Christ, a newer mission organization designed to reach military personnel and youth. In his 1949 crusade meetings in Los Angeles, Graham first became the magnetic evangelist and preacher that he would continue to be for nearly sixty years. From this point on Graham established a style of crusade meetings in cities throughout the world where attendees could respond by coming forward and filling out response cards. At the end of each meeting the response cards were given to local churches to follow up with individuals who made decisions to follow Christ. Graham's ministry acted both to serve local churches and to unite them in evangelism. His was a mission not to build up *a* church, but to see churches in each community built up through his preaching.

Graham's message was heard not only at crusade meetings but also through his radio ministry, *Hour of Decision*; his syndicated newspaper column, "My Answer"; and his monthly magazine, *Decision*. His Billy Graham Association also sponsored Worldwide Pictures, which produced and distributed more than 125 movies. In addition, along with his father-in-law, Dr. Nelson Bell, and the Christian philanthropist Howard Pew, Graham helped found the periodical *Christianity Today* (1956) as an evangelical parallel to the *Christian Century*. In 1969 Graham, with Harold John Ockenga and Pew, founded Gordon-Conwell Theological Seminary.[26] The 1950s was a time of evangelical resurgence in North America, and Graham was leading the way, bringing together many from both mainline and fundamentalist backgrounds who were ready to engage the culture and proclaim a Christian message centered on Christ, preached cooperatively. On the global stage Graham was the confidant of presidents, found ways to preach in the Soviet-bloc countries, worked to open doors with North Korea (where his wife had attended school), and in his later years spoke up about issues of racism and poverty. His organization sponsored international conferences on evangelism at Berlin (1966) and Lausanne (1974), and sponsored conferences for itinerant evangelists (1983, 1986). Graham, more than any other single figure, brought together evangelical streams within global Christianity. His sense of his own calling he has repeated many times: "My one purpose in life is to help people find a personal relationship with God, which, I believe, comes through knowing Christ."[27]

26. Earlier Ockenga helped to found Fuller Theological Seminary as a school that would promote good scholarship, reach the world, and avoid some of the isolationism of fundamentalism. Graham gathered around himself scholars who carried out theological work that would support his broadening evangelistic message.
27. http://billygraham.org/about/biographies/.

Whereas Billy Graham has been blessed with an unusually long life, **Martin Luther King Jr.** (1929–68) had his life violently taken from him before he was forty years old, yet his influence has been deep and wide across the globe. His leadership in bringing about social change on behalf of African Americans and for the poor at large was through or because of his Christian convictions. King was reared by a Baptist pastor and was also the grandson of a Baptist pastor. Raised in Atlanta, Georgia, he experienced segregation all his life. His studies at the black school, Morehouse College, then at Crozer Theological Seminary, and his doctoral work at Boston University, brought him into contact with many of the most influential theologians of his age, both African American and Euro-American. One of those influential personalities was Howard Thurman (1900–1981), who had been a friend of King's father and who had recently published the very influential volume on Christianity and society titled *Jesus and the Disinherited* (1949). Thurman was the dean of the chapel at Boston University when King was doing his doctoral studies. Critical to Thurman's theological development, and very influential by transfer to King, was Thurman's 1935 trip to India to speak on behalf of the WSCF. In that trip he had time to talk to Gandhi, who inquired of Thurman about the plight of the oppressed African Americans in the United States. The universal sense of oppression, linked with the gospel imperative that must respond to that oppression, was seen as a global concern that demanded local response.

King's experience in graduate school along with his experience as pastor in Montgomery, Alabama, and in Atlanta directed his thoughts toward social change. It was during the 1955 Montgomery bus boycott (in which African Americans refused to ride the buses because they were forced to sit in the back) when King began to rise as a leader of the civil rights movement. In 1957 he was elected president of the newly formed Southern Christian Leadership Conference, whose primary goals were to dismantle segregation and support voter education and registration. Theologically King moved from a liberal theology of his college and seminary days to a synthesis of liberal and neo-orthodox beliefs, always in service to the dispossessed. Reading Reinhold Niebuhr helped him to think clearly about social problems: "I realized that liberalism had been all too sentimental concerning human nature and that it leaned toward a false idealism. I also came to see that the superficial optimism of liberalism concerning human nature overlooked the fact that reason is darkened by sin. The more I thought about human nature, the more I saw how our tragic inclination for sin encourages us to rationalize our actions."[28]

28. Quoted in Carson, "Martin Luther King, Jr.," 159–77. This is from King's 1960 essay for the *Christian Century* on "How My Mind Has Changed" (April 13, 1960), 439.

King's preaching had power and attractiveness because he gave a clear and winsome message of moral standards and ethical conduct rooted in the knowledge of God. "I'm here to say to you this morning that some things are right and some things are wrong. (*Yes*) Eternally so, absolutely so. It's wrong to hate. (*Yes, That's right.*) It always has been wrong and it always will be wrong! (*Amen*) It's wrong in America, it's wrong in Germany, it's wrong in Russia, it's wrong in China!"[29]

As the civil rights movement gained momentum, King was the premier preacher. His speeches were memorable, repeatable, and empowering, as the following speech illustrates.

> One hundred years later, the Negro is still not free. . . . In a sense I have come to the nation's capital to cash a check. . . . America has given the Negro children a bad check. . . . We refuse to believe that the bank of justice is bankrupt. . . . Let us not wallow in the valley of despair. . . . I have a dream. . . . I have a dream that my four little children will one day live in a nation where they will not be judged by the color of their skin, but by the content of their character.[30]

King expanded his calls for justice to include all of the poor, and his critique of racism began to include issues of economic structures and militarism. His language, critical of US foreign policy, including the war in Vietnam, lost him many supporters and gained the interest of the Federal Bureau of Investigation. On April 4, 1968, he was assassinated while in Memphis, Tennessee, speaking in support of the garbage workers. His last speech, delivered to garbage workers, hinted that he might not "finish the journey." He had seen the promised land, and he was aware that he "might not get there" with those he was addressing. Like Romero twelve years later, King knew that he was confronting, with a message of peace and justice, powers that were both unjust and violent. Also, like Romero's martyrdom, King's became a catalyst for social change. His birthday has become a national holiday in the United States, and he too is remembered as a twentieth-century martyr along with Romero at Westminster Abbey.

Born about the same time as King was another Christian reformer and activist. **Letty Russell** (1929–2007) was one of the first women ordained to the ministry in the United Presbyterian Church. Early in her ministry she served in East Harlem, New York. In her church and community ministry she responded to the particular needs of African American and Hispanic members of the

---

29. Carson et al., *The Papers of Martin Luther King Jr.*, 2:251–52.
30. From King's "I Have a Dream" speech, delivered during the March on Washington, August 28, 1963.

local community. As she described it, the early feminist theologians pioneered gender issues through the civil rights movement. Russell would become one of the most innovative and pioneering thinkers in a theology of liberation for women. She would become a strong advocate for women, but, more important for Christian theological development, she developed her theology within the church and through her study of Scripture. One of the most important concepts she developed was the biblical concept of shalom, which she applied to hospitality and justice as well as peace.

As early as 1969, when working in Harlem and at the same time working on her PhD at Union Theological Seminary in New York, Russell recognized that the end of Christendom meant the end of traditional theological education. Theological education and the church it was preparing leaders to serve in had to change. Russell believed ministry that had developed in the West, in a Christendom context, became less and less relevant as we moved into a postmodern world. The monolithic approach that was dominated by WASPs (white, Anglo-Saxon, Protestants) was out of touch with the true nature of the church's calling in service to the *oikoumene*. Russell was thinking, along with her husband, Hans Hoekendijk, about missionary structures for the church. The two served on the study project of the International Missionary Council (IMC) on "missionary structure of the local church," she representing the US group and he the European. This was the era of "the church for others,"[31] as the final report called it in its title, and the era when missiologists, turning to the world, said it is not the church that sets the agenda for the future, but the world that sets the agenda for the church. Russell applied this thinking both to her parish ministry and to her life of advocacy for justice, especially for women.

Russell is a bridge figure for twentieth-century Christianity. Her conscientization regarding the needs of the oppressed, much like the same turn toward the oppressed that Câmara and Romero had experienced, came from her parish work. She bridged European and North American ecumenical and missiological thinking, and she bridged—or, more exactly, expanded—the civil rights movement in her inclusion of women and support of African American women. Russell was a formative theologian, and her many writings, such as *Becoming Human* (1982) and *Church in the Round* (1993), helped to liberate women, but, more important, they addressed the whole church. In one of her last lectures, Russell expressed the primary concern she had always had for justice: "Our struggle is to overcome the fear of difference and to break the bars that keep us apart. [Others] want what we

31. World Council of Churches, *The Church for Others and The Church for the World*.

want. They want to work, they want to change the social structure. They want hospitality with justice."[32]

Europe

The Christians of influence from Europe produced writings and led initiatives that ignited breakthroughs in theology and church practice in both the Roman Catholic and Protestant churches. Let us begin with the earliest European, the Catholic pope who did more than any other person in the twentieth century to redirect the Roman Catholic Church to a new openness to the world. *Aggiornamento* was the word he used to express the desire to open the windows to let God's Spirit blow through the church. **Pope Saint John XXIII** (1881–1963) not only made it possible for the Roman Catholic Church to better adapt to the modern world but he also made it possible for local communities to develop theologies, music, and liturgies that spoke to the heart of the many cultures of the world. He called for the first all-church council in more than one hundred years. The Second Vatican Council created a remarkable new ecumenical climate that brought Orthodox and Protestants, and even Pentecostals, into dialogue. His bold leadership in calling for reform in the Roman Catholic Church, a reform that helped to bridge the separation between Catholics and Protestants as never before, was nothing if not remarkable. Although we would not call him a major theologian himself, his call for the return of the exiled theologians of the *nouvelle théologie* to help lead the Second Vatican Council redirected Roman Catholic theology and especially its missiology and ecclesiology like nothing since the Council of Trent.[33] Two of the exiled theologians, Yves Congar (1904–95) and Henri de Lubac (1896–1991), were chosen to work on the preparatory commission for the council. When the council had completed its work, Congar was acclaimed as "*the* Theologian of Vatican II par excellence."[34] Thus John XXIII, in his choice of theologians to help guide Vatican II, was arguably the most influential pope of the twentieth century.

32. This was presented at the Paul Tillich lectures at Harvard University (May 2006) and was one of her last lectures. This can be found at the Harvard University Gazette website: http://news.harvard.edu/gazette/2006/05.11/09-other.html.

33. It could be argued that it was the greatest change in ecclesiology and missiology since the Fourth Lateran Council, for that is the council in which the way was prepared for both the Franciscan and Dominican orders, in which Jews and Muslims were to set themselves apart by their dress, and in which the doctrines of transubstantiation and *extra ecclesia, nulla salus* were approved.

34. Fouilloux, "Friar Yves," 83.

If Billy Graham was the greatest evangelist of the twentieth century, **Karl Barth** (1886–1968) was the greatest theologian of the century. Many will disagree with his particular theological positions, and yet his ideas continue to influence theology today. Much of Western theological development of the modern period traces Barth's theological biography. Barth was raised in a conservative Swiss Calvinist home and studied the theology of German liberals like Adolf von Harnack and Wilhelm Herrmann, completing his studies at Marburg. During his time as parish pastor preaching in Safenwil (1911–21), Barth found that he did not have a clear message to present to his congregation. He had learned a theology that came from the context of the world, a theology rooted in historical relativism, but he had no message to give back to the world. In 1919 Barth published a groundbreaking commentary on Romans. The response to this work, as Barth described it, was as if he had been

Figure 10. Professor Karl Barth

groping around in the dark and, in searching for something to hold on to, had grabbed the town church bell rope and woken up the whole town. The description is apt. Barth's radical Christocentric theology, with his devastating critique of nineteenth-century liberalism, initiated a theological reformation.

Barth went back and read Reformation authors like Luther and Calvin for himself and reappropriated their works on the other side of liberalism. Barth saw that the theologians with whom he had studied had no critique for World War I, and they had no reason to critique the Nazis' movement to reshape the church in their image. Barth's theology, often identified as neo-orthodoxy or crisis theology, fully recognizes the sinfulness of humanity, God's absolute transcendence, and human ability to know God only through his revelation in Jesus Christ. For Barth Christianity is not a religion that is either better than or similar to others. God is not human, and human religion, even the Christian religion, comes under the judgment of God because all religions are human strivings. Theology must not collapse the distance between humanity and God, for to do so is hubris and leads to the liberal theologies Barth was taught and to the wars that Barth experienced in the twentieth century.

Barth's greatest work, albeit never completed, was his *Church Dogmatics*, an extensive thirteen-volume work of major doctrines of the church. Barth was also the primary author behind the *Barmen Declaration* (1934). In this statement of the Confessing Christians of Germany, Barth's dialectic is unmistakable. Scripture is quoted, the meaning of the Scripture is given, and then the false teaching of the German church is rejected. Barth's theology has had a great impact not only on christological discussions but also on ecumenical and related missiological discussions. Barth believed that unity of the church was found only in Jesus Christ, but he also taught that election (in Christ) was for mission. Those whom God calls he sends. Barth's theology of the church (along with others) had a direct impact on the Second Vatican Council. For Barth, theology retains relevance and power to transform the world, but it does so on God's terms as revealed in the Word of God, Jesus Christ. While many theologies were emphasizing the immanence of God—God being very present in this world, very close to us—Barth offered the corrective that God is transcendent, a judge who is full of mercy. Our "no" to God can never be the last word. In Jesus Christ, God has said "yes" to us.

Christian unity, in the waning years of the ecumenical movement, remained a global Christian concern. A second concern, one that was limited to the nations of the North Atlantic region, was the very survival of the Christian faith. In the aftermath of World War II, Christianity began to decline sharply in the West, not because of attacks from without, but because of doubt, and its fruit disbelief, within. A number of apologists stepped in to defend the faith, but none was so unexpected or so effective as an Oxford scholar of Medieval English literature named **Clive Staples Lewis** (1898–1963), more commonly known through his writings as **C. S. Lewis**. Lewis is probably the most popular Christian author of the twentieth century. We would have to say that the most influential theologian was Karl Barth, but in terms of impact on the laity, families, and children, Lewis stands above all others.[35] More than 100 million copies of his children's book series The Chronicles of Narnia have been sold, and Lewis's books continue to sell more than a million copies a

35. There is even a "Narnia Center" in Russia (named for Lewis's fictitious land in his Chronicles series) that provides children's Christian literature and media materials.

year. His writings are not all explicitly Christian, but even his children's stories are written with the clear intent to engender Christian faith.

Lewis, who was born in Belfast, was baptized as an infant but did not come to real faith until he was thirty years old, under the influence of three other authors: George MacDonald, with his theistic fairy stories; J. R. R. Tolkien, author of *The Hobbit* and The Lord of the Rings trilogy; and G. K. Chesterton. Lewis was won first to theism and then to Christianity through aesthetic sensibilities as much as through rational arguments. When his conversion was complete, he turned to defend what he had discovered. As he noted in his autobiography, *Surprised by Joy*, "That which I greatly feared had at last come upon me. In the Trinity Term of 1929, I gave in, and admitted that God was God, and knelt and prayed: perhaps, that night, the most dejected and reluctant convert in all England."[36] Through radio addresses, children's fantasy, reasoned argument, and even autobiography, Lewis became one of the most influential defenders of the faith.

Mere Christianity, *The Problem of Pain*, and *Miracles* are three books that Lewis wrote as an apologist, defending the Christian faith at a time when theologians, in their search for the historical Jesus, discovered a Jesus who was very much bound by history and the historical process. Lewis gave to the world a Jesus who was present in pain and suffering, who was the design behind creation, and who was what he claimed to be. Through his winsome, and often humorous, words and his creative imagination Lewis has introduced many to the Christian faith and has bolstered the faith of many others. Lewis was another layman who became one of the most influential Christians of the twentieth century.

It has been suggested that the twentieth century, the century that should have been the product of the age of progress, produced more Christian martyrs than any of the previous Christian centuries. This would be difficult to prove, in part because there is much debate over what makes a Christian death martyrdom. However, a number of the most significant Christian figures in the twentieth century suffered for their faith, some of them unto death, including **Dietrich Bonhoeffer** (1906–45). A young German pastor, ecumenist, and theologian, Bonhoeffer contrasts greatly with the pacifist figures we looked at earlier in this chapter, for he responded to the Nazi holocaust against the Jews by participating in a plan to kill Hitler: one life for the lives of millions. However, the plot was discovered, and Bonhoeffer was eventually killed. Bonhoeffer is memorable not only for his resistance and his application of Christian ethics to a particular situation but also for the profundity of his writing. Though

---

36. Quoted from Dorsett, *The Essential C. S. Lewis*, 50.

he lived only thirty-nine years, his impact endures to this day through his *Letters and Papers from Prison* (English, 1953), *Ethics* (English, 1955), *The Cost of Discipleship* (English, 1949), and *Life Together* (English, 1954). His life and death have drawn attention to the ideas that supported and directed his decisions.

Caught in the midst of a Christendom tearing itself apart, Bonhoeffer, like Barth, was concerned that Christianity be real, that it not simply rubber-stamp the status quo. Bonhoeffer talks about "religionless" Christianity, by which he means a Christianity that has shed its aloofness and entered into the real human condition, as the weak and exposed community of Christ. In his doctoral dissertation (*Sanctorum Communio*, 1927), Bonhoeffer had already presented the idea of "Christ existing as church-community." The church community is "the present Christ himself, and this is why being in Christ and being in the church-community are the same thing."[37] Bonhoeffer learned from Barth, and in many ways reflects Barth, but Bonhoeffer seemed to have moved beyond Barth in seeing the end of Christendom, the collapse of a culture church, which means a new form of Christianity developing. In one of Bonhoeffer's most widely read books, *The Cost of Discipleship*, he discusses at great length the Sermon on the Mount, a collection of texts that have been central to other Christians who were resisting oppression and injustices in the world. Real discipleship is costly, and thus real justification is not a light thing, either for Jesus Christ or for his followers. Cheap grace, grace that makes no demands and does not change the person, is not real grace at all. Bonhoeffer is also one of the martyrs memorialized at Westminster Abbey.

Our final and most contemporary European life of great piety is another pope of great influence: **Pope Saint John Paul II** (1920–2005), a theologian in his own right. In many ways Karol Wojtyła was one of the most creative and important theologians of any church family of the twentieth century. We would do well to remember that popes are not necessarily creative theologians; most are not. Born in Poland, and caught between the violence and extermination policies of Germany on the west and Russia on the east, Wojtyła survived the war period during which 25,700 Polish military officers, landowners, civil servants, factory owners, and police officers were exterminated by Germans and Russians. Significantly, Wojtyła's dissertation was on the essence of faith in John of the Cross. Unlike past popes, he did not build his scholarship only around the writings of the great medieval theologian Thomas Aquinas. "Wojtyla contends that the mystical encounter with God is for everyone; we can know God through mutual self-giving, and the goal of the Christian life

---

37. Quoted in Wilson, *Introduction to Modern Theology*, 208.

is for us to become 'God by participation. . . .' We cannot know others unless we know them as persons in communion with God. . . . Take God out and we lose what is most truly human in us."[38]

It was his papacy, however, that propelled this idea into the ecumenical church and into the world. As Pope John Paul II created a more open and consultative papacy, he mended religious breaches, for example, by visiting the state of Israel and, earlier, by visiting a synagogue in Rome. One of the most important writings of his papacy was his encyclical *Ut Unum Sint* (1995, That They Be One). In this document, and with his follow-up afterward, John Paul II showed that it was his papal duty to lead all communions in prayer for unity. He lamented that the papacy, he himself, was one of the major roadblocks to church unity, and so he invited others to help reshape papal ministry with an ecumenical vortex. In this important encyclical he also praised "the courageous witness of so many martyrs of [the twentieth] century, including members of Churches and Ecclesial Communities not in full communion with the Catholic Church." Thus he received other martyrs as fully Christian, and he seemed to point to true ecumenism in the fellowship of the suffering church. In an age when the ecumenical priority seemed to have passed by, John Paul II did as much as any other church leader at the end of the twentieth century to remind the church of its unity and of the need for an ongoing struggle against the forces that resist that essential unity.

Orthodoxy

Christianity in Western Europe and North America began to wane in the twentieth century because of years of scholastic erosion and academic doubt. Two world wars simply accelerated the disbelief. In the Orthodox world of Eastern Europe the change was sudden, violent, and much more extensive. Orthodox theologians fled the Soviet bloc and continued to defend and define the faith in newer contexts in Europe and North America. The most significant Russian theologian of the twentieth century wrote from Paris and New York. **Protopresbyter Georges Vasilievich Florovsky** (1893–1979) spent his first twenty-seven years of life in the seaport city of Odessa, Ukraine, before his family was forced to leave in 1920. Although he never earned a formal theological degree, Florovsky became one of the most prolific, inspiring, and controversial of Orthodox theological writers. He taught at St. Sergius Orthodox Theological Institute in Paris, St. Vladimir's Seminary in New York,

---

38. Quoted in Kerr, *Twentieth-Century Catholic Theologians*, 165.

Harvard Divinity School, and Princeton University. A great defender of the Orthodox tradition, purified of Western and pietistic influences, Florovsky wrote extensively about patristic theology as living theology for the church today.

He was one of the most active of Orthodox theologians in the Faith and Order Commission of the WCC, bringing to the ecumenical meetings his approach of "forward to the fathers." The problem of church unity was one of the great problems of the age, he asserted. Christian existence, he wrote, is "a corporate reality": "Christian existence presumes and implies an incorporation, a membership in the community. This must be qualified at once: in the *Apostolic* community, i.e., in communion with the Twelve and their message."[39] The church need not be defined, but honored and lived as the Body of Faith and therefore as the source of faith. We have seen a similar apostolic emphasis in the ecclesiology of Bonhoeffer and

WCC Photo

Figure 11. Bishop Newbigin and Father Florovsky during the Committee of 25 at Bossey in 1953, presumably before the WCC Evanston Assembly

Barth and in the writings of the Second Vatican Council. Florovsky's Orthodox ecclesiology, born into the ecumenical family, gave a resilience to discussions of catholicity and a mooring to the vision of catholicity. "Christ conquered the world. This victory consists in His having created His own Church. In the midst of the vanity and poverty, of the weakness and suffering of human history, He laid the foundations of a 'new being.'"[40] The new being was in the church; we might even say it is the church, the sacrament of the world. Both the theology of Bonhoeffer and that of Vatican II reflect a similar view.

A number of other Orthodox theologians emerged in exile, including two former Marxists, Nicholas Berdyaev (1874–1948) of Kiev and Sergei Bulgakov (1871–1944), founder of St. Sergius in Paris. These and other theologians helped

---

39. Florovsky, *The Universal Church in God's Design*, 1:45.
40. "Catholicity of the Church," in Florovsky, *Bible, Church, Tradition*. Quoted here from Casiday, "Georges Vasilievich Florovsky" in *The Blackwell Companion*, 2:58.

to translate to the larger ecumenical community, especially in the French-, German-, and English-speaking worlds, the richness of Orthodox theology, and in their own way brought about a new era of catholicity that moved beyond Protestant ecumenical dialogue. Many of our great Christian leaders of the twentieth century had similar hopes and dreams, born out of suffering. It was a century of great suffering but also of remarkable saints.

When we look at the variety of global Christian leaders in the twentieth century, we can better understand the remarkable transformation that took place in global Christianity. Some of the people of greatest influence were Africans, Latin Americans, and Asians, and some of the models for Christian life were martyrs, or people who suffered to see the gospel proclaimed. With globalization in the twentieth century came global influences of Christian leaders. Oscar Romero is a model for Christians in China and Vietnam, not just Latin America. The writings of C. S. Lewis and Dietrich Bonhoeffer are available in Japanese, Korean, and Spanish, and Watchman Nee's works are readily available in English. Christianity developed in the writings and the blood of individual leaders in particular contexts of suffering and witness.

3

Politics and Persecution

How Global Politics Shaped Christianity

There is no God; there is no Spirit; there is no Jesus; there is no Mary; there is no Joseph. How can adults believe in these things? . . . Priests live in luxury and suck the blood of the workers. . . . Like Islam and Catholicism, Protestantism is a reactionary feudal ideology, the opium of the people, with foreign origins and contacts. . . . We are atheists; we believe only in Mao Tse-Tung. We call on all people to burn Bibles, destroy images, and disperse religious associations.

From a poster hung on the YMCA building in Beijing, 1966;
from Bush, *Religion in Communist China*, 257

After nineteen centuries, Jesus, who was rejected and crucified in western Asia, was still being rejected, persecuted, and martyred in the persons of his followers. The great irony is that in many of the places where Jesus had become most comfortable in society—places like Germany and Russia—he was most directly persecuted. Many of the most widely known twentieth-century Christian leaders were struggling against governments and movements that resisted Christian teachings. We think of Karl Barth and the *Barmen Declaration*, Dietrich Bonhoeffer and his role in the Confessing Church, Patriarch

Tikhon of Moscow[1] resisting the Communists, and many Chinese leaders like Wang Mingdao, whom we have quoted above. The single confession of Jesus Christ as Lord, coupled with the obedience such a confession requires, led to Christians being persecuted throughout the century and around the world. It would be hard to prove statistically, but few scholars have doubted the following assertion: the twentieth century was the century of the greatest persecution and martyrdom for Christians. A few snapshots from varied contexts show the pervasive theme of martyrdom in this time frame:

Russia: 600 bishops, 40,000 priests, and 120,000 monks and nuns killed.[2]

Korea: unknown number imprisoned and killed under the Japanese and then under the Communists.

Armenia: 1.5 million Armenian and other Christians killed by the Ottoman Turks.

Spain: seven thousand Catholic martyrs listed at the end of the Spanish Civil War.

South Africa: thousands died resisting the apartheid system.

Mexico: socialist revolution of 1917 caused the death of many priests.

Romania: the Soviet Gulag imprisoned and killed thousands.[3]

Germany and Poland: millions of Christians (mostly Roman Catholics) killed by the Nazis, including tens of thousands of priests and pastors.[4]

Egypt and Sudan: ongoing restrictions, imprisonment, killings.

China: Boxer Rebellion (1900), persecution under the Japanese and Communists.

Vietnam: persecution under Communists.

Uganda: up to four hundred thousand killed by Idi Amin, a convert to Islam.

Colombia: many Catholic priests have been murdered by revolutionary forces (FARC), as well as by government troops.

Albania: religion was outlawed, churches burned beginning in 1967.

1. "The balm accords with the relics," Patriarch Tikhon said when a sewage system leaked into the mausoleum for the Communist leader Vladimir Ilyich Lenin. http://sainttikhonroc .org/saint_tikhon.html.
2. McGuckin, *Orthodox Church*, 54.
3. See *Faith and Martyrdom: The Eastern Churches in 20th Century Europe*, a 520-page volume published by the Congregation for Eastern Churches, which contains proceedings from a contemporary church history gathering at the Vatican (October 22–24, 1998); quoted from a book review at http://www.indcatholicnews.com/news.php?viewStory=556.
4. See, e.g., Atkin and Tallett, *Priests, Prelates and People*, 244–64, on World War II.

Iraq and Iran: Islamic renewal has brought with it Christian persecution.

Myanmar (Burma): churches and schools were closed in the 1960s; ongoing persecution under the military dictatorship.

And this is only a partial list. When we look at the many countries where Christians have suffered, it is clear that nationalism and national ideologies (dictatorial fascism and Communist atheism) are the major causes. Christian loyalty to Jesus Christ and his teachings is a threat to those who would dominate people and cultures. It may be an exaggeration to say, as some have, that 70 percent of all Christian martyrdoms have occurred in the twentieth century, but it is quite accurate to say that efforts to systematically silence the Christian voice have been strongest in the twentieth century. This is not the only theme of the twentieth century, but it is one of the most obvious, if not *the* most obvious. In this chapter we look at the issues related to global political change, persecution, and Christian life. Key to this change was that the world map was transformed between 1946 and 1991, which meant that the global "Christian" empires dissolved and Christianity lost its privileged position.

A Statistical Survey of Twentieth-Century Christianity

Christianity developed in remarkable ways in the nineteen centuries of its history that we have traced, but in the twentieth century, or, more accurately, that century's last four decades, it underwent a dramatic, unprecedented shift of its center from the West (Atlantic world) to Africa, Asia, and Latin America[5] (the "non-West," for shorthand). This shift was caused by several forces. The decline of Christianity in the West we have traced in previous chapters; it was very much related to intellectual movements from the Enlightenment. The growth of Christianity in Africa and Asia, on the contrary, though also caused by several forces, was mainly catalyzed by the political changes we will discuss in this chapter. In short, we can say that Christianity, detached from colonialism and the supports of Western missions, stood on its own and became rooted in local social and cultural realities. Christianity became a Chinese religion and became an African religion. We will look at those political changes that were largely a result of decolonization, but first we will look at the statistics themselves.

5. Oceania was already 77.5 percent Christian in 1900, so the growth to 82.6 percent by 2000 is not so noteworthy. There was no percentage growth in Latin America during the century.

Asia is still the least Christian continent in the world, with only one country that could be considered a Christian nation, the Philippines. However, with the rapid growth rate of Christianity in many parts of East and Southeast Asia, significant Christian minorities (more than 5 percent) have developed in the following countries: South Korea, Kyrgyzstan, Malaysia, Singapore, Indonesia, Brunei, China, Vietnam, Myanmar, Taiwan, and Sri Lanka.[6] In Asia the percent of Christians during the twentieth century grew from 2.3 percent in 1900 (22 million Christians) to 4.7 percent in 1970 (101 million) to 8.5 percent in 2000 (350 million), but the growth was neither evenly distributed nor steady. In some countries, such as Malaysia, Indonesia, and Singapore, the faith grew from the 1960s through the 1980s, but then growth seemed to taper off. In China the growth was dramatic from the early 1980s on, after Chairman Mao died and China became more open to the world. In Cambodia there was rapid growth in the 1960s and 1970s until the devastating period under Pol Pot and the Khmer Rouge. In Thailand growth has been fairly strong among the minority groups, but almost imperceptible among the majority ethnic Thai. South Korea's Christian growth was dramatic at and immediately after the Great 1907 Revival, and then again after the partition in the 1950s. The largest churches in the world today are in South Korea: some are Pentecostal (e.g., Yoido Full Gospel Church, with more than nine hundred thousand members) and some are Presbyterian and Methodist.

Asian Christianity has grown more dramatically among traditional Protestants (from 5 million to 240 million) than among Catholics (from 11 million to 124 million). Pentecostal and newer independent churches have had the largest percentage of growth, but really all churches have been growing in Asia. In India the growth has been steady, but slow, from 1.7 to 6.2 percent of the population. Most of the growth has been among the Dalits (the "untouchables"), or those outside the caste structure. In Pakistan, Christian growth has barely kept pace with the growth in population.

China is a special category and still something of a statistical enigma. There are reasons for the great disparity among statistical accounts of Christians in China. The government's more open policy (freedom of religion) has not been trusted by all Christians. Decades of persecution and anti-Christian rhetoric, such as in the quotation at the beginning of this chapter, have made many Christians government-shy. The recognized churches—China Christian Council (CCC) and the Chinese Patriotic Catholic Association (CPCA)— have fairly reliable statistics, but these statistics count only Christians in

6. The statistics in this section come from three sources: United Bible Societies; Barrett, Kurian, and Johnson, *World Christian Encyclopedia*; and Mandryk, *Operation World*.

government-recognized churches. By 2000 the CCC estimated about 15 million Protestants in China, and the CPCA estimated about 14 million Roman Catholics. Both figures exclude unregistered churches. Estimates of the total Christian community in China go as high as 100 million, but 40–50 million would be more reasonable estimates. With more than 50 million Bibles printed and distributed in China since 1986, it is likely that there are more Christians in China than the combined total of 29 million estimated by the CCC and CPCA. We must remember that in 1949 there were fewer than 2 million Christians in China, which would make the growth rate greater in two generations than in any single nation in Christian history. Christianity continues to grow rapidly, but the largest religions in China are still the traditional Chinese religions (Buddhists, Taoist with ancestor worship), with an estimated 150 million practitioners.

Africa provides the most amazing statistical growth for the twentieth century, and it also provides the strongest evidence that Western imperialism hindered the growth of Christianity in the non-Western world. In 1900 Africa was much more Muslim and indigenously religious than Christian, even after centuries of Western missionary work. In 1900 there were 9 million Christians in Africa but 34.5 million Muslims—a nearly 1:4 ratio of Christians to Muslims. By 1962, in the middle of decolonization, there were 60 million Christians and 145 million Muslims, for about a 1:2 ratio. When colonialism was pretty much dismantled, Christianity had a remarkable growth spurt, so that by 2000 there were 360 million Christians and 317 million Muslims. Africa went from being 9 percent Christian to being 46 percent Christian in a century. It was estimated that by the end of the century there were more than sixteen thousand conversions a day. In contrast, about 4,300 people are leaving the church in Europe and North America every day, and not being replaced. In 1900 about 80 percent of the Christians in the world lived in Europe or North America, but by 2000 only 37 percent did. At the end of the first decade of the twenty-first century, Christianity was nearly two-thirds a non-Western—a majority non-Western—world religion. This shift took place beginning in the 1960s. No world religion has ever shifted its center so dramatically in human history.[7]

The number of adherents to the different forms or families of Christianity has also shifted. Orthodoxy suffered greatly during the twentieth century from Communist persecution. In 1900, 22 percent of the world's Christian population was Orthodox (116 million), but by 2007 it was only 10 percent (221 million). The massive persecution of Armenians by the Turks and the

---

7. The closest would be the rise of Islam, which in only one century spread to India, across North Africa, and up to central France. That rapid growth, however, was not global.

Communists severely stressed Orthodoxy globally. Roman Catholicism, in contrast, has been fairly steady during the whole century, at about 50 percent of all Christians in the world (from 267 million to 1.143 billion), growing only slightly from 16 percent to 17.2 percent of the world's population. Protestants, with the rapid growth of Pentecostals and independent churches, grew from 28 percent of the Christian population in 1900 to 41 percent (143 million to 947 million).[8]

Another great shift has been from Protestantism to the newer Spiritual churches (Pentecostal, Free Churches, and indigenous churches). It is hard to get statistics on the exact number, but it is reasonable to assume that by the end of the twentieth century about 15 percent of the world's population would be from this fourth stream of Christianity. There are a number of reasons for this rapid growth. First, many of the indigenous churches in Africa, Asia, and Latin America communicate the message in patterns that are more culturally appropriate for their neighbors. Christian growth in the latter part of the twentieth century was not from traditional Western churches. Second, most of the missionary work at the end of the twentieth century was done within continents by local, indigenous Christians. Among the Protestant Asian, African, and Latin American missionaries, Reformation-era distinctions (denominations) held little sway. Thus the Spiritual stream was the most active in missionary work outside the West.

In addition, Pentecostalism[9] and independent churches have always been strongly missionary in their identity, both in preaching a message of "fullness of the Holy Spirit" to Christians in the world (as a type of renewal) and in evangelizing the non-Christians. For example, by 2005, 3.5 percent (138 million) of Asia's population was Pentecostal; an additional 1 percent (25 million) would be identified as charismatics. This growth has been very rapid. As recently as 1970 the number of charismatic and Pentecostal Christians in Asia combined was under 0.5 percent of the continent's population. Thus even though the earliest Pentecostal missionaries arrived in Asia in the first decade of the twentieth century, it wasn't until the end of the century that Pentecostalism became a major theme.

In Latin America the spread was also very late (even though Pentecostalism was introduced very early) and extensive. More than two-thirds of Latin

8. These statistics are taken from Barrett, Kurian, and Johnson, *World Christian Encyclopedia*, 4; Johnson and Ross, *Atlas of Global Christianity*, 66–71.

9. Statistics on Pentecostalism in Asia are taken from the Pew Forum on Religion and Public Life (http://www.pewforum.org/2006/10/05/overview-pentecostalism-in-asia/). Pentecostals are distinguished from charismatics in two ways: requiring expression of "Spirit gifts" (usually speaking in tongues), or by their own Pentecostal denominations.

American evangelical Christians identified themselves as Pentecostals in 2000, and one-half of the world's "classic Pentecostals" were in Latin America. Brazil is both the largest Roman Catholic country and the one with the largest number of Pentecostals and charismatics.[10] In nineteen countries of the Caribbean and Latin America, Pentecostals number more than 10 percent of the population. In the largest country, Brazil, more than 45 percent of the population identifies itself as Pentecostal. In 1970 Brazil was only about 7 percent Pentecostal, indicating the rapid growth in the last few decades of the twentieth century.

The major shift from more traditional Orthodox, Roman Catholic, and Protestant families to the Spiritual family was a late twentieth-century shift. The decline in Orthodoxy (relatively speaking) was an early twentieth-century shift. Roman Catholicism has stayed fairly steady, losing many in Europe and some in Latin America, but growing substantially in Africa.

Wars and Rumors of Wars

We have spoken about persecution and martyrdom of Christians in the twentieth century, but we also need to look more specifically at warfare: Western nations, mostly identified as "Christian," were also responsible for some of the greatest violence. In fact, the decline of Christianity in the West and the rise of secular ideologies seemed to lead to some of the greatest violence in the century. Earlier we looked at World War I and the flu epidemic that followed. World War II, however, caused the greatest destruction of human lives in the century. An estimated twenty million soldiers died in that war, and even more civilians died. The war devastated Western Christianity. Christians were killing other Christians for what had become a higher loyalty: nation. In Japan, it was the Western, predominantly Christian, nation of the United States that dropped atomic bombs on Hiroshima and Nagasaki. Religion played a large role in the global conflict. Emperor worship inspired the Japanese in their militant conquest, and Germany's Hitler used the German church to support his expansionist plans and to support his program to annihilate the Jews. In the 1930s most of the German people, Catholics and Protestants, supported Hitler as a strong leader. Cardinal Bertram of Berlin, representing the Catholic bishops of Germany, sent "warmest congratulations to the Führer . . . with fervent prayers which the Catholics of Germany are sending to heaven on their altars."[11] In July 1933, Cardinal Secretary of State Eugenio

---

10. Information on Pentecostalism comes from Burgess, *Pentecostal and Charismatic Movements*. See the section on Global Statistics, 284–302.

11. Cornwall, *Hitler's Pope*, 209.

Pacelli, who would later become Pope Pius XII, signed a special agreement (concordat) with the Nazi government. This concordat gave legitimacy to the Nazi government and Hitler's rule. At the signing, the famous Protestant scholar Rudolf Bultmann was present, but he later found ways to resist the German church. Theologian Gerhard Kittel, in contrast, became a promoter of the German church's rejection of the Jews, providing academic support for national racism.

In the same year the concordat was signed, Hitler made a strong appeal for the Protestant church to fully support the National Socialists, and so through Hitler's direct manipulation, in their July 1933 elections a strong "German church" team was voted in, giving full support to Hitler. For his part, Hitler was a strong supporter of all the churches, if by support we mean co-opting them to serve his own ends. Through the years his "church" developed into a new "Christian-influenced" Aryan religion.

Resistance to Hitler and his social and military programs was not pervasive in the early years. A group of theologians and pastors, under the leadership of Martin Niemöller, began to resist the German church. Two of the main points of resistance to the German church were the new requirement that the church support the state without qualification and the exclusion of all non-Aryans, meaning pastors of Jewish descent. In 1934 a group of Protestant church resisters (both Lutheran and Reformed) met in Barmen and, under the leadership of Karl Barth, penned the *Barmen Declaration*. It is a clear statement that the authority of Jesus Christ, according to Scripture, must be the final authority for Christians. Any state that would claim ultimate authority must be resisted.

> In view of the errors of the "German Christians" of the present Reich Church government which are devastating the Church and also therefore breaking up the unity of the German Evangelical Church, we confess the following evangelical truths: "I am the way, and the truth, and the life; no one comes to the Father, but by me" (John 14.6). "Truly, truly, I say to you, he who does not enter the sheepfold by the door, but climbs in by another way, that man is a thief and a robber. . . . I am the door; if anyone enters by me, he will be saved" (John 10:1, 9).
>
> Jesus Christ, as he is attested for us in Holy Scripture, is the one Word of God which we have to hear and which we have to trust and obey in life and in death.
>
> We reject the false doctrine, as though the church could and would have to acknowledge as a source of its proclamation, apart from and besides this one Word of God, still other events and powers, figures and truths, as God's revelation.[12]

12. Cochrane, *The Church's Confession under Hitler*, 237–42. Available at http://www.sacred-texts.com/chr/barmen.htm.

Hitler's government turned more and more anti-Christian, imprisoning many pastors, confiscating the funds of the Confessing churches, and refusing to allow them to take further collections. Hitler's plan to "use" the church to promote anti-Jewish programs and to manipulate the church into complete compliance in his war effort proved unwieldy and unrealistic. Through both the compromise of some and the persecution of others, German Christianity was greatly weakened during the period of National Socialism. In the aftermath of the war, Christianity did not rebound in the European nations.

World War II was the largest and most destructive war of the century, but it was one of more than twenty regional conflicts, including the Korean War, Chinese Civil Wars (1927–37 and 1945–49), Vietnam War, Iran-Iraq War, Russian Civil War, Mexican Revolution, Spanish Civil War—and the list goes on. A few general statements need to be made about the impact that these wars had on Christianity in the twentieth century. First, in some cases Christianity survives and then thrives on the other side of war. This was clearly the case during the Korean conflict. The years of oppression under the Japanese were followed by the partition of the country, the northern half controlled by Soviet Russia. When the northern invasion of the south began, it was not yet clear just how anti-Christian North Korea would become. During and after the war, under the leadership of Kim Il Sung, hundreds of thousands of Christians were killed, many while in prison. However, even though northern Korea was where Christianity was the strongest, the persecutions and wars there have strengthened the Korean Christian resolve, and this has resulted in strong growth of Christianity in South Korea. Many pastors and elders were killed during the war, but those who survived planted new churches and doubled their efforts as a response. The same can be said of the Chinese War of Liberation (or Civil War), which culminated with the closing of most churches and seminaries. On the other side of the war and persecution, the Chinese church grew dramatically.

Second, at times war decimates the Christian community and cuts the life source of the church. World War II and the various wars in the Middle East, Iran, and Iraq would fit in here. European Christianity, we have already mentioned, was in rapid decline before the war. In the Middle East, each war seems to unleash both random (popular) and sustained (government) violence on Christian communities. Churches are burned and pastors are killed. As a result, Christians migrate to Europe or North America. The Spanish Civil War had an impact on Spain similar to that which World War II had on most of the West: it accelerated the decline of Christianity.

Third, wars have created Christian refugees, who have then diversified Christianity in the West. Christians fleeing war in the twentieth century would try to flee to safer regions, or if possible, to the West (the Iraq wars, Lebanon's civil war, the conflict in the Balkans, the Russian Revolution, civil wars in Rwanda and Sudan, etc.). For many reasons—but mostly for greater religious freedom, wealth, and opportunities—Western Europe and North America received a much greater diversity of Christians in the twentieth century. Armenian, Lebanese, Iranian, Pakistani, and Sudanese, among many others, diversified Christianity in the West.

Finally, when wars end, there is always a new order. Religions must always renegotiate their place at the table under new social and political order. It is helpful to ask at the end of a war or at the point of political shift, "How does Christianity fare in this new order?" The settlements after war either create stronger violence and restrictions against Christians (as in Russia, the Soviet Republics, Iran after the Iranian Revolution, Vietnam after the Vietnam War, etc.), or there is a new openness to missionary activity, Christian leadership development, and Christian participation in the public square. After the Korean War, the south was far more open to missionary work and leadership training. Christianity grew rapidly. In Vietnam, after the country was reunited in 1975, persecution picked up, churches were closed, and Christian activity was greatly hampered. Cambodia, after the war with Vietnam and the end of the Khmer Rouge's control of the country, returned to a policy of religious freedom. Christianity there has grown rapidly since the early 1990s, mostly through the witness of Asian missionary churches (Malaysian, Taiwanese, Singaporean, Korean, and even Indonesian and Filipino). Wars have had a great impact on the development of Christianity in the past century, but that impact has been as diverse as the battles and their illusive victories. The two great determinants of how Christianity survives are the overall health of Christianity before a war and the resulting social order after a war.

Communism and Christianity

One of the most important political forces in shaping Christianity in the twentieth century was the rise of Communism. We have already looked at how Communism in Russia brought about the rapid decline of Orthodoxy in West Asia and Eastern Europe. But Communist ideology, as envisioned by Marx and Engels, was always to be a global movement. In March 1919 the Comintern (Communist International) was founded in Petrograd (St. Petersburg, Russia) to promote international activities that would bring about revolutions across the globe. Well-financed and organized Communist cells were active in places as far off as China, Indonesia, India, and South Africa by 1921. Most of these early Communist activists accepted the Marxist teaching that in any society "the existence of religion is the existence of a defect."[13] "We do not change secular questions into theological ones. We change theological questions into secular ones. History has for long enough been resolved into superstition: we now resolve superstition into history."[14] Even with the strong anti-Christian rhetoric, the impact on Christianity was not always negative. However, the spread of Communism was a major factor in the development of Christianity in all of Europe and Asia as well as in many countries of Africa and the Americas.

In Indonesia, for example, the Partai Komunis Indonesia (PKI, Communist Party of Indonesia) was established in 1920; after some premature rebellions, it was outlawed in 1927. However, by the end of the Japanese occupation of Indonesia, there were three Marxist parties there, including the PKI. Marxists were working in an unfriendly territory, however, for the Indonesian government under President Soekarno (Sukarno) affirmed that it was not a secular nor a religious state, but a *Pancasila* state. *Pancasila* means the country would be built upon five principles, the first being the mandatory belief in "the one almighty lordship." Even though the country was overwhelmingly Muslim, it would not become a Muslim state, but it would require belief in God. Thus atheistic Communism was not welcomed in such a country. In 1965 there was a Communist coup in the country, but it was quickly put down. It was a major political shock, and in the aftermath of the military takeover, religious commitment was encouraged. This encouragement to religious belief in the mid-1960s marks the beginning of rapid church growth in certain areas of the country. In Timor as well as in Java there were revivals, many of which seem to have been triggered by the fear of atheistic Communism and the encouragement to theistic belief in the country.

Nearby in Malaysia, Communist activity also began in the 1920s, directly from China and through Chinese immigrants coming to Singapore and to the Malay Peninsula. The Malayan Communist Party (MCP) was formed in 1930 to oppose British rule and bring an economic revolution in the means of production in the region. The MCP gained little local support until the invasion by the Japanese, when the Communists then fought alongside the British to turn back the Japanese. In the aftermath of Japanese aggression, MCP continued its struggle, and by 1948, with more than eight thousand armed Communist fighters in the jungles of Malaya, the government declared an emergency. Under emergency conditions suspected Communist organizers could be imprisoned

13. This oft-quoted phrase is from Karl Marx's "Zur Judenfrage," *Werke*, 1:352. Quoted here from New York University's website on Marx: http://www.nyu.edu/projects/ollman/docs/a_ch18.php.
14. McLellan, *Karl Marx*, 51.

or even executed without trial. Since so many of the Communists were living in the jungles, on the edge of villages, the government also began a resettlement program, setting up about six hundred "new villages," which would be closely monitored by the government. As the villagers were in need of basic services such as schools and clinics, the British (who ruled until 1957) requested the help of mission societies, who would then set up schools as well as churches in many of the new villages. Thus, ironically, evangelization was actually enhanced by the Communist threat and British relocation programs. With the Communist liberation of China, many Chinese as well as missionaries migrated to Southeast Asia, and these Christians aided in the work in the new villages. Although the Malaysian government continues the policy established by the British of protecting the ethnic Malay (mostly Muslim) from evangelism, the Malayan Emergency did help to advance Christianity in the region among the Chinese. Thus the threat of Communist advances in most of Southeast Asia has been more of a help than a hindrance to the development of Christianity.

China is a special situation, since Communism spread slowly throughout the country beginning in 1920 and eventually was victorious under the leadership of Chairman Mao (Mao Zedong, 1893–1976) in 1949. China, like Russia, had always been a very religious country, with large peasant populations. In the early months after the Communist liberation it was not clear what the future would hold for Christianity in China, for the Christians individually, and for missionaries working to rebuild their work after the Pacific battles during World War II. When the Communist victory was assured, two of the key Chinese Christian leaders were in Europe. K. H. Ting (Ding Guangxun, 1915–2012) and Y. T. Wu (Wu Yaozong, 1890–1970) actually met in Prague, Czechoslovakia, in the spring of 1949 and discussed the new situation in their homeland. Both were very involved in global Christianity through the ecumenical movement; Ting's involvement was through the World Student Christian Federation. Reflecting from Europe on the events in China, "Wu brought enthusiastic reports of the new life of people in the Liberated Areas of China, and, referring to Matthew 25, he said that the Communists were putting love into practice."[15] Wu had studied extensively in the West (Union Theological Seminary and Columbia University, both in New York), where he eventually developed distaste for Protestant Christianity's partnership with capitalism. He was very politically aware and knew many of the top leaders in the Chinese Communist Party (CCP).

As a result, he promoted a Christian way to work with the Communist order, beginning with a key article published in March 1949 titled, "Christianity under

15. Wickeri, *Reconstructing Christianity*, 79.

Anthony E. Clark, China Mission History Archive, Whitworth University (Spokane, WA)

Figure 12. Y. T. Wu and Mao Zedong

the People's Democratic Dictatorship," where he argued that the new order supported freedom of religion, but that religion must serve society, it must not be "reactionary," and it must not support superstitious beliefs. Wu helped to organize the Three-Self Movement (later the Three-Self Patriotic Movement, TSPM) and encouraged Chinese Christians to "Love Country—Love Church" as a way of promoting self-support, patriotism, and an end to foreign missionary control. By 1952 most of the missionaries had been expelled from the country or were held in prison. In 1950 a "Christian Manifesto" was published, penned mostly by Wu with the approval of Zho Enlai and other CCP officials. After some minor changes it was sent out to the churches, and an estimated four hundred thousand signatures were collected. However, Christianity's place in the new Communist order was not firmly set. During the decades of Mao's rule the churches suffered greatly, even with the creative and diplomatic work of people like Wu, Ting, and others. The "Great Leap Forward," beginning in 1958, during which the government wanted to quickly transform China from an agrarian to an industrialized society, was a period when many churches were closed, combined, or taken over for government use. During the "Cultural Revolution," even the most compliant church leaders were sent to "reeducation camps" or imprisoned. It is impossible to quantify the suffering of the Chinese, not just the Christians, during these periods. Famines caused by the economic disaster caused the deaths of between twenty million and forty million people.

Many Christians saw any type of cooperation with the new government as a compromising of the gospel. Most of those who sought ways to work with the CCP had come from Anglican, Episcopal, Congregational, and some Presbyterian and Methodist missions and churches. The YMCA and WSCF provided much of the leadership of the TSPM. Those Christians who resisted cooperation came mostly from Baptist churches, independent churches (including indigenous churches), and China Inland Mission churches. Individuals made their own decisions, but in general, the leaders of the TSPM, people like Ting and Wu, were better educated, Western educated, and fluent in English. Those Christians who refused to sign the "Christian Manifesto" soon lost their churches, many of their pastors were arrested, and they had to begin to meet secretly. By the end of the Great Leap Forward the Christian colleges (all 13) and the seminaries and Bible colleges (210 total) had all been closed. Only one seminary, in Nanjing, remained open, and church attendance, even under the "freedom of religion" policy, had slowed down to a trickle.

Left on their own—cut off from foreign money, leadership, or training—Chinese Christians found ways to survive and pass on the faith. When the Cultural Revolution was finally over and Christians slowly began to worship publicly again, the world was surprised to learn that Christianity had not only survived, but grown far beyond what any had expected. Bibles had been hand copied and passed on for others to copy. Meetings were held during the night, and baptisms were held at streams or lakes in the middle of the night. In prisons, many church leaders had remained faithful, and they became evidence of the suffering gospel for the world. The work of the TSPM and the CCC made it possible to negotiate the reopening of church buildings, the opening of clinics, and, eventually, a return to printing Bibles again in China. The difficult experience of the Chinese church under Mao's form of Communism did more to promote Chinese Christianity than 140 years of Protestant missions. Interestingly, both the missionary work and the Communist persecution were necessary.

Decolonization: New Nations in Africa and Asia

It was the oppressive experience of colonialism and Western capitalism and imperialism that had tilled Chinese soil for a Communist revolution. The dismantling of colonial structures, like the advent of Communism in Asia and Africa, had complex results for Christian development. Without detailing the process of liberation in each particular place, a few generalizations can be made about the impact of decolonization on Christianity. First, the process of liberation from colonial powers, or decolonization, was a sudden global change that took place in about twenty-five years.[16] From 1945 to 1969 more than 99 percent of the non-Western world that was under colonial control was liberated: Ralph Winter calls it the "unbelievable 25 years."[17] Colonization and reformatting the global map had taken centuries. But soon after World War II ended, the colonial powers began to make arrangements to leave, holding on to as much political and economic influence as they could. The sudden change in geography and international relations led to great instability, dramatic changes, and ongoing conflicts. Multiple factors fed into the new national divisions, including language, ethnic identity, natural resources, and colonial "leadership." All of the new national boundaries cut across indigenous languages and cultures, and so decolonization initiated the largest migration in modern history. Millions fled to regions that were perceived as safer or were places of "their own people." Millions of others fled back to the colonial home. We will talk more about these migrations in the final chapter.

Second, decolonization was a time of rediscovery of national or ethnic (linguistic or religious) identity. Thus many countries returned to a local language for education and commerce, and some for their national language. Myanmar uses the Burmese language in much of its lower education and in all of its newspapers and public discourse, though in higher education people in Myanmar often use English. The religion of Myanmar is Theravada Buddhism, which is a recovery of long cultural heritage. Sierra Leone uses English as its national language, but Krio (Creole), a mixture of English and a number of local languages, is the most commonly spoken language in the country. Many countries reclaimed their dominant religion as a state religion (Buddhism in Myanmar, Sri Lanka, and Cambodia; Islam in most countries of North Africa, the Middle East, and Central Asia). A few Asian countries, like India, Turkey, and Indonesia, did not claim a state religion, but upon independence either limited or outlawed foreign missionary activity. The recovery of cultural heritage, more often than not, made Christian participation in nation building and participation in the ecumenical church more difficult. However, the emphasis on local cultures accelerated the indigenization process of Christianity, which aided in its acceptance in local contexts.

Third, colonial residue, both good and bad, remained. The colonial heritage included the use of a European language for education or government.

16. See the appendixes at the end of this book for dates of decolonization of African and Asian countries.
17. Winter, *25 Unbelievable Years*, 3.

In countries like India, where there are more than one thousand languages, thirty of which are spoken by at least one million people, the use of a common language helped to unite the nation. However, Indian cultural and social concepts were originally given in Hindi, or Tamil or Punjabi, or Bengali. So even though English helped to unite people, it sacrificed much of the richness of local cultures.

The end of the British Raj in India was no surprise, but even after the country had been moving toward independent rule for decades, the transition immediately erupted into violence between Hindus and Muslims. In other British territories, British law was retained, with some local adaptation. The Internal Security Act in Malaysia was a British tool of indefinite detention without trial used against the Communists during the Emergency.[18] The law continues today in both Malaysia and Singapore, and it can be used to deal with any type of perceived national security issue, such as religious disruption, political activism, or possible terrorist activity. Other colonial residue includes trading partners, agricultural and mineral development, and religious policies.

Some of these colonial institutions and practices were of great benefit to Christianity in particular countries, but other colonial residues were less helpful. For example, was the common use of an imperial language good for the development of the church? Yes, if it comes to higher education, such as in seminaries. But the use of a colonial language in pastors' education, after which pastors would go out to villages and have to speak a Chinese dialect or Bantu, Urdu, Swahili, or Amharic, created new problems. Christianity was expressed and taught as a foreign religion in a foreign language. Contextual issues have been delayed by the convenience of a commonly understood colonial language, with all of its valuable books and resources.

Finally, most of the decolonization left the colonized countries poorer. Empires generally used their colonial holdings to provide raw materials rather than to help the indigenes become producers of modern products. In tropical countries the scars of colonial presence can be seen in miles of coconut palms, pineapple trees, or rubber plantations. Colonialism turned to a newer type of dependency, neocolonialism, under which the newer nations of the world depended on the Western countries to buy their raw materials and for cultural innovation. In this situation, most of the former colonies have remained among the poorest countries in the world. It is in these countries, however, where Christianity has been growing most rapidly, whereas the Christian populations

---

18. Called the Anti-British National Liberation War by the Malaysian Communists, the Emergency was the British term for their struggle against Communists in Malaysia from 1948–60.

of the neocolonial countries, dependent on the resources of these former colonies, are rapidly declining.

These are some of the major themes in the process of decolonization, but what has this meant for Christian development at the end of the twentieth century? It may be too early to make clear summary statements, but one conclusion is clear. Where the new nation developed a strong national or religious identity in opposition to Christianity (Muslim or Buddhist), Christianity has struggled to survive at all. In most of the Muslim nations of North Africa and the Middle East, even where there was a strong Christian presence in the past—such as in Lebanon—Christianity has declined. Little else can be said as a generalization.

Israel and Palestine

One country that was created out of the ashes of World War II and from the decolonization that followed needs to be looked at individually. That country is Israel. The formation of no other single country has had such a global impact. Although the original idea of a homeland for the Jews goes back to as early as the conclusion of World War I, it was the League of Nations "Mandate of Palestine" that gave Great Britain the power to administer the Palestine part of the former Ottoman Empire. The original mandate (dated 1922) made it clear in the preamble that it was the purpose and responsibility of Britain to work for the "establishment in Palestine of a national home for the Jewish people, it being clearly understood that nothing should be done which might prejudice the civil and religious rights of existing non-Jewish communities in Palestine, or the rights and political status enjoyed by Jews in any other country."[19]

This mandate to form a nation for the Jewish people became intensified in the aftermath of the Holocaust, when an estimated six million Jews were killed under Nazi Germany. In 1947 Palestine was partitioned, allowing for a Jewish homeland. The nation was born in conflict, the partition being accepted by the Jewish representatives but rejected by the Arab counterparts. The history of the nation has been one of conflict, redefinition, global alignments, and larger and smaller regional conflicts. Furthermore, many Christian groups, such as dispensationalists[20] who were looking for signs of Jesus's return, found

19. Quoted here from "The Balfour Project" website: http://www.balfourproject.org/britains-betrayal-of-the-sacred-trust-in-palestine/.

20. Dispensationalism, a theological belief of a small strand of Western Protestants, has had a disproportionate influence on Middle Eastern politics. J. N. Darby pioneered the beliefs,

1947 as an interpretive key for their eschatology. As a result, dispensational groups from the West, and now from around the world, have developed a theology that uncritically supports Israel, seeing Israel as a sign from God. "Christian Zionism" is the term for those Christians who see support for Israel as support for God's plan for Jesus to return and take home those who are his. Christian Zionists encourage Jewish resettlement of Israel and even raise money to build homes and settlements for Jewish emigrants. This unqualified support of some Christian groups for Israel has further alienated many Muslim nations from the United States and England, the homelands of most of the Christian Zionists. The meaning and value of the Jews have been a major issue throughout Christian history because their lives, theologically and historically, have been lived in close proximity to Christians. Only since 1947 has Jewish history been important to Christian hope because of a Jewish nation that for many is a sign.

Most Christians, however, do not look to Israel as a sign. It is important to see the great variety of Christian belief and practice that developed further during the twentieth century. One way of viewing the major Christian families in the twentieth century is to compare their responses to Israel. But we also need to look at patterns of worship, engagement in Christian mission, and ways of living in a world that seemed increasingly antagonistic to the teachings of Jesus. The four major families of Christianity mentioned in the introduction had diverse patterns of growth and decline between 1900 and 2000. Pentecostalism grew from infancy to a major family of Christianity, but Orthodoxy suffered great losses. With all of the persecution of Christians in the twentieth century it is interesting how persecution and warfare caused a great decline of certain families of Christianity, while others seemed to thrive in the midst of great suffering.

---

but it was C. I. Scofield in his annotated King James Version of the Bible who spread the ideas that there will be a central place for Israel and especially for Jerusalem for Jesus's return. The final dispensation of God's grace will take place on the Temple Mount in Jerusalem, according to dispensational theology.

4

Confessional Families

Diverse Confessions, Diverse Fates

> The World Council of Churches is a fellowship of churches which confess the Lord Jesus Christ as God and Saviour according to the Scriptures and therefore seek to fulfill together their common calling to the glory of the one God, Father, Son and Holy Spirit.
>
> "Basis" of the World Council of Churches, 1961

In this book we have been looking at the great reversal of Christianity in the twentieth century. Few people recognized at the time that such a great transformation was taking place. Lesslie Newbigin, an English Presbyterian, was a missionary bishop of the church of South India who also worked during part of that time for the International Missionary Council and then the World Council of Churches (1959–65). In 1953 he wrote a very important book that clearly identified some elements of great transformation of Christianity in the twentieth century: the breakdown of Christendom, the missionary experience of the churches, and the modern ecumenical movement. The book was *The Household of God*, and here is part of what he said about the "breakdown of Christendom":

> By this phrase I mean the dissolution—at first slow, but later more and more rapid—of the synthesis between the Gospel and the culture of the western part

of the European peninsula of Asia, by which Christianity had become almost the folk-religion of Western Europe. That synthesis was the work of the thousand-year period during which the peoples of Western Europe, hemmed in by the power of Islam to east and south, had the Gospel wrought in the very stuff of their social and personal life, so that the whole population could be conceived of as the *corpus Christianum*. That conception is the background of all the Reformation theologies. They take it for granted.[1]

Most Christians recognized the dissolution by the end of the century, but few recognized so early both that it was a fact, and what this fact meant. We have traced the gentle reshaping of Christianity that was occurring at the turn of the century, and we have hinted at the sudden tearing away of the Christian threads from the fabric of Western society. Wars and ideologies have been prime movers in this transformation.

In this chapter we want to look at this transformation of Christendom, as well as the *global* transformation of Christianity, by looking at the four main streams, or families, of Christianity: Orthodox, Roman Catholic, Protestant, and Spiritual. We will look at the major developments in the Christendom West as well as in the growing churches in the non-Western world. Not all families enjoyed the same fate. Not all regions embraced the same hope.

The Orthodox Family

It has generally been appropriate to speak of Orthodoxy as both a stream of Christianity and an approximate geographic location.[2] However, this is no longer true after the events of the twentieth century. Most of the Orthodox churches that we might study in earlier centuries were identified by an ethnic group or nation, and that nation or ethnic group was in a particular place: Greek Orthodox, Coptic (Egyptian) Orthodox, Russian Orthodox, and Serbian Orthodox, among others. The transformation of Orthodox Christianity in the twentieth century is most visible in the new Orthodox churches outside West Asia, the Mediterranean, and Eastern Europe. But this visible transformation is one of a number of changes. Here we will look at the major changes that took place in Orthodoxy, as seen through the twin lenses of persecution and globalization.

The twentieth century began tragically for Orthodox Christianity. Even though the Muslim Ottoman Empire was dying a slow death, its suffocating

---

1. Newbigin, *Household of God*, 11.
2. This is the approach in Irvin and Sunquist, *HWCM*.

impact on Christian life in West Asia and Eastern Europe had already taken its toll. In the final years, the Young Turk Revolution only increased the animosity toward non-Muslims and set the stage for the new Turkish government. That government, though building on "enlightened pragmatism," still resisted Greek occupation of "Turkish" lands, and so in 1922 the Turks invaded Smyrna, killing close to thirty thousand Christians. Many other massacres of Orthodox continued throughout the twentieth century, causing Orthodox believers to migrate, seeking safer lands. These persecutions and others, such as the Armenian Genocide and the Bolshevik Revolution, accelerated the decline of Orthodoxy during the century. Symbolic of this decline of Orthodox Christianity was the place and role of the patriarch of Constantinople. Once the glorious head of Orthodox Christians throughout the region, numbering to more than eight million, under the new nation of Turkey the patriarch had his direct oversight limited to the seventy thousand or eighty thousand Greeks residing in the capital of Constantinople. Greek Christians were not welcomed in Turkish lands, and so there was a mass exodus of Christians from West Asia. Between 1907 and 1926 the population of Greece grew from 2.6 million to more than 6 million, many of them Asian refugees who spoke Russian or Turkish.

With the change of governments in the region, the spread of Communism, and the rise of nationalism, Orthodox national churches were reconfigured. In some places a national church was developing, but the national governments generally opposed the church formulating a patriarchate. In Bulgaria, even with a growing Christian population, the monarch refused to allow the church to develop an order that might be perceived as a threat to the state, and so the church gradually (in the pattern of nineteenth-century Russia) came under state control. In the end Bulgarians became more and more secularized.

The decline of Orthodoxy in Lebanon is unique. The largest Lebanese church has always been the Maronite Church, an indigenous church founded in the fourth century by Saint Maron (d. 410). In the twentieth century this church declined from 73 percent to about 30 percent of the population of Lebanon. In its struggle to maintain a Christian national identity in the twentieth century, the mostly Christian nation (French protectorate from 1918 to 1943) suffered from the external onslaught of Muslim Arab resurgence and from internal Christian divisions. More than any other single issue, the formation of Israel set in motion a series of disruptions. In and around 1948, more than one hundred thousand Palestinian refugees flooded into Lebanon and were never allowed to return to their homeland. Then in 1975 a fifteen-year civil war broke out, resulting in a greater alliance of Lebanese elements with an international entity, the Arab League. Invasions by Syria and internal fighting among Christians,

Druze, and various Muslim (Arab, Palestinian) elements tore the fabric of Lebanese society and sent many Christians abroad for their own safety.

In many other countries in the region the Orthodox population declined. The Coptic Church in Egypt, about 17 percent of the population in 1900, was estimated to be only 10 percent (six million) in 2000. Many Copts moved to the West (two million), while others remained under great pressure to convert to Islam. Thus we see here, as well as with Lebanon, the twin themes of persecution and globalization (nearly 25 percent of the Copts now live outside of Egypt) most clearly. Each nation and context is unique, and yet some common features of twentieth-century Orthodoxy are evident from the Egyptian example. Nationalism, or a rising Egyptian identity vis-à-vis British imperialism, was one of the major factors in the treatment of Christians. The British favored Islamic identity over Christian rights, and so under Sir Eldon Gorst, British high commissioner from 1907 to 1911, the British effectively barred Copts from higher-level positions in government. Egypt's Muslims were encouraged further to argue for Egyptian identity as Muslim identity; to be Egyptian was to be Muslim.

When the Christians demanded greater participation in government and greater freedom for their religion, they were rebuffed. Christian-Muslim relations improved during the 1920s after the 1919 Revolution/Egyptian Revolution of 1919, when all Egyptians cooperated in resistance to the British occupation. Muslim leaders like Ahmad Lutfi al-Sayyid (1872–1963), journalist and academic, argued for Egyptian solidarity against the forces of colonialism. His arguments were modern and secular, but his approach later lost out to the Islamist influences. During the 1930s through the 1940s Copts were further marginalized under narrow Islamic nationalist movements. The 1952 revolution led to the independence of Egypt and further limitations for its Christian community. The 1971 constitution, ignoring the voice of Copts, instituted "Islam as the religion of the state, Arabic its official language and the principles of Islamic Shari'a as a principal source of legislation."[3] In effect, Christians in Egypt returned to the narrow and limited *dhimmi* status of "protected" non-Muslim natives living in an Islamic state, and the modern concept of a secular and pluralistic state was rejected.

And yet in the midst of this marginalization of the Copts, Christian women began to become involved politically in the 1919 protests against British rule, and they began to be acknowledged through their poetic writings and other scholarship. Pope[4] Cyril V (1874–1927) received the poetry of Coptic women

---

3. The text of the 1971 Constitution of Egypt can be found on the following website: http://www.constitutionnet.org/files/Egypt%20Constitution.pdf.

4. Although "pope" is most commonly understood as referring to the bishop of Rome, the patriarch of Alexandria in the Coptic church also receives the title "pope."

during his tour of Upper Egypt, and, along with rebuilding men's monasteries along the Nile, he rebuilt women's monasteries in Cairo. He was also an advocate for women's property rights and equal rights in marriage, contradicting Islamic law. Pope Cyril VI (1901–71), who reigned from 1959 to 1971, redeveloped ties with the Ethiopian Church and presided over the epochal Oriental Orthodox Conference in 1965 (convened by Ethiopian emperor Haile Selassie), which brought together Armenians and Syrians along with Egyptian and Ethiopian representatives. As a result of this conference, at a time of great persecution, these churches united in confirming that the Orthodox faith is based upon the Bible and the "sacred tradition" from Saint Mark. Later Cyril VI laid the foundation stone for the majestic Cathedral of Saint Mark (Anba Ruways). Thus, Cyril VI developed a reputation for church renewal through rebuilding and repairing churches. During his reign renewal also came through reported sightings of Mary in and around Zaytun, which fanned the flames of devotion to Mary beginning in 1968.

As Orthodoxy was suffering under both Communist ideology and growing Islamic and Arab revival, ecumenical relations helped to provide a new global identity as well as needed support for Orthodox churches. For the persecuted Christians, ecumenical ties were a way of saying, "We are all part of this global fellowship." One of the great ecumenical Orthodox leaders was Athenagoras I (born Aristokles Spyrou; lived 1886–1972), ecumenical patriarch from 1948 to 1972. Athenagoras, in the tradition of Cyril VI of Egypt, strongly supported Orthodox unity, but in addition he reached out to other Christians to repair many centuries-long divisions. He may have cultivated his passion for Christian unity during his seventeen-year tenure as archbishop of North and South America (1931–48), where he had to unite the various streams of ethnic Orthodoxy and at the same time work within Roman Catholic and Protestant contexts. One of the most remarkable moments in his life was when he met with Roman Catholic pope Paul VI (r. 1963–78) and they jointly lifted the anathemas of 1054. Thus the main and great division that had separated these two great churches was, at least symbolically, put aside.

The twentieth century has been the century of Orthodox diasporic communities because of persecutions and the threats of persecutions.[5] We have noted that Greece received Orthodox Christians fleeing the new Turkish nation and Soviet Russia. Most of the Russians, however, fled first to Baltic nations, Germany, France, and eventually (after World War II) to North America. In 1950 New York became the new headquarters for the Russian Orthodox Church Outside of Russia. Two Russian intellectuals, one a priest who stayed

5. See chapter 3 for a discussion of persecution and genocides of the twentieth century.

in Russia and one a revolutionary existentialist who fled the Bolsheviks, represent two of the major responses to the Bolsheviks. They also reflect the revival of Orthodox thought in the West. Basil Preobrazhenskii (1875–1945) was consecrated a bishop in 1921, in the midst of the great Soviet persecution of the church led by the secret police. Preobrazhenskii continued to lead the church and preach even during this anti-Christian campaign, and when this was not possible, he found ways to secretly provide catechetical instruction for children. This did not go on for long, for in 1923 the faithful bishop and his followers were imprisoned and then sent into exile, where he eventually died. His crime, like the crime of most exiled or executed bishops and priests, was his unwillingness to sign a loyalty pledge to the Soviet government. Thus he spent his last twenty-two years in exile.

Nikolai Berdyaev (1874–1948) was involved with revolutionary intellectuals in Kiev University, and his protests and agitation eventually led to imprisonment and internal exile. Later, his criticisms of the Orthodox Church Synod led to his being labeled a heretic, and only World War I prevented his further exile, this time to Siberia. When the Bolsheviks took over, he resisted them, not because of their Marxist analysis but because of their totalitarian rule. Exiled, he found himself first in Germany, and then in Paris, where he lived and eventually endured German occupation before his death. Berdyaev remained an Orthodox Christian, but he became an important bridge figure between Orthodoxy, modern social analysis, and existentialist philosophy. Influenced by Orthodox spirituality (mainly from Vladimir Solovyov), Berdyaev also made connections with mystical Christian spirituality and modern Western philosophy. His influence has been tremendous. The Catholic Worker Movement, founded by Dorothy Day and Peter Maurin in 1933, was greatly influenced by the writings of Berdyaev. Here we see Berdyaev's critique of the dominant nineteenth-century Christian philosophy of progress. This Western philosophy, he says, has a great moral contradiction in that it denigrates its own religious past while worshiping a future that is unfulfilled.

> It is this fundamental moral contradiction that invalidates the doctrine of progress, turning it into a religion of death instead of resurrection and eternal life. There is no valid ground for degrading those generations whose lot has been cast among pain and imperfection beneath that whose pre-eminence has been ordained in blessedness and joy. No future perfection can expiate the sufferings of past generations. Such a sacrifice of all human destinies to the messianic consummation of the favoured race can only revolt man's moral and religious conscience.[6]

6. Berdyaev, *Meaning of History*, 189.

We see here in the life of Berdyaev just a small example of the tremendous contribution Orthodoxy began to make to the global church outside its traditional lands as a result of its own forced migration. Roman Catholic studies and Reformation studies began to benefit from the new ecumenical dialogue forced upon the various Christian families, especially the modern reengagement with the patristic tradition.

Athenagoras I, one of the great ecumenical leaders of the century, began his vocation as a truly "ecumenical" patriarch providing leadership in the Americas. The diaspora way of life has been a gift to the Western world, but it has been a deep challenge to the Orthodox existence. Ethnic communities that no longer live in their homelands still live under the rule of their own self-governing (autocephalous) patriarch from their homeland. The problem of jurisdictions is an ongoing issue. In the early stages these diaspora groups are considered "missions," but over time they become more a part of their new context (China, Japan, North America), and such oversight becomes difficult. The situation of the Orthodox in the United States may be unique. With its origins in Russian missions to Alaska, a large influx of highly educated Russian Orthodox came to the United States even before the Russian Revolution. Over a twenty-two-year period the archbishops in "America" split from the highly compromised Orthodox Church in Russia, but their division also precipitated an internal division among the North American diasporic Orthodox. One of the groups, the Greek Catholic Russian Orthodox Church in America (later the Orthodox Church in America), was led by some of the most influential Orthodox theologians of the century: Fathers Georges Florovsky (1893–1979), Alexander Schmemann (1921–83), and John Meyendorff (1926–92). Under the leadership of these theologians the struggling Russian Orthodox seminary in New York, St. Vladimir's, became a notable center of global Orthodox theology. In 1970 the Moscow patriarchate granted both autonomy and autocephalous status to the Orthodox Church in America. This has not been universally accepted by Orthodox globally because any particular country can have only one autocephalous church. Greeks, Armenians, and others resist such an identity coming from Russian emigrants and pronounced by a compromised patriarchate. Orthodoxy in America remains a diverse community coming from every stream of Orthodoxy in the world, and some of those streams, such as the larger Russian and Greek streams, have attracted many young people from other ethnic backgrounds.

In its diaspora existence Orthodoxy has encountered the modern and pluralistic world. In this encounter we should not expect to see changes in worship or liturgy as we will observe with other confessional families. However, Orthodoxy has responded to many of the same social and cultural winds that

Christopher Humphrey Photography, 2014

Figure 13. Baptismal service for an infant at St. George Antiochian Orthodox Cathedral in Pittsburgh, Pennsylvania. The baby being baptized, along with his godparents and some of the priests involved, are non-Syrian members of this Antiochian Orthodox Congregation.

other Christians have encountered. The Orthodox have always had a vigorous theology of marriage and family, and so they resist all intrusions that would destroy the traditional sanctity of the family as expressed in Scripture and in the liturgy. Orthodoxy rejects any forms of contraception or birth control that involve abortifacient methods, and they resist all influences that would desacralize the mystery of marriage and the family life it engenders. Such respect for marriage and family allows barren couples to seek scientific or medical fertility aids that, honoring the sole union of husband and wife, will bring about future children. In this we can see that Orthodoxy is finding its way among modern movements and technologies, while remaining rooted in tradition.

Additionally, Orthodox women today have a larger role in the church than in previous centuries. Academic study of early texts that reputedly restricted women are now being interpreted within the larger Orthodox tradition as protecting and positioning women for various roles of leadership, often as ascetics. Today there are women Orthodox theologians who are leading the way in recovering some of the lost traditions of women in Orthodoxy. For example, for the past eight hundred years the female diaconate in Orthodoxy has been lost, but now there is discussion of recovering this lost office. Other discussions regarding women include removing the Levitical rules about blood and ritual cleanliness for women in liturgical practice and treating girl and boy infants equally at baptism. These and other discussions reveal some of the tensions within Orthodoxy in the present world but also the promise that Orthodoxy holds in finding answers in their ecumenical tradition for present realities.

Roman Catholicism in the Twentieth Century

Roman Catholicism entered the twentieth century in what appeared as a defensive mode regarding Western cultures, but today we can see that for most of the century, globally considered, Catholicism was engaging the world in new and creative ways. It is best to start with Pius X (r. 1903–14), the first pope since the sixteenth century to be canonized. Often considered the "antimodern" pope, a century later he is being understood as the pope who paved the way for Roman Catholicism to survive in the new context of the modern world, a world in which the church was no longer one of the two crowns of political authority. By the middle of the twentieth century Christendom would be breaking down. Modern nation-states would leave the Roman Catholic Church hierarchy without a royal partner (or antagonist) with whom to validate their authority. It was Pius's contribution, through his Code of Canon Law (promulgated after his death by Pope Benedict XV, 1917), to provide the means, or the path, for the church to reform and find a place in the modern world. In a rapid transformation never seen before, the global network of national churches (and religious schools) were all unified under the Holy See.

This can be thought of as counterrevolutionary, reductionistic, or reactionary, but it provided the order needed for modern Catholicism to be a global movement connected as a universal church, rather than as a conglomerate of national churches working in tandem with the (no longer existent) royal rulers. Even the apparently heavy-handed "Anti-Modernist Oath" (*sacrorum antistitum*)—required to be signed by "all clergy, pastors, confessors, preachers, religious superiors, and professors in philosophical-theological seminaries"— should be seen both as a common Christian response to the challenges of the modern world and as a way for Catholicism to survive the new movements of nationalism and modern secular assumptions.[7] The statement, signed by almost every priest from the time of its promulgation in 1910 until its abolition in 1967, can be summarized in the last affirmation: "Lastly, I profess myself in everything totally averse to the error whereby modernists hold that there is

---

7. The Anti-Modernist Oath can be found at http://www.papalencyclicals.net/Pius10/p10 moath.htm.

nothing divine in sacred tradition . . . [and] . . . I most firmly retain the faith of the Fathers." As with the Protestant fundamentalists, the earliest response was to strongly affirm the tradition, including the reality of "miracles and prophecies." As we will see, the second step was to find ways to hold on to that tradition and engage the world in new ways.

It was the religious orders, not the papacy, that continued to be the vanguard of innovation and global engagement of the Roman Catholic Church. Although not as prolific as those in the nineteenth century, new religious orders did spring up for specific missional ministries in the twentieth century as those ministries moved out into new social and intellectual frontiers. The new orders, going back as far as the nineteenth century, had the effect of both centralizing and globalizing the Roman Catholic communion. Newer orders, or "congregations," were mostly "exempt" orders, meaning that they were not under the direct supervision of a local bishop; they looked to Rome for permissions and guidance. Most of the missionary work in the nineteenth and twentieth centuries was done by these missions, and so they became, as it were, collaborators with the Vatican, giving Catholicism a more centralized global outreach and development.

New orders continued to emerge in the twentieth century. The Daughters of St. Paul, founded in 1915 in Italy, was one of a number of new orders founded by Fr. James Alberione to promote the Word of God, through teaching, preaching, and modern means of communication. The year before, he had founded the Society of St. Paul (Paulists) to work specifically in media. His concern was to respond to the modern world by using all modern means available to communicate the gospel of God. Later he founded other orders and societies to reach all sectors of society. By the end of the century, the Paulists had become well known for their publications and other media ministries. Other newer orders followed the example of more modern missionaries. The life of Charles de Foucauld (1858–1916), who lived in Algeria among the Tuareg people, became an example of Christian presence and compassion for nineteen other religious orders founded in his train. Charles died alone in the desert, having been shot by passing Bedouins, but not before he had become well known for both his Christian witness and his translation of the Tuareg language. Some of the orders that were founded through his inspiration include Jesus Caritas, the Little Sisters of Jesus, and the Little Brothers of Jesus.

Another example of twentieth-century orders is the Franciscan Brothers of Peace, founded in 1982 in St. Paul, Minnesota, with a special concern for protecting the lives of the unborn and seeking peace. This is an interesting order in that its initial inspiration came from a prophetic word delivered at a National Charismatic Renewal Conference held at the University of Notre

Dame. The modern Pentecostal movement began to influence Roman Catholic and Protestant churches in the 1960s. February 18, 1967, is considered the birth date of the Roman Catholic charismatic movement, which now claims to include more than 100 million Roman Catholics. On that Saturday in 1967 a group of university students from Duquesne University in Pittsburgh, Pennsylvania, were on a spiritual retreat, led by theology professors. Two professors had recently experienced the "baptism of the Holy Spirit," as they called it, in the small home of a Presbyterian woman, Florence Dodge. Influenced by the Pentecostal movement and the recent growing presence of the charismatic movement in the Episcopal Church, Dodge and others prayed for the Catholics. It seems that God answered the Presbyterian prayers, for within the year the experiences in the Holy Spirit were spread to the University of Notre Dame in Indiana, to campus ministers in Lansing, Michigan, and soon around the world.

This movement was very much Roman Catholic, emphasizing the celebration of the Eucharist and prayers to Mary, but now with greater lay involvement and with more study of the Bible. By the end of 1970 more than ten thousand North American Catholics had met at charismatic meetings, and soon the movement was spreading in New Zealand, Australia, England, and parts of Latin America. Influenced by Protestant charismatics and Pentecostals, the Roman Catholic charismatic movement blurred the lines between different Christian families, while maintaining Roman Catholic piety regarding Mary and the sacraments. Brazil is a case in point. Pentecostalism bridged Roman Catholic and Protestant churches as millions of Roman Catholics became involved in grassroots Catholic charismatic renewal groups (CCRs). At about the same time (in the 1970s) many Catholics joined "basic ecclesial communities" (*communidades ecclesiais de base*, CEBs). The CEBs were more focused on responding to local social realities, but both CEBs and CCRs drew Catholics together in worship and fellowship in the pattern of past Catholic lay associations. Many Catholics still participate in both and attend worship that may involve both traditional and Pentecostal elements. These dual movements of vitality in Roman Catholicism occurred in Asia as well, bringing about a global Catholic matrix of grassroots theological developments that expressed new charismata and local engagement. This was possible because of the most important Roman Catholic event of the century, the Second Vatican Council.

When Pope John XXIII (1881–1963) was elected pope in 1958, it was assumed by most people that, at seventy-eight years old, he would be a transition pope, steering the church on a straight course for a few years. The global public was mistaken. In less than three months of his election, on January 25, 1959, he announced that he would call for a general council of the church to "bring the Church up to date" (to bring about an *aggiornamento*). He also used the language of "opening up the windows."[8] Fresh winds did blow into the Roman Church as a result of the Second Vatican Council (1962–65), but in addition, it appeared to many people that some unwanted matter also blew in.

At the end of the last meeting, on December 8, 1965, the council (between 2,100 and 2,540 bishops) had met in 168 plenary sessions, in 10 public assemblies over a total of 36 weeks. The council approved four core documents (on liturgy, *Sacrosanctum Concilium*; on revelation, *Dei Verbum*; on the church, *Lumen Gentium*; and on the church in the world, *Gaudium et Spes*) as the foundation for twelve other documents.

The council was the twenty-first council (by Roman Catholic counting), and with only 1,041 Europeans included, it was the first time the Europeans and West Asians could not control the decisions of the church. There were 956 bishops from the Americas, 279 from Africa, and 300 from Asia. It was an all-male conference with (eventually) twenty-two women "auditors" invited, but the changes in women's religious orders were far greater than their representation would indicate. Non-Catholic observers—including Methodist Albert Outler, Lutheran George Lindbeck, Presbyterian Robert McAfee Brown, and Orthodox Nikos Nissiotis of the World Council of Churches—gave the council a healing and ecumenical aura.

Figure 14. Vatican II Assembly by Lothar Wolleh

Lothar Wolleh/Wikimedia Commons

A number of changes blossomed from this council, but we would like to focus on just four that have had a lasting impact upon all of Christianity into the twenty-first century. First, one of the core concerns of the council, which ended up producing sixteen documents,[9] was the unity of the church. To that

8. Sullivan, *Road to Vatican II*, 40.
9. Four "Constitutions," three "Declarations," and nine "Decrees."

The Maryvale Institute, *The Sower* 23, no. 1 (2002)

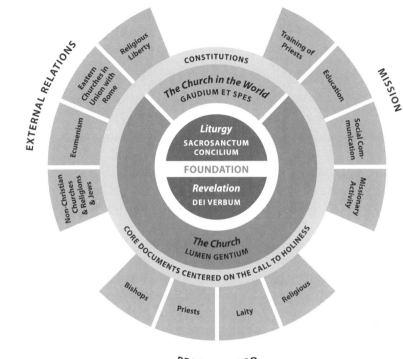

Figure 15. Chart of the documents of Vatican II, highlighting the interlinking themes and teachings

end, a Dominican priest who had been shunned by the church for decades, Yves Congar (1904–95), was specially appointed by John XXIII to help write the documents. As much as any other single person, Congar, with his concern and commitment to church unity and his theology of church as communion in the Triune God, provided the strong theological structure for the two core documents on the church: *Gaudium et Spes* (*Pastoral Constitution on the Church in the Modern World*) and *Lumen Gentium* (*Dogmatic Constitution on the Church*).

Congar, raised among Reformed Protestants and Jewish neighbors in northeast France, developed relationships with young Protestants in the World Student Christian Federation—many of whom became Protestant ecumenical leaders—and wrote an important work on the church when he was just thirty-three, *Chrétiens désunis* (*Divided Christendom: A Catholic Study of the Problem of Reunion*). Although he had been sent into exile by Pope Pius XII for his controversial writings, he was revived by Pope John XXIII and, along with Jesuit Henri de Lubac, was brought to Rome to help write preparatory material for the upcoming council. His irenic theology of the church drew deeply from biblical, liturgical, and patristic sources and rooted the church's identity in the Trinity. The church is communion, the "Body of Christ, a communion in which humanity shares in God's own communion through the mediation of Christ."[10] With the new emphasis on sharing in communion and relationship with the Triune God, Congar and the Second Vatican Council moved away from a primarily hierarchical understanding of the church. The repercussions would be dramatic.

Second, as a result of Vatican II the liturgy and Scriptures were put in the local languages. In the council's foundational document on divine revelation (*Dei Verbum*) we read in section 6, "But since the word of God should be accessible at all times, the Church by her authority and with maternal concern sees to it that suitable and correct translations are made into different languages, especially from the original texts of the sacred books. And should the opportunity arise and the Church authorities approve, if these translations are produced in cooperation with the separated brethren as well, all Christians will be able to use them."[11] Here two important themes of Vatican II—Christian unity ("separated brethren") and common access to Scriptures—are expressed together. Throughout the sixteen documents non-Catholic Christians are not identified as "outside of the church," but now as "separated brethren." Brethren are people of the same family, so the nomenclature was very important in beginning to turn back the divisions of the sixteenth century. As a result of the shift to the vernacular in the use of Scripture and in literature, religious practices and beliefs were brought into the lives, families, and villages of Catholics throughout the world. The Latin Vulgate Bible had been commonly used in the West and became the official Catholic Bible during the Council of Trent in 1546. After four hundred years the Latin Vulgate Bible was replaced by translations of the Bible in the various mother tongues of Catholic believers all over the world. The insistence on Latin for worship had been a major issue dividing Catholics from Protestants. Now it became another reason for traditionalists among the Catholics to become more and more concerned.

Third, after Vatican II a different missiological understanding became a dominant theme in ecclesiology. The new constitution of the church begins with the words *Lumen gentium*, or, in the English translation, "Christ is the light of the nations." Thus the church, from the first sentence, is identified with the mission of Christ for all nations. Again, in the first chapter (paragraph 5) the missionary nature of the church is affirmed from its genesis:

10. Ruddy, *Local Church*, 41.
11. http://www.vatican.va/archive/hist_councils/documents/vat-ii_const_19651118_dei -verbum_en.html.

When Jesus, who had suffered the death of the cross for mankind, had risen, He appeared as the one constituted as Lord, Christ and eternal Priest, and He poured out on His disciples the Spirit promised by the Father. From this source the Church, equipped with the gifts of its Founder and faithfully guarding His precepts of charity, humility and self-sacrifice, receives the mission to proclaim and to spread among all peoples the Kingdom of Christ and of God and to be, on earth, the initial budding forth of that kingdom. While it slowly grows, the Church strains toward the completed Kingdom and, with all its strength, hopes and desires to be united in glory with its King.[12]

Even the *Constitution on the Sacred Liturgy* (*Sacrosanctum Concilium*), in its first paragraph, has a missiological (and ecumenical) concern: "[This sacred Council is] . . . to foster whatever can promote union among all who believe in Christ; to strengthen whatever can help to call the whole of mankind into the household of the Church. The Council therefore sees particularly cogent reasons for undertaking the reform and promotion of the liturgy."[13] Unity of all believers and inclusion of all of humanity—important missiological themes—are twin concerns guiding all of the council's decisions.

A fourth major change is actually more of a trajectory that Vatican II sent the Roman Catholic Church as a result of its greater engagement in ecumenical and social dialogue. The church became more directly engaged in the world, and the world became more a part of the church. Nuns began to shun habits (religious clothing), worship was conducted in the vernacular, laypeople began to participate more in worship, bishops and priests began to oppose economic and political oppression more openly, and old patterns of ecclesial and political alignments began to break apart. Not everyone was pleased with this greater openness to the world and the search for greater unity with other (separated) Christians. Some blamed the late twentieth-century decline of Roman Catholicism on the decisions of Vatican II, and not without reason. In England and Wales the attendance at Mass dropped from 2.1 million to just more than 1 million from 1966 to 1999. In that same period the number of newly ordained priests dropped from 230 to just 43. The statistics in North America and throughout Europe are similar. However, the reason for the drop in Roman Catholic activity and vocations seems to be part of the much larger trend of secularization of the West. In the same period, Roman Catholicism grew in Africa from 12 percent to 15 percent of the population. Vatican II did not stem

12. http://www.vatican.va/archive/hist_councils/ii_vatican_council/documents/vat-ii_const _19641121_lumen-gentium_en.html.

13. http://www.vatican.va/archive/hist_councils/ii_vatican_council/documents/vat-ii_const _19631204_sacrosanctum-concilium_en.html.

the tide of secularization in the West, but it did open viaducts for Christianity outside the West. There is no argument that Vatican II facilitated the development of Christianity outside the North Atlantic world. Catholicism became more African, more Asian, more Latin American, and more Pacific Islander.

For decades after the closing of Vatican II there was much interpretation about how the council had opened up the church to the world (the progressives) or, conversely, how the council restated Catholic theology and ecclesiology in new language (the traditionalists). In Latin America, a continent-wide council of bishops (CELAM: Latin American Episcopal Conference) that was formed in 1955 had prepared the Latin American church to respond as a continent to grave injustices and ongoing poverty. The Second Vatican Council's new emphasis on the church as being "the pilgrim people of God"[14] was seized upon by the CELAM 1968 gathering at Medellín, Colombia. Using emergent themes from liberation theology, the conference of bishops denounced the scandalous inequities and "the oppression of institutionalized violence"[15] in the Americas. After centuries of walking closely with kings, governors, and landowners in Latin America, the bishops, as it were, broke ranks and sided with the poor and oppressed. The new theological understanding was reaffirmed at later meetings in Puebla (1979) and Santo Domingo (1992). The unwelcome response from the Vatican was a recommendation of restraint, and from military governments it was persecution and martyrdoms. More than 850 priests and nuns were killed in the 1970s, and hundreds more into the 1980s.[16] In a similar fashion, after the visit of Pope Paul VI to Manila in 1970 a Federation of Asian Bishops' Conferences (FABC) was established, giving structure to Asian Catholic theological and missional concerns. The FABC was formed not only to address concerns about injustice (especially in the Philippines) but also specifically to carry out the mandates issued by, and address the new concerns engendered by, the Second Vatican Council. Because of the unique situation of the church in Asia, the FABC has as one of its seven main concerns "to foster ecumenical and interreligious communication and collaboration."[17] Vatican II should be considered the most significant council of the church since the Reformation period. Seldom do a council's decisions so immediately affect believers in local churches or affect their weekly practices.

However, Vatican II was not the only major influence in Catholicism in the twentieth century. We have already mentioned the charismatic movement

14. http://www.vatican.va/archive/hist_councils/ii_vatican_council/documents/vat-ii_const _19641121_lumen-gentium_en.html.

15. http://www.mercaba.org/Pastoral/C/celam_documentos. Translation by Juan Martinez.

16. See the discussion of Oscar Romero and Dom Hélder Câmara in chapter 2.

17. http://www.fabc.org/about.htm.

beginning soon after Vatican II. Much earlier, another movement that influenced both laity and clerics started in Spain. The Sociedad Sacerdotal de la Santa Cruz y Opus Dei (also called simply Opus Dei, meaning "work of God") was founded by José María Escrivá de Balaguer (1902–75) in 1928 in an effort to bring the disciplines and holiness of the Catholic to all people in everyday life, both priests and laypeople together. As Escrivá explained it, his vision from God to found Opus Dei was given as a way to help ordinary Christians "to understand that their life, just as it is, can be an opportunity for meeting Christ: that it is a way of holiness and apostolate [evangelization]. Christ is present in any honest human activity. The life of an ordinary Christian, which to some people may seem banal and petty, can and should be a holy and sanctifying life."[18] In its early years the work was very much marked by Spanish austerity, discipline, and even nationalism, but over the decades it has become a global movement with its main concern being to deepen the spiritual life of Christians in everyday circumstances. The movement has had its critics, but Pope John Paul II recognized Escrivá's contribution of bringing holiness to everyday life and had him beatified in 1992. The charismatic movement, Opus Dei, and the Second Vatican Council are all twentieth-century paths that the Roman Catholic Church has traveled that have brought greater involvement of the laity and have increased ecumenical and global outreach.

A few issues in the Roman Catholic Church continued to be controversial at the end of the twentieth century, issues such as birth control and the male celibate priesthood. Almost all Christians opposed birth control at the beginning of the twentieth century, both for theological reasons (God commanded humanity to "be fruitful and multiply") and because most abortifacients were either dangerous or unreliable until the middle of the century. The Roman Catholic Church reaffirmed this broadly Christian position with the 1930 encyclical of Pope Pius XI (*Casti Connubii*); then this was later defined and explained by Pope Paul VI in 1968 (*Humanae Vitae*), and by the Congregation for the Doctrine of the Faith in 1987 in its *Instruction on Respect for Human Life in Its Origin and on the Dignity of Procreation. Replies to Questions of the Day*. With the rapid advances in science, the greater variety of contraception, and the rising rates of abortion, the Catholic Church responded with the 2008 instruction titled *Dignitas Personae*. Consistent with earlier statements, this instruction makes it clear that Catholics are not to support artificial means of preventing pregnancy, or artificial means of ending a pregnancy, or even

18. This quotation has been misused and misquoted in many contexts, but on the "Escriva Works" website it is given under conversation #60 as shown here: http://www.escrivaworks.org /book/conversations/point/60.

artificial means of creating a pregnancy. Although the Roman Catholic position on birth issues is clear, it became increasingly difficult for most Catholics to follow. Many Catholics do use birth control, even though most lay Catholics stand with the Vatican in opposition to all forms of abortion.

The second issue that has created much tension in the Roman Catholic Church is the issue of the celibate (and male) priesthood. During the Second Vatican Council there were good Catholics who hoped that the aggiornamento ("bringing up to date") that Pope John XXIII had spoken of would include allowing priests to marry. However, on the day before the council ended, December 7, 1965, Pope Paul VI released a decree on the priesthood (*Presbyterorum Ordinis*) in which the theological, biblical, and practical reasons for celibacy are given in section 16. The celibacy requirement in an age when sexuality is emphasized seems to have made it harder to recruit priests. It is difficult to say if the celibacy requirement or the general decline of Christianity in the West is at fault, but from 1990 to 2003 the number of active priests (both religious and secular) fell 22 percent in the United States. This is a very rapid decline. In contrast, the number of African priests increased from 1985 to 2005 by 55 percent.[19]

Roman Catholicism entered the twenty-first century more diverse than ever, reflecting in reality the globalization it began in the fifteenth century. By the end of the century, people were talking about the possibility of a Nigerian pope, something that could not have been imagined before 1962. The election of a Brazilian pope in the early twenty-first century seemed possible, but unlikely, when it was suggested. The election of the Argentinian pope now seems unsurprising. It is expected that African and Asian leadership in the Vatican will continue to outpace Western leadership in a church that continues to decline in the West.

Protestant Churches

Protestant Christianity, starting late in the modern mission era, greatly outpaced Roman Catholicism globally in the twentieth century. But by the end of the twentieth century the growing edge of Christianity was suddenly passed on from the Protestant churches to the Spiritual churches, especially the Pentecostal, African Indigenous Churches, and unregistered churches in China. Protestantism's main themes after 1920 were the tandem issues of ecumenical unity and mission. At different times and places one or the other would be the leading

19. Dean R. Hoge, "Facts and Figures: The State of the Priesthood," in *The Boston College Magazine*, Summer, 2005. http://bcm.bc.edu/issues/summer_2005/c21_hoge.html.

partner, but throughout the century these two themes dominated. A number of subthemes—church independence, ordination of women, liturgical renewal, contextualization—flow out of the impact of the missionary experience and the struggle for Christian unity. Here we look briefly at these major themes.

We can say that the 1910 Edinburgh Missionary Conference marks both the end of the "Great Century for Missions" and the beginning of the ecumenical century. The design of the conference was to study carefully how to best evangelize the remaining areas of the world, by which the attendees meant that the church should have witnessing communities in all regions of all countries of the world. With the disruptions of World War I and rise of Communism, churches redirected their cooperation to finding ways to work for peace and then to help rebuild Western societies and churches. Missions were often orphaned, and most took a long time to recover; many never did. Still, the concern for Christian unity grew in the midst of social upheavals and missionary decline. The concern for unity began on the "mission field," but the theory and conferences were mostly European and North American endeavors until after World War II.

In the 1920s three important international church conferences were held, symbolizing the major areas of concern in Christian unity. Unity was sought through a conference on "life and work" (Stockholm, 1925), through another on "faith and order" (Lausanne, 1927), and through a third on international mission (Jerusalem, 1928). These conferences were marked by the broader Western theology of the twentieth century coming from the social gospel, theologies of religion, and liberal theologies. Tensions within the ecumenical movement were evident beginning in the 1920s. We now look first at the missionary conferences.

At the Jerusalem Conference of the International Missionary Council (IMC), for example, the specter of secular Marxism in Russia was so great a concern that many delegates called for all religions to unite against the rising tide of Marxism. The common human experience of religion was emphasized, whereas in the past, as recently as at the Edinburgh Conference in 1910, other religions were understood to be the "mission field." Ten years later another IMC conference was held, this time in Tambaram (Madras), India. The Tambaram Conference marks a major shift in Protestant thinking in mission. Mission was now described as the task of the whole church, not just of professionals, priests, or preachers. When the ecumenical movement now used the phrase, "Let the church be the church,"[20] it meant, in part, let the church—meaning all Christians—participate in God's mission to the whole world. The church

20. It was John McKay who first coined the phrase at the Oxford Conference of Church, Community, and State in 1937. See his book, *Ecumenics, Science of the Church Universal*, 5, 6.

had a witness-bearing responsibility that was understood as part of its very nature. This was a very forward-looking rediscovery, for even at the end of the century many of the churches in the West had not fully grasped this concept. The findings of the conference expressed it clearly: "It is the church and the church alone which can carry the responsibility of transmitting the gospel from one generation to another, of preserving its purity, and of proclaiming it to all creatures. . . . The place where this task is centered is the local church or congregation."[21]

The missionary nature of the church was rediscovered, but from the Americans came a challenge to the meaning of that missionary task. Supported by the expansive resources and great generosity of John D. Rockefeller, seven mission boards backed a large study on the Western missionary work in representative countries in Asia: China, Japan, India, and Burma. Their report, produced under the leadership of Harvard professor of philosophy William Ernest Hocking, was published in 1932. In short, the report, *Re-Thinking Missions, A Laymen's Inquiry after One Hundred Years*, prescribed a new approach to mission that called on the church to "be willing to give largely without any preaching, to cooperate whole-heartedly with non-Christian agencies for social improvement."[22] American optimism, progressivism, and pragmatism drove the theology of the report, and it created a major upheaval in mission circles. This common search for truth and social improvement, dislodged from basic and traditional words about Jesus and the Trinity, was troubling enough that Hendrik Kraemer, Dutch missionary to the East Indies, was commissioned to prepare a biblical and theological study prior to the 1938 meeting. His study, *The Christian Message in a Non-Christian World*, was a strongly argued 450-page study built largely on a "biblical realism." "The realism of the Bible . . . simply takes seriously, on account of a robust and sane intuition, the fact that God is God and that if He is God, his Will is the Ground of all that is."[23] The two positions—continuity of Christian faith with other faiths (Hocking's report), on the one hand, and absolutely no continuity between God's revelation and our beliefs (Kraemer), on the other hand—were outlined in these two works. Protestant Christianity was greatly polarized regarding its mission and view of non-Christian religions before World War II.

Other Protestant mission conferences were held after the war, but dialogue continued between those advocating the centrality of the Christian message for all people and those emphasizing the need to cooperate with all religions

21. Quoted in Bassham, *Mission Theology, 1848–1975*, 24.
22. Hocking, *Re-Thinking Missions*, 326.
23. Kraemer, *Christian Message*, 68.

in works of justice and social healing. The 1960s was the decade when many of these positions came to a head. The 1961 World Council of Churches (WCC) General Assembly, held in New Delhi, India, brought the IMC into the broader ecumenical movement. This integration, it was feared by some, would mean that the missionary task of the church would be overwhelmed or absorbed by other ecumenical tasks. Many Protestants in the West sensed the divide much earlier and began to set up their parallel missionary and ecumenical organizations. The rise of groups like the National Association of Evangelicals in 1942 and the Evangelical Foreign Missions Association (both in the United States) just four years later marked the division in Western Christianity and the shift of balance of Protestant Christianity to North America. A new form of missionary cooperation began in 1974 with a major conference in Lausanne, Switzerland, headed up by the Billy Graham Association. The Lausanne Conference in some ways was a parallel ecumenical movement, based not on faith-and-order discussions but on cooperation for worldwide evangelism. Many people in the movement claimed to be recovering the heritage of the 1910 Edinburgh Missionary Conference. This first meeting involved 2,300 participants representing 150 countries, and it marked the rise to international prominence of a new generation of evangelical leaders like Billy Graham and John R. W. Stott. These were not official church delegates, but self-appointed or self-selected leaders who spoke only for themselves. Nonetheless, the enduring quality of the Lausanne Covenant and of many other later documents and statements from the Lausanne movement suggests that Lausanne and other evangelical groups were speaking the language and expressing the concerns of a large number of Protestants as well as Pentecostals.

After the polarized positions of the 1960s the winds shifted, and during the late 1970s and 1980s, some talked of consensus or convergence between the ecumenical and evangelical movements, especially after the 1975 Nairobi Assembly of the WCC. John Stott, a champion of evangelicalism, spoke up at this conference and said that the WCC needed to recover recognition of the lostness of humanity, confidence in the truth and power of the gospel, conviction about the uniqueness of Christ, the urgency of evangelism, and personal experience of Christ. By the end of the century the WCC maintained a broad involvement in mission, with much greater emphasis on peacemaking, environmental issues, and justice. The evangelical groups also maintained a broader involvement of mission than before, but with greater emphasis on evangelism and church planting among "unreached people groups." At particular times and places the divide seems to expand or contract, but it was no longer just a Western discussion. As the Western institutional structures promoted ongoing discussions, most of the missionary work had become the prerogative of Asians, Africans, and Latin Americans after the 1980s. Thus, the first area of ecumenical cooperation was in the area of missionary work and mission theology.

The second important area of ecumenical cooperation revolved around the issues of Christian life and work. Many people, after the centuries of division over theology and liturgy in the Protestant churches, argued that "theology divides, but service unites." In fact, the 1925 Conference on Life and Work, held in Stockholm, Sweden, with six hundred delegates from thirty-seven countries, adopted this phrase as their watchword. Participants in the Life and Work movement found they could agree on many issues and need not allow differences over definitions of the Eucharist or married priests to prevent cooperation. Feeding the poor, caring for refugees, and intervening for reconciliation and peace were issues on which all Christians could agree. The "Message" from the Stockholm Conference stated concerns for common unity, and it outlined areas of concern for society:

> The sins and sorrows, the struggles and losses of the Great War and since, have compelled the Christian Churches to recognize, humbly and with shame, that "the world is too strong for a divided Church. . . ." [We have] accepted the urgent duty of applying [Christ's] Gospel in all realms of human life—industrial, social, political and international.
>
> Thus, in the area of economics we have declared that the soul is the supreme value, that it must not be subordinated to the rights of property, or to the mechanism of industry. . . . Cooperation between capital and labour should take the place of conflict, so that employers and employed alike may be enabled to regard their part in industry, as the fulfillment of a vocation.[24]

"Service" as an abstract noun can unite, but once it becomes necessary to act in specific ways (supporting labor unions, or promoting socialization of human services), it is harder to keep Christians united. This first conference followed a more classical liberal approach to social issues, but the next conference, one of the most significant conferences ever for social ethics, was quite different. This one, the Oxford Conference in 1937, was led by theologians like Reinhold Niebuhr, whose public address became a signpost of biblical realism as a Christian social concept. Held in the shadow of the rising Nazi movement in Germany, the conference spoke clearly about racism, social order, international order, and the need for church unity as "society goes to pieces." J. H. Oldham, the main organizer of the conference, expressed the basic approach in social ethics that the conference espoused as "middle axioms."

---

24. For the whole "Message" from Stockholm, see Bell, *Stockholm Conference 1925*, 710–16.

The Gospel is not a code of morals or a new law. But the new mind which is formed in those who have responded to the revelation of a new reality in Christ must express itself in new forms of behavior. . . . Between purely general statements of the ethical demands of the Gospel and the decisions that have to be made in concrete situations there is a need for what may be described as middle axioms.[25]

Many of the later discussions about the role of the state, racism, war, and peace would return to discussions and statements that came out of the Oxford Conference of 1913.

Not until the momentous 1960s did Protestant thinking about social ethics and global issues shift significantly. The 1920s and 1960s had common features for Western Christianity. During both decades social thinking in the church shifted, divisions hindered the church's work, and the church grew greatly in many parts of the world. Engaging a rapidly changing world called for radical responses, and many of these were seen as unfaithful to the church's great tradition, even as others saw the responses as being faithful for the contemporary contexts. More liberal social policies and theological approaches split churches in the West as well as in the East (the 1920s mark the rise of independency in China), and in the 1960s some of these responses used Marxist analysis, while others contained much stronger responses to ongoing racism. Again, churches split over whether to support the ecumenical movement in its social engagement. Two conferences highlighted the new social engagement of the ecumenical movement: the 1966 World Conference on Church and Society (Geneva) and the 1968 Fourth Assembly of the WCC (Uppsala, Sweden).

The Geneva Conference was the first major ecumenical conference whose delegates were mostly non-Western and were mostly nonclerical. It was an important departure from past conferences also in that it was commissioned to speak *to* the WCC rather than speaking *for* the WCC. With participation from Archpriest Vitaly Borovoy of the USSR, and in the context of revolutionary situations in Latin America and with international attention on the United States' involvement in Vietnam, the conference made strong, often revolutionary pronouncements:

As Christians we are committed to working for the transformation of society. In the past we have usually done this through quiet efforts at social renewal, working in and through the established institutions, according to their rules. Today, a significant number of those who are dedicated to the service of Christ and their neighbour assume a more radical or revolutionary position. . . . They

25. Hooft and Oldham, *Church and Its Function*, 209–10.

are searching for a new strategy by which to bring about basic changes in society without too much delay.[26]

Behind this language was a new theology that saw God's action in revolutionary movements of the age. Christians were called to participate in these movements and to recognize the "'incognito Christ' . . . working through technology and secularity."[27] The conference expressed an impatience or "urgency" regarding the slow global changes taking place and a confidence in human ability to recognize where God is at work and to bring about kingdom changes. Some ecumenists saw the last decades of the twentieth century as "decisively shaped by the experience of pluralism (i.e., by the dialogue of cultures and ideologies with the now global church)."[28] It is true that within the ecumenical movement there was a much larger and more open engagement with social movements, liberation movements, and technology. The theology undergirding these responses was based more on a realized eschatology and a secularized kingdom of God. Evangelicals and fundamentalists criticized this theological development, and yet ecumenical Protestantism was continuing the ongoing concern for the poor, oppressed, and marginalized.

The Uppsala Assembly of the WCC (1968) carried these concerns further, under the shadow of violence (Martin Luther King Jr. was to be a speaker but was assassinated before the assembly), but still with unquenchable optimism about what revolutionary Christians could do. The official report, seen from the twenty-first century, makes humanity seem strangely felicitous. "For the first time in history we can see the oneness of mankind as a reality. . . . The new technological possibilities turn what were dreams into realities."[29] Later ecumenical meetings were more realistic as to what could be accomplished, but the decades of social witness that focused on personal responsibility to bring about revolutionary changes damaged the ecumenical witness. Direct involvement in revolutionary situations such as the struggle against apartheid in South Africa meant supporting refugees and others who were fighting for justice. Some of the money ended up in the hands of liberation fighters. Direct involvement in such struggles involves such risks, but the global Christian community is not always forgiving. One of the more constructive statements in the area of society came from the 1990 WCC Convocation on Justice, Peace and the Integrity of Creation. Linking the three issues together—with specific statements on the poor, racism, women's rights, and

26. Mosley, *Revolutions of Our Time*, 49.
27. Schall, "Revolutionary Challenge," 25–32.
28. Kinnamon and Cope, *Ecumenical Movement*, 4.
29. Goodall, *The Uppsala Report 1968*, 45.

youth—has given Protestant Christianity a way to constructively engage global issues. The concerns for creation, ecology, and global warming have become global Christian concerns that have helped to unite all four Christian families.

The third major area of ecumenical concern has been faith and order, or working toward agreement in areas of Christian belief and religious practices. In this realm one of the most difficult issues is the most basic: what is the ecumenical goal? Is the goal to reverse the effects of the Reformation so that a single united universal church will evolve? Or is the goal some type of global association or union of different churches such that each accepts the others as equal? There is still no consensus, but there is common consent that churches must continue to move closer together in all areas of shared faith and practice. The earliest efforts of cooperation and union occurred in missionary contexts. Mission societies working in Asia and Africa fully recognized one another's ministries, and so comity agreements were made, dividing territories for missionary work. One of the most famous of these was the meeting held in New York as Protestant mission societies prepared to enter the formerly Spanish-controlled Philippines. In India various Presbyterian societies united in their work in 1904, a year later they added Congregational churches, and in 1908 all of these formed the South India United Church. After decades of work this Reformed union was expanded to include Methodists and Anglicans when the Church of South India was finally formed in 1947. This union and others like it (Church of Christ in Thailand, United Church of Christ in the Philippines, etc.) were organic unions.

In the West, with its much longer-standing traditions and divisions, such consolidation has been more difficult. In the earliest conferences the hope was expressed that by talking about differences, churches could move toward consensus. Later conferences realized that the focus should be on what holds Christians together. We should start with the common faith that Christians share. From this foundation, so it was reasoned, church leaders could build toward greater and broader unity. Some Western churches (more precisely, "denominations") did unite, or began to unite. In 1925 the United Church of Canada, one of the earliest Western church unions, was formed out of the Methodist and Congregational churches and 70 percent of the Presbyterian Church of Canada. As with all unions, it brought together Christians, but it also created divisions in the process. The Uniting Church of Australia (UCA) was formed in 1977 from the smaller non-Anglican or non-Catholic churches: Presbyterian, Methodist, and Congregational. Both the United Church of Canada and the UCA view themselves as in a process of "uniting," seeking further unity with other churches through time.

Some church unions have been forced by political decisions completely out of the hands of church leaders. During the Japanese imperial period, the Japanese "Religious Organizations Law" (1939) was part of a total effort of Japan to create two churches: Protestant and Catholic. The same policy was pursued in other nations in East Asia. However, in Japan there was already great progress toward Protestant unity, beginning with the 1923 Christian Alliance of Japan. Across the East China Sea, in 1922 about one-fourth of the Protestant Christians in China united, creating the foundation for what would later be the Three-Self Patriotic Movement, or the state-recognized Protestant Church in China. As an interesting side note, the founder and first moderator of the Church of Christ in China (not to be confused with the 1980-initiated China Christian Council) was Cheng Jingyi, who spoke memorable words at the Edinburgh Missionary Conference in 1910: "Your denominationalism does not interest Chinese Christians." From the beginning, this union had the two goals of complete independence and Christian unity. This unity was later supported (or enforced) through the Religious Affairs Bureau of the Chinese government. Christian unity often has political implications.

Where unity has been sought, some of the major hurdles have been forms of church order (and therefore ordination) and worship or liturgical practices. When women's ordination began to be a central concern (in the 1950s and 1960s), this created a further division, since not all churches were ready or willing to recognize women church leaders. The search for unity in faith (or common confession) and order (including the titles for those ordained) led Protestants and Orthodox back to the Bible and the earliest church councils. Up until the 1960s discussions mostly focused on differences or divisions, but beginning with the Third Assembly of the World Council of Churches in 1961 (New Delhi), the focus was on "the nature of the unity we seek," which was to be "all in each place."[30] This meant the focus would be on what holds Christians and Christian communions together, not theoretically or spiritually, but really in every local context. Two of the major documents that were produced toward that end were the Lima Liturgy and *Baptism, Eucharist and Ministry* (BEM; "The Lima Document," 1982). The *BEM* document revealed that it was much more difficult to agree about ministry and ordination than about the sacraments of Baptism and Eucharist. The *BEM* document that was approved at the Lima General Assembly of the WCC, the culmination of more than fifty years of faith-and-order discussions, brings various communions closer together by using language closer to the Bible and the early church writings. Denominational distinctives are played down,

---

30. Visser 't Hooft, "Reports of the Sections," 116–22.

and the common ground of biblical language and patristic theology helps to bring greater unity.

The ecumenical movement is not the only way of tracing twentieth-century Protestantism, but it does reflect much of the larger Protestant church. Theologically, liberalism of the nineteenth century continued to express itself in the inclusive missionary theology of the Hocking Report and in many of the seminaries of the West. However, the optimism, confidence, and even pragmatism of much of liberal theology was challenged by the tragic unfolding of the Great War, the economic collapse that came about twelve years later, and the challenges that came from the "mission fields." The largest theological challenge came from the prolific and incisive pen of Karl Barth, whom we looked at in chapter 2. Outside the West, converts to Christianity in Africa, Asia, the Pacific Islands, and Latin America also resisted liberal theologies. Kikuyu, or Cambodian, converts had the Bible, but liberal theology was a much more nuanced reading of history, tradition, and the biblical texts. The clear and simple reading of the Bible called for repentance, conversion, and transformation. Africans or Asians reading the Bible found the biblical world closer to their own world. The more liberal reading usually called for mutual cooperation for social transformation and a more secular (this-worldly) reading of the Bible. In addition, the divisions that existed in African Christianity, Latin American Christianity, and Asia-Pacific Christianity were mostly exports from Europe and North America. These non-Western Christians found their own voice in the twentieth century, and in many instances they refused many of the Western divisions and Western theological assumptions.

It was from this non-Western world that the great world Christian leaders arose during the twentieth century. We have mentioned the 1910 prophetic address of V. S. Azariah, but he was only one of thousands who had led and were now leading the growing edge of Christianity by the end of the century. Leaders like Philip Potter, from Dominica in the West Indies, and M. M. Thomas from Kerala, South India, became the key leaders in the global ecumenical movement. D. T. Niles from Ceylon (now Sri Lanka) led globally but also helped to organize regional Christian associations and evangelistic conferences. Others became great Christian scholars: Christian B. K. Baëta of Ghana, Lamin Sanneh from Senegambia, Kwame Bediako of Ghana, Paul David Devanandan of India, Choan-Sen Song of Taiwan, and Kosuke Koyoma from Japan. Thousands of others began to provide the primary theological writings in Bahasa (Indonesia), Vietnamese, Portuguese, Spanish, and Amharic. Building stronger churches, and led by theologians and church leaders in their own languages, Protestant Christians in the non-Western world not only resisted older colonial models of missionary involvement but also quietly developed their own theology, liturgy, and music even as Western theologians and Christian institutions struggled to find their new place as partners in missionary obedience. By the beginning of the twenty-first century, Christianity, which was rising from the "South," was more biblical in orientation, more evangelistic, more diverse, and more like the early church. Tensions with the West and with more liberal traditions could not be avoided. This greater confidence in the Bible and the biblical world was expressed by Philip Jenkins simply as "Power in the Book."[31]

Another important theme of the twentieth-century Protestant movement is the proliferation of renewal and missionary movements throughout the globe. Some individuals were identified with major renewal movements. Bishop Azariah of Dornakal not only was known as one of the major promoters and designers of what would be the church of South India but was also the creative force who founded the Indian Missionary Society in 1903 and then the National Missionary Society in 1905. As much as any other single person, he promoted the evangelization of Indians by Indians. Billy Graham was a single evangelist, and yet through the latter half of the twentieth century he was the head of a whole evangelistic movement that saw many other evangelistic organizations created. Student evangelism had been a priority of the Student Volunteer Movement and its close cousin, the Student Christian Movement (SCM), in the early twentieth century, but by the middle of the century newer groups became the dominant forces for evangelizing students globally. The International Fellowship of Evangelical Students (Inter-Varsity Christian Fellowship) started as a student-led movement in Cambridge and then spread to Canada, the United States, Australia, and eventually through most of the student world. Campus Crusade for Christ, started by a businessman, Bill Bright, began working with students in the 1950s but quickly expanded its work to pioneer evangelism throughout the world in hundreds of languages, through literature, meetings, and the use of the "Jesus Film," which was translated into more than one thousand languages. Student ministry was also taken up by Youth for Christ (founded to reach young soldiers in 1944) and the Navigators (founded in 1933 to reach sailors). These groups began to reach university students globally much as the SCM did earlier in the century.

Other types of Protestant renewal can be seen through liturgical development, especially the proliferation of Christian music. In most of the Reformation churches, worship music became much more diverse through the addition of music from around the world. In the 1960s a younger generation began to write Christian music, especially worship songs, using guitars and percussion

31. Jenkins, *New Faces of Christianity*, chapter 2.

instead of the organ. By the 1980s, music or worship wars began to develop because of the diversity of music and the proliferation of new songs. Many of the newer churches, both in the West and in the former "mission lands," were producing Christian music following tunes and styles that were more culturally familiar to them. With global travel and communications, this music traveled quickly to the far corners of the world, so that songs written in Australia might be sung in Hong Kong, Harare, or Houston. Whereas before the 1950s Christians in most of the world might have recognized many of the same hymns (Western hymns that were translated into Chinese or Portuguese or Tamil), by the end of the century this was not the case. The diversification created some communication problems, but all in all this was a sign of renewal and vitality as Christians in each place, inspired by the gospel, took up the pen and began to write songs of praise. In fact most of the newer music coming from the diverse new languages should be classified as praise music.

An important theme that we have seen among the Orthodox and Roman Catholics in the twentieth century has been the increased role of the laity, especially of women. This theme is much more important in Protestant Christianity, and even more significant (or radical) still among the Spiritual family (Pentecostals and independent churches). As is often the case, the movement was more significant from the margins, not from the center. The impetus to full inclusion of women in church leadership became the measuring stick of the women's movement in the twentieth century, but the more radical (Baptist, missionary, and Pentecostal) churches paved the way. The Salvation Army fully included women in leadership in the 1860s, and the founding of the Women's Christian Temperance Union (WCTU; supporting the prohibition of alcoholic drinks) also gave women full admission to Christian leadership. Thus it was in missionary organizations and on the missionary frontiers of the church that women first found full inclusion in leadership positions.

Clara Celestia Hale-Babcock (1850–1925) was ordained mostly for evangelistic outreach and WCTU leadership in the Disciples of Christ Church. Her ordination in 1888 (or 1889) at the age of thirty-nine marks one of the earliest ordinations of female pastors in the modern era. Other women were ordained for full ministry soon after, but not from the larger Protestant churches until after World War II. In 1904 Minnie Jackson Goins was ordained as the first African American woman cleric in northwest Kansas by the United Brethren in Christ (later to become part of The United Methodist Church). In England the Congregational churches began to ordain women in 1917; but the Assemblies of God, one of the larger Pentecostal churches, began to ordain women from their earliest history (1914).

Women's ordination became much more important in Protestant churches in the West when the women's missionary societies began to be consolidated and the leadership taken over by men in the first decades of the twentieth century. Women had initiated and led in numerous societies in the nineteenth century, but the consolidation that took place in the "big business" approach to church order in the twentieth century cut women off from leadership. After World War II, women's ordination occurred in rapid succession in the Reformation churches in the West. Interestingly, the first ordination of a woman in a Reformation-era church probably took place in Japan, not in the West, on December 5, 1933, when Takahashi Hisano was ordained by the Nihon Kirisuto Kyokai, or the Presbyterian and Reformed Church of Japan. In 1936 the newly formed United Church of Canada (1925) ordained its first woman. But ordination in most mainstream Reformation churches came later:

1947: Czechoslovak Hussite Church

1948: Lutheran Church of Denmark

1956: Presbyterian Church (USA) and Methodist Church (USA)

1960: Lutheran Church of Sweden

1967: Presbyterian Church of Canada

1971: Anglican Communion (Hong Kong)

1992: Church of England

Although ordination was not the only measure of full inclusion of women in Christian leadership, it was an important measure. However, it is important to remember that it took the Spiritual churches, or the newer and less institutionalized churches, to pioneer the place of women in church leadership, and it is to these churches we now turn.

Spiritual Churches: Independents and Pentecostal

Of all of the transformations and themes we might discuss concerning Christianity in the twentieth century, the single most important is the rise of "fourth-stream" churches: those that are independent and rise up, or suddenly spring up, in local contexts. As important as the ecumenical movement may seem to those in the West, those discussions were among family members trying to reverse the divergent flow from the Reformation. The dramatic rise of Spiritual churches (including independency and Pentecostalism) is a new movement that begins to shape a whole new global Christian reality. Before the twentieth century the Spiritual churches were smaller and marginal (Quakers, Menno-nites, etc.), but the twentieth century is the century of the Spiritual churches. Most often these churches do not have a link with the Spiritual churches of the Reformation period, but they are of the same genetic makeup. It is the nature of Spiritual churches to spring up, or be initiated, not through a tradition but by direct inspiration of the Holy Spirit.

The Azusa Street Revival and Its Legacy

Pentecostal churches expect direct revelations from God through the Holy Spirit. They expect healings, exorcisms, and speaking in tongues as part of the normal Christian life. The origin of the modern Pentecostal movement is difficult to date since many of the elements that would become normative were observed before the beginning of the twentieth century. However, in terms of lasting impact, and the development of a distinct Pentecostal theology, the global movement is usually recognized as beginning with the Azusa Street Revival in Los Angeles (1906–15). This revival was led by several preachers, most notably Charles Parham (a former Methodist from Kansas) and William J. Seymour (a Southern black Holiness preacher). In the spring of 1906 they traveled to Los Angeles, where the ground for revival had been plowed by the broad influence of the Great Welsh Revival (1904–5). Los Angeles was a city ripe for revival, growing at a rate of 15 percent a year, mostly through immigrants from Japan, Russia, China, Korea, and, of course, Mexico.

With William Seymour as the leading preacher, a movement of the Spirit both attracted people from across the country and sent people beyond the nation. The movement that started in a former African Methodist Episcopal church turned horse stable in Los Angeles spun off churches and missions that touched the far corners of the world. Almost mystically, or even providentially, the *Los Angeles Times* recorded on April 18, 1906, that a speaker the day before had "prophesied awful destruction to this city unless its citizens are brought to a belief in the tenets of the new faith." At 5:12 a.m. on April 18 all of California shook and San Francisco crumbled under the Great Earthquake of 1906. In some ways the Azusa Street movement validated and consolidated other, similar movements around the world. It was deeply local in its engage-ment, prophetically intercultural, and immediately global in its expression. Not only California but also all of Christendom shook and was repositioned by this inauguration of the Pentecostal movement.[32]

---

32. See Bartleman, *Azusa Street*, 44–54. Bartleman's original book was published in 1925 under the title *How "Pentecost" Came to Los Angeles—As It Was in the Beginning*.

A number of new denominations or associations of churches began in the aftermath of the Azusa Street Revival. Additionally, numerous missions were established, some more formal than others. The first mission that was founded was the Apostolic Faith Mission (AFM), which had its headquarters on the top floor of the small building at 312 Azusa Street, the location of the revival. AFM missionaries went throughout the world with little more than zeal and vision to carry them through. Missionaries were sent from Azusa Street to India, China, and South Africa. How rapidly and uniquely this movement spread can be illustrated by one of the most significant missions, the small group that went to South Africa. The Azusa Street Revival occurred in April 1906, but by 1908 the Schneiderman family (Jewish converts), the Hezmalhalches, Lakes, and Lehmans, along with Ida Sackett, were headed to Liverpool, England, and then to South Africa. In May 1908 they led a service in Doornfontein with about five hundred in attendance, where about half the people had "the Spirit of God" fall upon them and they prayed all at once, to the chagrin of the Congregational missionaries and the joyous acceptance of the Pentecostal missionaries.

Not only did missions head out around the world from among those who had participated in the Azusa Street Revival in 1906 but new churches and missions, inspired by what had happened on Azusa Street, also formed just as quickly. The first missionary group that formed from people who had participated in the Azusa Street revivals was simply called the Apostolic Faith Mission, recognizing that this was the faith of the apostles. The Pentecostal Assemblies of the World trace their beginning to 1906, but they split from other Pentecostals in denying the traditional language of the Trinity, saying that Jesus is God and baptism should be only in the name of Jesus. Other "Oneness" Pentecostals followed. The Assemblies of God Church was formed in 1914, in large part because in the predominantly black Church of God in Christ (COGIC) denomination, blacks and whites had been unable to work together. Early Pentecostalism was color-blind, but racial differences quickly became visible. As they moved to the southern United States, the new, mostly white Assemblies of God denomination was started. The Pentecostal Church of God in Christ, which had organized as a Pentecostal denomination in 1907, separated from the Assemblies in 1919, and many others followed. Another Pentecostal church shows how the apostolic, or primitive, impulse meshed with modern twentieth-century communications and marketing. The International Church of the Foursquare Gospel was founded by a Canadian woman with a Salvation Army background, Aimee Semple McPherson (1890–1944). "Sister Aimee," as she was known, pioneered radio preaching, large megachurches, and modern religious drama, along with slick marketing and patriotism. She first articulated her Foursquare Gospel in 1922:

full Gospel evangelism,

the whole Bible as divinely inspired,

the second coming of Christ and

the return of Apostolic healing.

Her life was a confusing mixture of holiness and devotion to preaching and healing on the one hand, and failed marriages, a mysterious absence, and very materialistic and carefully organized marketing for her mass meetings on the other hand.

The growth of Pentecostalism, however, has not depended on marketing or large buildings like the Angelus Temple in Los Angeles or a "Gospel Car."[33] Pentecostalism is most notable in how it has attracted the least, the lost, and the lonely with nothing but a message and a promise of spiritual power. This reliance on spiritual power often comes in conflict with the need to think through and/or reason about theological or even practical issues. Thus Pentecostalism was slow to develop schools around the world beyond basic education. However, since its very nature was evangelistic, it spread very rapidly, and, because of the varied contexts where it soon found a home, its evangelistic nature soon became much more broadly missionary. One example of this transformation can be found in the early work of Pentecostal missionaries in India. Before their arrival, an indigenous mission was already in place, the Mukti Mission of Pandita Ramabai. Many of the early Pentecostal missionaries, coming to convert Hindus in India, were voluntarily accompanied by Ramabai's women of her Mukti Mission. In some ways this legitimated the foreign missionaries. As they traveled with the Indian missionaries, the Pentecostals learned of their work rescuing young widows, destitute women, and orphans. Soon the Pentecostals were expanding their missionary work by caring for destitute young women, providing housing and food, and teaching basic skills. Pentecostal mission, in like manner, developed broader missionary labors throughout the world and began to be a major dynamic in development work in poorer countries.

Other churches within the broader Spiritual Family of churches that formed in the early decades of the twentieth century were not technically Pentecostal in experience or theology, but they too started up independent of established churches (Protestant, Catholic, or Orthodox), finding their inspiration directly from biblical witness and the Holy Spirit. None of these churches would say

33. These horse-drawn vans and automobiles with Scripture verses and related gospel slogans written on them served as traveling evangelistic outposts for many early Pentecostal preachers.

Figure 16. The African Inland Church of Oreteti, Kenya, is situated on a prominent hill overlooking the Great Rift Valley.

that they find their heritage in the witness of Martin Luther, John Calvin, John Wesley, or any other Protestant figure. Churches with names like the China Independent Christian Church, or the Jesus Family, or the True Jesus Church reveal that their heritage and identity are found with Jesus more than with tradition. Independency in Christianity sprang up roughly one-half century before political independency took place. Christian identity, we might say, paved the way for national and ethnic identity, in large part through the translation and education projects of Western missions. Of course, independency was working the opposite direction of the ecumenical movement with which it was contemporaneous, and yet the independent and other Spiritual churches have found ways to work together, often, but not always, in opposition to the Western churches.

One of the themes of Spiritual churches is the spiritual life that Christian faith engenders and even requires. The spiritual life may be a matter of exhibiting spiritual power or uncommon gifts, but often it is seen in transformed behavior. Many of the Spiritual churches come out of or reflect the Holiness tradition. The COGIC, founded by Charles Harrison Mason in 1897, can be understood as a Pentecostal church before Pentecostalism. One of the identifying characteristics of the COGIC women was that they lived sanctified lives and were identified as doing so by being called "Saints." "For COGIC women, the goal was not to present a respectable public figure, but to remove the sin from their lives in order to move in the power of the Holy Spirit."[34] The sanctified life of Spiritual churches becomes the witness to others and proves the existence and power of the Holy Spirit. It is not always necessary to speak in tongues, for a consecrated and transformed life is evidence enough that the Spirit of God is present. Spiritual churches generally do not have distinct or elaborate liturgies or sacramental practices and are thus often set apart by their spiritual power and sanctified lives.

34. Butler, *Women in the Church*, 66.

Spiritual Churches in Africa

Another important theme of Spiritual churches is their independence. The early decades of the twentieth century mark the rise of African Independent Churches (AICs) in Africa.[35] These churches are often initiated by two elements: resistance to foreign (colonial) control of the churches and inspirited African leaders. Some of the churches were catalyzed by foreign elements such as the Zion and Apostolic churches in South Africa that were inspired by Pentecostal missionaries from Zion City, Indiana. Zionist churches developed from South Africa, spreading outward with African symbols and liturgies. Pentecostalism seemed to give the freedom in the Spirit to develop truly African Christian worship and life. Other churches were inspired by independency and African identity revealed in the history of the great Christian kingdom of Ethiopia. "Ethiopianism became a movement of cultural and religious protest. It delved back into its history to recover and re-contextualize its black traditions of emancipation. . . . It breathed the hope that Africans would bear the burden of evangelization and build an autonomous church devoid of denominations and free of European control."[36] "Independence" meant that the strength of these churches—independency and contextual identity—would favor their growth and influence. The growth of these churches has meant a great deal for indigenous Christian leaders, some of whom went on to become important political voices in the period of decolonization.

In the AICs there was also a new place for women in religion in Africa. In many places of the world women outnumber men in active Christian participation, but in the AICs the role of women seems to be even more important than is commonly seen elsewhere. In the AICs women are given creative space to be actors and leaders in local cultures. They have spiritual resources to help resolve family conflicts and power to speak and act against many of the oppressive structures of traditional life. AIC women are also bridge people, connecting traditional patterns of life to more modern—even cosmopolitan— life.[37] Many of the AICs are founded by a prophetess, or the primary leadership may be that of a woman. Revivals are more democratic than the church life of hierarchical churches, and so a woman can easily become a healer, or a prophet, leading the church. Independency often opens access to women as well as the marginalized.

Often local politics, disasters, and conflict have focused attention on the spiritual and opened up greater opportunities for AICs to grow. Revivals from

35. Often called African Initiated Churches.
36. Kalu, "Africa, Christianity in," in Bowden, ed., *Christianity*, 10.
37. See Mwaura, "Women in African Instituted Churches."

the Protestant churches (such as the mostly Anglican East Africa Revival) produced or stimulated other indigenous movements. In the 1930s the East Africa Revival was the catalyst to the indigenous *Balokole* ("saved ones") movement in Uganda and the surrounding countries. In the twentieth century these AICs grew from about forty thousand converts to an estimated fifty-four million at the beginning of the twenty-first century. Their influence has been even greater than the remarkable growth to 15 percent of the Christian population of the continent. In 1913 there were only thirty indigenous churches in Africa, but by 1990 there were more than six thousand. In patterns of worship, in singing, in the use of instruments, in the freedom to situate Christian theology and practice in local African cultures—in all of these ways the AICs have influenced the more traditional Orthodox, Protestant, and Catholic families in Africa.

Spiritual Churches in Asia

In Asia too independency and resistance to colonial control of churches often combined to bring about movements of Spiritual churches. In most countries Spiritual movements were initiated by Pentecostalism from the West, but in China a number of indigenous Spiritual movements sprang up, whether directly catalyzed by Western missionary contact or not. Early twentieth-century revivals from Wales (1904–5) spread to Korea, northeast India, and China. Soon missionaries who were converted and inspired by the Azusa Street Revival began traveling to these regions with their own understandings of the gospel. In some regions the influence from these movements promoted new lines of development in mainline churches. In China new independent movements were imitated by Chinese leaders. A few examples will illustrate what happened in hundreds of separate locations.

A movement in Shandong Province called the Great Shandong Revival was initiated by contact with Pentecostalism from the West. The impact was felt across all denominations—public confession of sin, healings, conversions, and reconciliation of enemies were all recorded. The movement spilled out beyond the Western church structures. An indigenous church was started called the Jesus Family (c. 1927), a communal form of New Testament Christianity that borrowed elements from Chinese Confucianism and Taoism while calling people to holiness in life and witness. The Spiritual Gifts Movement (Ling'en Yundong) also developed throughout northern China and Manchuria. While its followers sought after spiritual gifts, the movement also had strong elements of millennialism during a time of great national turmoil. Chinese leaders, in effect, took leadership of a single spiritual movement that was initiated outside China and helped to shape it into several movements that can be considered the earliest Chinese forms of Christianity. It would be hard to disagree that these indigenous spiritual movements (including the revival movements of groups like the Bethel Worldwide Evangelistic Band of John Sung; see chap. 1 under "Non-Western Transformations of Christianity" and chap. 2 under "Asia") prepared Chinese Christians to endure Japanese occupation, civil war, and Communist oppression of the church.

Other Spiritual movements developed during the years of Japanese disruption. The True Jesus Church, the Little Flock of Watchman Nee, and important Chinese pastors like Wang Mingdao provided indigenous Chinese Christian leadership that would become the foundation for a large percentage of Christianity that germinated during the Mao years (1949–76). These Spiritual movements, coming from the soil of China, often have Confucian concerns for a moral and ethical life mixed with a Daoist openness to the mysterious and mystical. Out of Chinese Spiritual churches have come new indigenous hymns and spiritual writings. Evangelistic and missionary concerns for China have always been part of these movements, but by the end of the twentieth century concern for missionary work to western China and to non-Chinese cultures began to appear.

Spiritual Churches in Latin America

Spiritual Christianity grew tremendously in Latin America as well. The earliest movements were directly or indirectly connected with India, the United States, Sweden, and Italy, all before 1910. In all cases where Pentecostalism grew in Latin America, it had very limited contact with North American Pentecostals. The first major movement of Pentecostalism occurred within the Methodist Episcopal Church (MEC) in Chile. After twenty years of missionary work, an American missionary in the MEC (and former physician) named Willis Hoover received a copy of Minnie Abrams's booklet *The Baptism of the Holy Ghost and Fire*. Abrams, a Methodist missionary in India, read her booklet while working with the Mukti Mission of Pandita Ramabai and revised it in 1906 in light of the news that came from Azusa Street. Three years later (1909) the Hoovers were reading the booklet in Chile and began praying for the same experiences. The result was a Pentecostal movement that grew out of a Methodist church and became the first Spiritual church in Latin America: Iglesia Metodista Pentecostal (Methodist Pentecostal Church). As with many of these Spiritual churches, this one has split a number of times, but it has retained its strong emphasis on missionary work through planting churches. By the end of the twentieth century it was estimated that 95 percent of the Protestants in Chile were actually from Spiritual or Pentecostal heritage. Thus the major drain on the Roman Catholic Church in Chile is not mainline Protestants, but Spiritual and other indigenous churches that have sprung up there.

In Brazil we see again how the global nature of Spiritual churches combines with local or indigenous features to generate rapid growth. The first Pentecostal preaching in Brazil was done by an Italian and former Waldensian from Chicago named Luigi Francescon. After becoming Pentecostal in 1907 and traveling widely in the United States and Canada preaching a Pentecostal message, Francescon arrived in Buenos Aires, Argentina, in 1909 and established a Pentecostal church there. In 1910 he began preaching in Brazil, at first only to Italian speakers. By 1935 the church, Congregação Cristã (Christian Congregations), was developing Portuguese ministries.[38] At almost the same time that Francescon came to Brazil (1910), two Swedish Baptists, a pastor named Gunnar Vingren and a layman named Daniel Berg, received prophecies independent of each other that they were to go to "Para." After finding where it was, they obeyed the prophecy and went to northeastern Brazil, preaching Spirit baptism. Soon the two Swedes learned Portuguese and founded churches called Assembleia de Deus (Assembly of God). Within three years they were sending out missionaries to other Portuguese-speaking countries—the first to Portugal itself, beginning in the city of Porto. Today Assembleia de Deus is the largest Pentecostal denomination in the world. One of the splits from this church is Igreja O Brasil para Cristo (Brazil for Christ Church), another very large Spiritual church with a global outreach.

With the rapid growth of Spiritual churches in Latin America since the 1960s, several themes have surfaced. First, Spiritual churches have been attracted to the poor. Although some popular Pentecostal preachers have preached health and wealth and some have misused money, in general Spiritual churches in Latin America have emphasized ministry to the poorest people, and they lead the continent in that type of ministry. Even in small *favelas* (slums or shanty towns) attached to major metropolitan areas, small groups of Pentecostals meet to pray and discuss their social needs. Pentecostals were originally strongly premillennial and therefore pessimistic about this world. However, today Pentecostals in Latin America are engaged in educational work, orphanages, and even politics (with mixed results).[39] They are important people for the future development of Latin America.

38. McClung, *Azusa Street and Beyond*, 47–48.
39. In most regions Pentecostal church members resist the established rulers and vote for candidates who are more socialist in their leanings. However, at times the Pentecostal leaders of these same churches have had a history of supporting military dictators (Ríos Montt in Guatemala). In contrast to the support of a military dictator in the 1980s, in the twenty-first century

Another important theme is the greater involvement of women in the church and broader society. Women in Latin America, excluded from most church leadership in the Roman Catholic Church, became preachers and teachers in Pentecostal culture, and many became politically involved. In Brazil, some of the first Afro-Brazilian women to be involved in leadership in church and society were Pentecostals.[40]

Unquestionably the same is true of independent and other Spiritual churches in Latin America and Asia. Spiritual churches, it can be argued, have been the main story in the transformation of the world Christian movement in the twentieth century. Of all the unexpected themes that, like colorful threads, have made up the fabric of twentieth-century Christianity, none was so unexpected as the rise of Spiritual forms of Christianity. These expressions seem to germinate below the surface of the Christian story and then suddenly grow and even blossom with little planning and no real strategy. They are spiritual to the core, starting with a vision, a dream, or a prophecy, and moving people to travel across the world or to preach a new message of spiritual power.

Divergent Family Histories

All of this transformation of the families of Christianity began between the years of 1904 and 1910. In those brief years, immediately preceding the Edinburgh Missionary Conference, Spiritual forms of Christianity began on all continents. The Great Welsh Revival developed in 1904–5, and missionaries from Wales spread the revival's spirit to Korea, India, North America, and eventually China. In 1906 in Los Angeles a Pentecostal revival began on Azusa Street, and missionaries spread out to Asia, Africa, and across the Americas. Before this time there were some indigenous movements, some more orthodox than others, but the foundations that were laid in this period of six years proved to be solid. Pentecostalism from outside and indigenous movements from local contexts multiplied during the century from this brief period, and they continue to grow today. What began as small spiritual meetings, prophetic messages, and evangelistic preachers has grown to be the most dynamic and growing family of Christianity into the twenty-first century.

Orthodoxy was severely persecuted during the twentieth century, and as a result it was scattered to far regions of the world, and the percent of Orthodox in the world declined from 22 percent of all Christians in 1900 to 12 percent

the founder of the El Shaddai Ministries, Harold de Caballeros, started a reforming political party and later became the minister of foreign affairs of Guatemala.

40. See Anderson, *To the Ends of the Earth*, 179.

in 2000. Again, this was not at all expected in 1900. Political events further hedged in a form of Christianity that was tied to the governments under which it flourished. Roman Catholicism fared well during the twentieth century, even while suffering losses to Pentecostals and other Protestant groups in Latin America. In Asia and especially Africa, Roman Catholicism continued to grow. In Europe all Christian families (except Spiritual) declined in the twentieth century, but for Roman Catholics the loss was greatest. Protestantism entered the twentieth century strong and with a growing missionary zeal expressed in new institutions and numerous conferences on mission. The decline of Protestant forms of Christianity in the West was more than made up by the rapid growth of Protestantism in Asia, Africa, and Latin America. Protestant Christian leaders may often still have white faces, but that is less and less the norm as Protestantism deepens its impact in non-Western cultures.

Thus the different families of Christianity experienced different fortunes and different gains and losses of territory in the twentieth century. None of these changes, however, was so surprising as the explosion of Spiritual and other indigenous forms of Christianity, brought about by the remarkable movements of people. Modern science made such movement easier, but modern economics and politics made it necessary.

5

On the Move

Christianity and Migration

The significance of local and global networks among African churches in both home and host contexts cannot be overemphasized. Such networks are assuming increasing importance for African migrants. . . . The "flow" between the links is two-directional, sending and receiving—globally and locally.

Afe Adogame, "Contesting the Ambivalences
of Modernity in a Global Context," 21

At their best moments Christians recognize that they are sent in the pattern of Jesus Christ, to go into the world—to all nations—proclaiming redemption and exhibiting the coming kingdom of God on earth. In the twentieth century this missionary identity underwent an odd twist, based on a false assumption. From the eighth through the sixteenth centuries, when Christianity had become cornered in Western Europe, with only small surviving Christian communities in India and Africa, it had been assumed that Christianity was really a European religion. Slowly, as Europeans moved out to the Americas, Africa, and Asia, a new belief came to be assumed, that missionary work was "from the West to the rest." This assumption, though false, endured even after the Edinburgh Missionary Conference in 1910. This is quite understandable: in 1900, 82 percent of the world's Christians were in the West. Christianity was a Western religion with some fragile outposts. Thus, though it was theologically false that Christianity "came from" the West, factually it was to a large extent true.

Christianity: Apostolic and Migratory

From the very beginning Christianity was a missionary faith in two ways: apostolic individuals being sent out from a church center *and* migrations of people carrying the cross of Jesus into new cultures and nations. The second type of growth of Christianity, from region to region, has always been just as important, but not as closely followed or studied until recently.[1] One of the earliest examples of this was that when Christians were persecuted in the Roman Empire, they often fled to the East and found protection in the Persian Empire. The exact opposite happened after the early fourth century, because the Persian Empire was antagonistic to Christian life, and therefore many Christians fled to one of the "Christian" empires to the West (Armenia or Rome). As we will see, persecution is one of many causes of movements of people. From the beginning of time humans have been on the move, carrying their possessions as well as ideas and religious beliefs with them.

In the early modern colonial period migration became one of the major causes of the spread of Christianity, bringing many forms of Christianity to colonies, and later empires, overseas. True, in most colonies Christianity did not spread, because the populations of Christian immigrants there remained small. For example, in India the French, British, and Danish did not much affect the spread of Christianity to the subcontinent except in their own European communities. Similarly, the British in Malaya (now Malaysia and Singapore), Burma (now Myanmar), and Ceylon (now Sri Lanka), as well as in East Africa, did not spread Christianity much at all. In these regions, only small communities of Europeans and a few local people continued to practice the Christian faith before the twentieth century. In places where European immigrants overwhelmed the local indigenous populations, however, Christianity did spread. In North America, most of the continent became so thoroughly Christian that a new type of Christendom developed in which Christianity was not monolithic or uniform. There, and also in Australia and New Zealand, a new form of pluralism of Christian expression—denominationalism—became the norm. Migration, not intentional missionary activity, mostly explains this spread of Christianity.[2]

1. See, e.g., Hanciles, *Beyond Christendom*, among others.
2. It is true that a minority of European immigrants to North America showed a concern for reaching various indigenous people once they crossed the ocean. (See Irvin and Sunquist,

Migration Reversals and Upheavals

The twentieth century, a century filled with reversals and upheavals, brought two odd twists to this global understanding of mission and Christian identity. First, after centuries of Europeans going out, "the nations" began to come back to the old Christian homelands of Europe and the Americas. When European colonialism collapsed after World War II, millions of Europeans and westernized Africans and Asians migrated to Europe from those two continents. Although missionaries were still going to "the mission fields," the nations, in a sense, were not waiting. Asians and Africans began coming to Europe and then to North America. Migrating largely from Hindu and Muslim cultures, they were coming to live in the shadow of cathedrals and monasteries. Before World War II and the collapse of Western empires, most of the global migration was from the West to the non-Western nations and between colonial nations. Between 1800 and 1925, one in five Europeans moved out of Europe. This was the largest migration of all time, up to that point. Europeans and North Americans were also recruiting Chinese and Indians to Africa and the Americas to provide cheap labor for their empires and nations. About two million Chinese were brought as contract workers to places like South Africa, Malaya, Guyana, and the United States. Nearly five times that number of Indians were brought as contract laborers by the British to the far corners of the British Empire. Empires, by their very nature, require and enhance the movement of peoples.

After World War II, however, Western empires were collapsing, and the direction of migration reversed. Indonesians began migrating to the Netherlands; Indians and Pakistanis were coming to Britain; and for similar reasons, Vietnamese and Filipinos began (and continue) to flood into the United States. Nearly one million legal foreign-born people immigrate each year to the United States. Most of these immigrants speak Spanish (about 300,000), but more and more speak Chinese or one of many Indian languages. In Western Europe the concept of "reverse mission" is even clearer. Nearly 20 million Muslims from North Africa, Iraq, Turkey, and the Balkans as well as from West Africa have settled in Western Europe, so that in France about 10 percent of the population is now Muslim[3] and in Britain about 4.4 percent.

HWCM, 2:256–57, for a discussion of one of the most interesting and tragic cases of this type of early outreach, John Eliot.) However, most of the national missions work began after people migrated to North America. Migration made local outreach an interest.

3. Accurate statistics on religion in some countries are difficult to come by. France does not allow a census to question religion, but surveys do provide some of this information. According to a profile of France published by the US Central Intelligence Agency (CIA), France's Muslim

The second part of this strange twist to Christian mission relates to the missionaries themselves; most of them are no longer European or North American. Just as the missionary movement up to the twenty-first century could be seen as an undercurrent of modern migrations, we can also understand the modern, non-Western missionary movement as an undercurrent of present migration trends. In the case of non-Western missionaries, however, the link is not so clear. By the year 2000 more than 62 percent of the Christians in the world were non-Western, and more than 70 percent of the missionaries were non-Western.[4] In the past, the flow of people and missionaries was from the West to the South and the East. The present missionary movement does not follow the mass movements going mostly to the West. Many Korean, Brazilian, and even Singaporean missionaries are working in the West, but most of the African, Latin American, Pacific Island, and Asian missionaries are working within their regions. More than one hundred Protestant mission agencies in India are sending about twenty thousand missionaries, but most of the missionaries are working in India, Nepal, Bhutan, or in different language groups within South Asia.

Economics determines much of this twenty-first-century missionary movement, as it did in the past. Taiwanese and Korean missionaries can afford to send missionaries to Russia, Brazil, and Bolivia, and so they do. There are more than 140 Korean missionary societies sending more than 12,000 missionaries to about 60 countries. The strong East Asian economies have opened up the world to Korean missionaries, and more recently to Chinese missionaries. This is not true for nations in Latin America, Africa, and the rest of Asia ("Lafriasia"). It is difficult (far too expensive) for Tamil believers in South India to send missionaries to Singapore or San Francisco. In most African nations, missionaries work in adjacent cultures or countries. However, more and more missionaries from West Africa, especially from Nigeria, are planting churches in Eastern and Western Europe as well as in the Americas. These are the major new twists of migrations and missions at the beginning of the twenty-first century. The result is a much more culturally diverse Christianity and a much broader missionary engagement with cultures and societies than the world has ever known.

---

population is between 5 and 10 percent and growing. The country's Protestant population is about 2 percent. Most of the statistics above are from *The World Factbook*, a CIA publication that documents a variety of facts on nations of the world: https://www.cia.gov/library/pub lications/the-world-factbook/.

4. In 1800 about 14 percent of the world's Christians were found outside the West. See Haniles, *Beyond Christendom*, 378. The statistics in this chapter come from ibid.; Barrett, Kurian, and Johnson, *World Christian Encyclopedia*; and Central Intelligence Agency, *World Factbook*.

Causes of Migrations

It has been said that "migration is an irrepressible human urge."[5] This is true, but it has only been in the nineteenth and twentieth centuries (and now the twenty-first) that people have migrated on such a global scale.[6] In the year 2000 more than 200 million people were living outside of their country of origin. This means there are enough people scattered in seminomadic, multi-religious communities to fill up a country all their own. Some of these people are seeking a more prosperous life, but most are seeking a safer or healthier life. Kurds who have migrated to Germany, Sudanese who have migrated to Minnesota, and Karen from Myanmar who have migrated to Sweden are all moving to save their lives and the lives of their families. Most of the migrants of the world are intensely religious people, and at times the experience of migration magnifies the religious commitment.

> Migration, then, takes many forms: people migrate as poor peasants, day labourers, industrial workers, skilled professionals, students, talented entre-preneurs; or as refugees and asylum seekers. They migrate alone, in families, or in large groups. Most are young adults, but many migrant flows, such as refugees, contain a substantial number of children and older people. People migrate for short or long periods. Or, like refugees, they may have no control over how long they are away; they may never be able to return, or they may be forced to return.[7]

The causes of migration are complex and interrelated, but the reasons for the great increase are simple: communications and transportation. People are able to find out where they can receive refugee status, and then they can get there. The causes of migration can easily detain us, but we should briefly look at the major issues that both push people off their lands and pull them to other lands. In general migrations develop for sociological, economic, political, religious, and environmental factors.

Urbanization

One of the causes of migration in the West in the twentieth century relates to the ongoing urbanization of the planet. The development of new industries and the need for cheap labor have drawn laborers to the cities. This mass movement of

5. Böhning, "International Mission and the Western World," 18.
6. A wonderful visual description of modern migration, with brief explanations, is given in King, *People on the Move.*
7. Ibid., 14.

peasants, farmers, and small-town residents to the major cities of the world has brought together different ethnic groups and religions to cities in the Americas, Asia, and, to a lesser extent, Africa. China, still a mostly agrarian country, now has five of the largest cities in the world, and more and more farmers are coming to the cities looking for jobs. The largest internal migration in history is now occurring in China: from the rural areas to the cities. In North America there is now a reverse trend. In some cities managers and white-collar workers are moving out of the city to large suburban areas, taking their money with them. Many of the American urban centers are dying, and many of the large churches that used to serve the urban population are also dying. Consequently, the religious landscape of North American cities has become less mainline, less Euro-American, and more religiously diverse. Immigrant churches and African American churches are springing up as the large cathedrals are emptying or being sold.

Economics

Economics has been a much greater cause of migration and has been the major pull factor in the African, Asian, and Latin American brain drain. Many of the best and the brightest from Lafriasia study in the West and then stay in the West. A medical doctor can be a rich woman or man in Los Angeles or London, but a doctor will struggle to stay above the poverty line in his or her home village in Pakistan, Peru, or Palestine. The end of the twentieth century saw many Chinese captured trying to sneak into the United States (even through Mexico) to get manual labor jobs hoping for a better life for their families. Turks, Iraqis, Lebanese, and Moroccans migrate to Europe seeking better jobs. East Europeans travel west for the same reasons. Poverty pushes and hope pulls in this economic migration piece. Some of the greatest doctors, research scientists, and professors in the West come from the poorer nations of Lafriasia. Some of the best and brightest from China are also migrating to East and Southeast Asia. These scholars come from all religious backgrounds, but while passing through the secularization curtains to the West, many drift away from the religion of their childhood, and some become Christian. There is a much higher rate of Christian practice among Chinese, Korean, or Indian professors in the West than in China, Korea, or India. Migration often enhances religious vitality.

Politics

Politics has always been a great cause of migration, but the twentieth century set all records for political migration. The highly strict and controlled societies of Soviet Russia (and its possessions), China, Vietnam, and North Korea caused a flood of political refugees, "boat people" (from Vietnam, Cambodia, and Laos), and asylum seekers. The rise of Russian Orthodox scholarship in the West can in large part be attributed to the Bolshevik and then Soviet policies regarding religion. As the White army was being defeated in Russia in 1920, about ninety thousand Russian Orthodox escaped to the East, either passing through or remaining in China (Harbin, Shanghai, etc.). Thus Russian Orthodoxy spread to "the West" in part by going east to the Pacific and then to the United States and Europe. Chinese flooded out of China to Southeast Asia as well as across the globe after the victory of Mao's Red Army in 1949. With these Chinese immigrants also came Western missionaries who had been working in China. Thus Mao's political policies helped to spread Western missionaries—most of whom were fluent in Chinese dialects—and Chinese Christians to Southeast Asia. Again, politics played an important role in one of the two greatest miracles of Christian growth in the twentieth century: the explosive growth in China.[8] The persecution of Christians and the removal of foreign support strengthened the small Christian community in China. Once greater openness was allowed, it was discovered that Christian witness throughout the 1950s, 1960s, and 1970s had been strong and healthy, though almost imperceptible to the outside.

War

The role of politics has been most clearly seen in migrations caused by war. One of the great lies that was finally exposed in the twentieth century was that modernity would create a more civilized humanity. Social religion and human ability, as expressed through modern science and technology, was to save humanity. It seems that the exact opposite has happened. The increase in scientific and technical knowledge has proved a social devolution rather than social evolution. Even a brief list of regions suffering conflicts during the twentieth century, often involving genocide (attempted annihilation of a whole people or of a race), will remind us of the millions of unwilling migrants as well as the more direct casualties of war: Armenia, Korea, Vietnam, Kosovo, Rwanda, Afghanistan, Iraq and Iran, Somalia, Sudan, India and Pakistan (over partition), El Salvador, Biafra, Cambodia (oppression by Khmer Rouge), and, of course, all the nations involved in World War I and World War II. The greatest number of deaths and dislocations of people in the century resulted from political decisions of secular, Communist political rulers: Stalin's political purges, which

---

8. The other great miracle of Christian growth is Africa, which grew from 120 million Christians in 1970 to more than 350 million in 2000.

may have caused the death of some thirteen million people, and Mao's "Great Leap Forward" and "Cultural Revolution," which together caused the death of about fifty million people. With all of these wars and internal conflicts, the numbers of refugees and unwilling migrants increased so rapidly that they could not be counted. Many "political refugees" end up in Western nations, but most of these migrants are always among the poorest of the poor and have no means of escape. They wander to another country or region seeking safety and food. They lose hope, and ultimately millions die due to political decisions that prevent them from receiving necessary food and water.

Religion

Religion is also a major push factor in migrations. Religious wars, never far from the center of global events, arose in the wake of the secular massacres and starvations. Thus the third cause of migration, religion, has created a volatile mix with modern warfare. The partition of India and Pakistan became a forced migration of millions, and the violence continues. Among Shi'a and Sunni Muslims, religious and various tribal loyalties have mixed to create the largest number of refugees in Asia: Muslims. Regional Muslim jihads have been part of Islamic history from the earliest Muslim centuries, but in recent centuries they have occurred in places like the Balkans, Ethiopia, and North and West Africa. Toward the end of the twentieth century Islamic jihads globalized along with the economy, communications, fast food, and fashions. The struggle for purity within Islam and the spread of a more pure Islam became subthemes in most areas of Islamic conflict. In Indonesia, Muslims migrated into predominantly Christian parts of the Moluccas and sought to Islamize the area through violence. The movement of Muslims to spread more fundamentalist teachings or to Islamize areas has also created greater violence, although mostly it has been Muslims killing other Muslims. However, the greatest number of Muslims have migrated not to bring violence (such as to Afghanistan) but to escape Islamic violence and seek greater economic advantages in places like Europe and North America. France has received millions of Muslims from Algeria and adjacent regions of North Africa. This is all part of the major migration movement mentioned at the beginning of this chapter: the nations began to come to the home of missionary outreach.

Environment and Disease

Finally, millions of people became refugees because of environmental stresses and disease. With overpopulation in many regions, the poorest of

Nancy S. Sunquist

Figure 17. Stateless children of migrant workers in Sabah, Malaysia, are gathered for a time of instruction at an independent "school" run by Christians in the area. This is the only formal instruction they are able to receive.

the poor live on floodplains or move into more marginal climates. Every year the monsoon rains flood large sections of Bangladesh and Pakistan, displacing millions of people and spreading disease. Hurricanes (cyclones or typhoons), tsunamis, earthquakes, famines, and even the flu (1918 pandemic, killing more than fifty million) displace people even as they take millions of lives. Again, massive movements of people magnify religious devotion and spread the same. Sometimes people never return to the ravaged region, for disease usually follows disasters, but other times new people move into the region, bringing new religious practices.

The role of environment, including such factors as drought and soil erosion, often combines with political realities to create massive poverty and starvation. At the opposite extreme, these same factors, combined with globalization and "free market" competition, have created pockets of extreme wealth. Often the two extremes are found in the same countries or even in the same cities. Regional poverty is a strong push factor, for those who can move. Many of the poorest people are trapped by geography or political realities and cannot migrate to better lands or to jobs. In Asia, for example, the poor, coming from countries like India, Sri Lanka, Indonesia, or the Philippines, look for labor in wealthier countries.

Construction workers from India are found in Dubai and Saudi Arabia. Household servants from Indonesia and the Philippines are found working in the homes of the wealthy in Malaysia, Singapore, and Hong Kong. When migrant workers are Christian, they often develop churches in their temporary homeland. When non-Christian laborers find themselves in Christian households, or Christian regions, they are often evangelized by the locals. Thus the extremes of wealth and poverty create new ethnic churches in far-off lands. Filipino congregations are found wherever Filipinos find jobs in foreign countries. New congregations of Sinhalese and Tamils are found in Singapore and Kuala Lumpur.

Migration and the Development of Christianity

Our concern is the impact of these migrations on the development of Christianity. Christianity develops, for the most part, along the borderlands, or along the overlapping folds of cultures. Where cultures and peoples collide, intermingle, and share, Christian teaching and life have to be retranslated into local parlance. In this translation and retranslation the gospel is presented afresh and greater openness to the message of Jesus appears. "Migration movement has historically been a prime factor in global religious expansion—preeminently so in the case of Christianity—and . . . current patterns of migration will have an incalculable impact on religious interactions in the course of the twenty-first century."[9] In the very retranslating of the gospel message a new vitality may be (most often is) unleashed. All cultures are reinvigorated by trade and cultural exchange, but Christianity, unlike other religions, seems to exist within or on the missional edge. Thus migrations of people are very important for Christianity, and at the end of the twentieth century these migrations became more complex and extensive.

One example may help. The history of China has been one of an empire becoming more open to the world and then turning inward, closing off to the world. During these cycles, Chinese have moved out in trade, and then when this was not possible, they would move out permanently (migrate) to foreign lands for business purposes. At the end of the twentieth century, as China was once again opening up to the world, Chinese began moving out. Most of the Chinese moving to other Asian countries or the West to study have only a rudimentary understanding of Christianity. Unexpectedly, however, many

9. Hanciles presents the main argument of his book *Beyond Christendom*, 378.

Chinese who have encountered Christians in their adopted countries have been converted. Many of these Chinese return to China, either permanently or on visits, with their newfound faith. This is not a planned strategy of a church or of a mission agency, but many Christians who receive Chinese in their countries do what they can to enhance the movement.[10]

Migration and the Loss of Christian Presence

The word "migration" always carries pain and loss. A person or family moving from home is leaving friends, family, and often an identity rooted in a particular place with local language and local customs. Even when people migrate of their own free will to seek a more prosperous future, they suffer loss. One of the places of greatest pain and loss, both for families and for the Christian presence, is Lebanon. Official records placed the Christian population in Lebanon in 1926 at 84 percent. Most of these Christians were from the ancient Maronite tradition (Eastern rite Catholic), but others were Orthodox, Roman Catholic, or Protestant, with the last group growing. However, by the end of the twentieth century the Christian population declined to about 36 percent of the total population. Why such a decline, and why has Lebanon, like other countries in the Middle East, been a country marked by massive Christian emigration?

At the beginning of the twentieth century Lebanon was ruled by the Ottoman Empire, and therefore Christian participation in society was limited. Toward the end of the nineteenth century there were migrations out of the region due to the expanding of economies in the later period of the Industrial Revolution. Ottoman rulers did not make room for the new middle-class merchants and business innovators.[11] These people, mostly Christian men, emigrated at the rate of thousands a year until the formation of modern Lebanon in 1920. At that point many of the Christian middle class remained in Lebanon, and others returned from cities like London to which they had migrated to develop businesses. However, two of the largest periods of emigration from Lebanon occurred after World War II and during and after the Lebanese Civil War (1975–90). The end of World War II redrew the map of the Middle East. British and French protectorates were ended, and local rule created new instabilities. Christians were a minority in the former Ottoman Empire, and religious tensions rose.

10. My wife and I have witnessed local Chinese in Sabah, East Malaysia, reach out to Chinese students who are studying in Malaysian universities. We then watched as a number were baptized on Easter, preparing to go home to witness to their families in China.
11. See Tabar, "Lebanon."

The greatest cause of emigration, however, was not the rise of independent states in the Middle East but the formation of Israel. As we noted in chapter 3, the formation of Israel, out of mostly Muslim Palestine, was one of the greatest causes of persecution and now of emigration of Christians in the latter half of the twentieth century. The Palestine Liberation Organization established many bases in southern Lebanon for fighting against Israel. This violence and economic instability, on top of the Lebanese Civil War, left the economy in shambles with an unemployment rate of nearly 25 percent in the late 1980s. In this seemingly hopeless situation many of those who had the means connected with relatives who had migrated earlier, and they joined those relatives in North America, South America, Western Europe, and Australia. Large numbers of Lebanese businesses sprang up in urban areas, and the Orthodox, Catholic, and Maronite churches followed. The decline of Orthodoxy in the Middle East was matched by Orthodoxy's growth in the West.

Other areas of the Middle East also declined in Christian presence after decolonization. What little protection of Christian communities was possible under British and French protectorates was lost after World War II. Religion became a major factor in the modern social formation of countries like Iran, Iraq, Syria, and Egypt, and of others across North Africa. For example, Algerian independence in 1962 initiated a flood of European colonists and European-educated Algerians (called *pieds-noirs*, "black-feet") to France. An estimated nine hundred thousand came to Europe. European presence, even if the Europeans were not strongly committed to missionary work, did provide the environment for ongoing Christian life in the Middle East and North Africa. The migration of Middle Eastern Christians out of the land of Jesus's birth meant greater diversity of Christianity in lands of migration. During the twentieth century 2.7 million Lebanese, mostly Christians, came to the Americas. Coptic churches sprang up in major cities of Europe and North America as well.

Christian Migration

When I lived in the East End of Pittsburgh, Pennsylvania, my wife and I attended an urban Presbyterian church. Near the end of the twentieth century we noticed some newer ethnic groups in our area of the country, an area that had traditionally been black and white. Signs written in Spanish began to appear, and Pentecostal church vans, with writing in Spanish and English, began to be seen at intersections. Ethiopian restaurants—three in a four-block area—opened up, and soon our church leadership was asked to host a French

West African worship service. More Chinese and East Asians began to attend our worship service, and then we had two or three Egyptian families. All this happened within a decade. What was happening?

The United States, unlike Europe, is becoming more Christian by migration, but less Christian by attrition of Euro-Americans. Most of the immigrants to the United States today (about 75 percent)[12] are Christian. There are three basic reasons for this. First, the United States has a large border with Mexico, which is mostly a Christian country. Most of the immigrants to the United States, both legal and undocumented, are from Mexico, Central America, or the Caribbean. Second, immigration to the United States is related to our history. We have a large number of immigrants who came from Korea because of the Korean War and from Vietnam because of the Vietnam War, and a much larger percentage of these immigrants are Christian than of people who remain in the immigrants' home countries. For example, the Christian population of Korea is only about 20 or 25 percent, but about three-fourths of immigrants to the United States from Korea are Christian.[13] Third, Christians seeking asylum from persecution (Sudan, Russia, Ethiopia, Armenia, Iraq, Iran) have often come to the United States. Orthodox communities that have been persecuted in Russia and the Middle East have found a home in the United States, strengthening the Orthodox presence there.

Chinese are a special case here. Many Christians from Hong Kong migrated to North America (Vancouver and Toronto were major settlement areas), anticipating persecution once 1997 came and Hong Kong was returned from British to Chinese rule. The persecution never came, but neither did the migrants move back. Hundreds of Chinese fellowships and churches were planted in North America, and these churches now have ongoing relationships with family members (and sometimes with churches) back in China. Chinese outreach to Chinese students and businesspeople in North America created another missionary dynamic in the twentieth century. Not only Chinese but also other immigrant groups (Koreans, Nigerians, Egyptians, etc.) reach out to people from their country of origin. Christian migration is a two-way street with multiple levels of influence.

12. According to Pew Research Religion and Public Life Project, *Religious Affiliation of U.S. Immigrants*, the percent of legal (green card) immigrants who are Christian is slowly declining because of the increase in Asian and Middle Eastern immigrants. Today only about 61 percent of legal immigrants are Christian. However, the undocumented immigrants from the Americas are about 83 percent Christian. Most of the immigrants to the United States (38 percent, including legal and undocumented) are from Mexico and Central America and are almost all Christians.

13. According to Pew Research Religion and Public Life Project, "Religious Affiliation," 71 percent of Korean Americans are Christian, and only 6 percent identify themselves as Buddhist. Twenty-three percent of Koreans in South Korea are Buddhist.

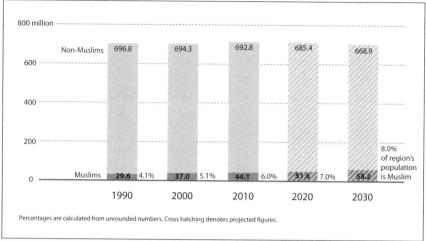

Pew Research Religion and Public Life Project,
The Future of the Global Muslim Population, 2011

Figure 18. Muslims as a share of the population of Europe

The decline of Christianity in Europe is caused not only by secularization of institutions and ideas; unlike the United States, Europe is also de-Christianized by migration.

> In 2010 approximately *47 million people* lived in the European Union . . . who were born outside the EU country where they live. This corresponds to 9.4 percent of the **total EU population**. Of these, 31.4 million (6.3% [of the total EU population]) were born outside the EU. The largest absolute numbers of people born outside the EU were in Germany, France, the United Kingdom, Spain, Italy, and the Netherlands. This leads to a multicultural environment, where immigrants do not stand out, and can integrate more easily.[14]

As we noted above, the postcolonial situation in the Middle East has encouraged Middle Eastern Christians to migrate to both Europe and North America. In addition, the proximity of Europe to North Africa and the Middle East has made possible two other types of migration to Europe: economic and political. Many Muslims are leaving regions where there is ongoing warfare within Islam. Remember that the largest number of refugees in Asia—often living in tents—are Muslims. When possible, they seek asylum in Europe. They are seeking asylum in any country of Europe, not just in proximate regions.

For example, in the past twenty years the two European countries from which the most people have immigrated to Norway have been Poland and

14. From a website designed to help people in their migration to EU countries: Move Europe (http://www.artiszelmenis.lv/moveeurope), emphasis original.

Sweden. This is not a surprise if you look at a map. However, more Muslims from Pakistan, Iraq, and Somalia immigrated to Norway than all the Poles and Swedes who did, combined.[15] According to the Pew Research study on Islam in Europe, the trend toward an increasing Muslim population will continue. The Muslim percentage of Europe's population is not large (predicted to be only 8 percent by 2030), but the point is that as the Christian trend continues to decline, the Muslim trend increases through migration (see figure 18).

Thus the Christian population of Europe has been rapidly declining both for internal, ideological reasons and for external reasons. At the beginning of the twentieth century no one dreamed that by the end of the century Europe's most vital and growing religion would be Islam. But with Muslim birthrates much higher than European birthrates (whether Christian or not) and the continuing migration patterns, nothing short of a great Christian revival and missionary outreach will temper or reverse this trend.

Shifting Centers, Centering Shifts

How do we make sense of these global shifts in religion caused by migration rather than by missionary activity? Let's step back for a moment and put this in perspective. In the story of Christianity since the life, death, resurrection, and ascension of Jesus Christ, his followers have moved from Jerusalem to Antioch and Alexandria, from Edessa and Nisibis to India and China, from Rome to Ireland, and from York to New York. For centuries the theological center of Christianity was in the Mediterranean basin; Constantinople, Alexandria, and Rome would have been the centers of Christianity. Later, Christian vitality was in France, with new monastic orders being founded and major theologians residing in places like Paris and Cîteaux. With the rise of the modern mission movement, the center of Christian vitality seemed to be in Germany, the United Kingdom, and North America.

As we have seen, all of this changed with the collapse of European colonialism and the rise of indigenous Christian movements in Lafriasia. As we can see in figure 19, the global statistical center of Christianity was in West Asia and Europe for the first nineteen centuries. It moved from West Asia to Europe about the time of the Crusades (1000–1100), and at the time of the Reformation the statistical center of Christianity was in Austria, in Eastern Europe. As late as 1900 Christianity was still dominated by Europe: its center

15. Thorud, "International Migration."

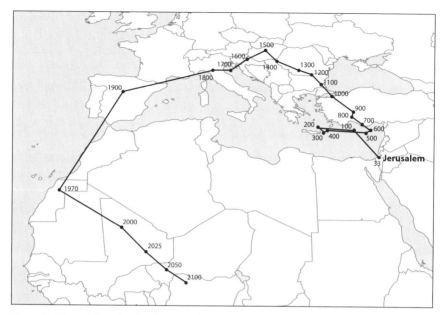

Figure 19. Map tracking the global statistical center of Christianity

"Trajectory of the Statistical Center of Global Christianity, AD 33–2100," *International Review of Mission* 33, no. 369 (April 2004): 166–81. Map made by Global Mapping International.

was in Spain, and eight of the top-ten Christian countries were in Europe. Asians or Africans could be forgiven for thinking that Christianity was a European or white religion. But in the twenty-first century this is no longer the case. The last four decades of the twentieth century marked a tremendous change, something no one was ready for and few people even imagined. Suddenly Christianity went from mostly Western (1960) to more than 50 percent non-Western (late 1980s), and today Christianity is only one-third white and two-thirds people of color.

This is significant for both what it says about Christianity and what it says about world cultures. First, Christianity is more and more a religion practiced as a minority faith without "Christian" government support. In countries like Nigeria, Malawi, China, Vietnam, Indonesia, and Nepal, Christianity is vital and growing even though the governments vacillate between benign tolerance and active persecution of Christians. There is a much larger *percentage* of the general population worshiping weekly in Brunei, Singapore, Egypt, and Lebanon (not to mention Ghana, Nigeria, and Uganda) than in any country in Western Europe. All of these Christians in Africa and Asia (except in the Philippines) do not have the Christendom comfort that European Christians had in the past. One of the countries with the largest numbers of Christians is China, a country that has had very contentious relations with religions.

Ever since the conversion of the early kings like Tiridates of Armenia, Christianity has seemed to prosper after the conversion of rulers or even has seemed to depend on such conversion for its survival. Early Jesuits in China, Vietnam, and India always had in view the need to reach the ruler. Today, however, Christianity is developing quite apart from royal conversions. As the Christian West becomes less and less Christian, the number of Jesus followers continues to grow in countries where the religion is marginalized. It appears that Christendom Christianity—Christianity spreading with the support of governments, societies, and popular customs—is coming to a close. This bears repeating: it seems that the 1,700-year-old model of Christianity prospering most under Christian rulers is at an end. Christianity will now penetrate cultures and societies from barrios, farms, and neighborhoods rather than from castles, palaces, and parliaments.

Second, and closely related, is the shift away from Western religious hegemony. Many historians and Christian leaders in the West assumed a basic pattern for Christianity. The Western model, like Western culture, would slowly spread, now on the coattails of Western technology. This hegemonic view has proved false. Christianity, even (or especially) when scattered and persecuted, does not slowly conform to Western liturgies, theologies, and practices. Christianity is not beholden to Western cultures, much to the chagrin of Western Christian leaders and secular historians. Jehu Hanciles says it well:

> The popular and entrenched notion that the values, ideals, and institutions of modern Western societies are destined to dominate the world, at the expense of autochthonous or indigenous forms, is one of the most pervasive myths of the contemporary era. Yet it has a certain allure. It is patently self-serving. . . . It promises a certain future based on a fixed, supposedly universal, ideal.[16]

Hanciles notes that an ideology of a "single global culture or universal model based on Western liberal secular values" is nothing new. In the past it was expressed as "*padroado*," "manifest destiny," "divine providence," and "white man's burden." The history we have described here reveals that Christianity in the twentieth century broke out of its Western Christendom expression and is entering into African religious cultures and Chinese Confucian cultures, and in each context the local cultures are, as it were, being remade, not overwhelmed. This is a transformation shaped by local people, not foreign leaders. There is continuity with local religious culture, rather than a radical

---

16. Hanciles, *Beyond Christendom*, 374.

discontinuity. This new awareness about Christianity has been forced on the West in light of the massive migrations of people and the surprising fruitfulness of Western Christian missions. Both have been important.

Third, this proliferation of Christianity that is village based, locally based, without political or elite protection, places Christians in a precarious but important place on the global stage. Will government officials and religious leaders recognize the conversions and growth of Christian institutions as something that is good for society as a whole or rather as a threat to the social order? We have seen both in the past. Without political clout and with only a small, quiet political voice, will Christian presence in societies continue to be seen as threatening or as hopeful? Will the terrible growth in Christian martyrdom that we saw in the twentieth century, martyrdom that came from both secular ideologies and religious motives, continue or even grow further?

With so little political voice, there would seem to be little to deter such violence, a violence that has continued into the twenty-first century. The former Christian nations seem concerned for tolerance, freedom, and human rights in general, but as these definitions become farther and farther detached from their Christian heritage, will any nations speak up for Christian welfare and Christian witness? On the one hand, the future does not look bright for Christians as we see less and less political and institutional power to protect it. On the other hand, it was such an alliance with power that gave Christianity its darkest blots in the historical logbook. Today Christianity is still the largest religion in the world, but its places of greatest growth, practice, and overall health are more from the fringes of global political and economic health. So it was from the beginning of Christian existence with the earliest followers of the homeless prophet, Jesus the Christ. As always, Christianity is centered on the person of Jesus, not in a culture, nation, city, or ethnic group.

6

One Way among Others
Christianity and the World's Religions

A Hindu friend of mine said to me one day, "We shall put an image of Christ into every Hindu temple, and then no Hindu will see the point of becoming a Christian. . . ." For the Hindu attitude toward Jesus Christ is to accept him and make him at home in Hinduism. . . . Mahatma Gandhi once said, "I think of Christ as belonging not to Christianity alone, but to the whole world, to all its people, no matter under what name they may worship."

D. T. Niles, *Stone of Stumbling*, 17;
1957 Lyman Beecher Lectures

Evangelist and ecumenical pioneer Daniel Thamyrajah Niles understood the major issue regarding Christian faith and other faiths for the twentieth century. How would Jesus be appropriated or rejected by the people of other faiths? By the middle of the twentieth century most peoples of the world had been introduced to the life of Jesus. There were many from the non-Western world who respected Jesus, or at least many of his teachings, but who could not abide by his call to absolute loyalty. And there were many Christians in the West who began to respect other religions and who also could not abide by Jesus's call to absolute loyalty. What was happening?

The missionary encounter of the nineteenth century set the stage for three related movements in the twentieth century: religious pluralism, religious conflicts, and the conversion of many from one religion to another. We have already looked at some twentieth-century conflicts in chapter 3 and noted that many were religious. In the context of a century of religious violence, many Christians argued for greater tolerance and pluralism in practice and belief. Under these same conditions other Christians became anxious and belligerent about the growing pluralism. Some in this second group became intolerant of diversity; others became more committed to missionary work among other religions.

In between the pluralists and nonpluralists, newer religions and religious movements developed from unique encounters and mixing of religious beliefs and practices. During the twentieth century it became more and more unlikely that a village could live with a single religious culture or "web of significance."[1] Modern migration, missionary work, and empire building forced villages to live with other cultures and religious practices. Muslim villages in Upper Egypt that had developed ways of living with Muslim and Coptic Christian communities side by side now found Protestant churches springing up, formed out of former Muslims and former Orthodox. Buddhists and indigenous worshipers in northern Thailand found more and more churches springing up in village after village. Christians were now living in close proximity to Hindus, Muslims, Buddhists, Sikhs, and even Zoroastrians.

But it was not just Christianity's spread to Asia that brought about the new religious proximity. Muslims were moving to North America and Europe. Wealthy Hindus, mostly from upper-caste families, were attending universities in the West and staying after graduation. Increasingly Asians, Africans, and Latin Americans from families of means were coming to the West for better education and better jobs. A doctor in Egypt or in Myanmar makes a fraction of what a doctor makes in New York or London or Munich. These communities from India or Iran or Turkey began building Hindu temples, Buddhist temples, or Muslim mosques in their new hometowns. Religious architecture in the West was changing. Muslim schools for children were set up in urban areas to help parents keep children away from the secular and Christian influences of public school education. Religious schools and buildings that once seemed out of place in the West were spreading. Most of these new

---

1. From Clifford Geertz, whose understanding of cultures and beliefs is very helpful in discussing the relationships between people of various religious beliefs and practices. It is best to talk about religious people and practices rather than about "religions," as if a religion is a static "thing" we can study. Religions are always dynamic communal ways of living. See Geertz, *Interpretation of Cultures*.

interreligious relationships were brought about because of decolonization and globalization. As a result, the major faiths of the world came to be practiced and perceived very differently. Thus, as we noted above, it was a remarkable century of religious conflicts, religious pluralism, and conversions.

Migration and Religious Developments: New Religious Movements

One type of conversion that accelerated in the twentieth century was that of religions themselves, not just of individuals. It may be more accurate to talk about the transformation of religions. Rapid and complex patterns of migration and globalization did more than simply bring Christians into non-Christian villages and bring non-Christians into Western cities. At the same time these global movements have fragmented both religious patterns and religious communities. As a result, new religious movements, many appearing as genetic mutations of Christianity, have erupted in the last century, creating a whole new field of study: new religious movements (NRMs).[2] One way to explain this phenomenon is to say that "globalization has blurred boundaries among realms of human activity, allowing traditional religious expressions long considered to be waning to take center stage alongside commodified consumer culture."[3] Christianity has proven to be a catalyst for many of these new religions. In the 1960s liberal secular ideologies predicted the global collapse of religions,[4] but those who so prophesied have all proved to be false prophets. Christianity has been renewed and reconceived on the global stage, and at the same time older as well as newer religions are languishing less and living more.

Christianity, Islam, Buddhism, and Hinduism—what are often called the world religions—have all survived and, in particular regions, are doing quite well. Globalization and migrations have mixed these religions in newer contexts, and at times whole new religions have evolved. Buddhism in Southeast Asia is transforming itself and spawning newer "evangelical" expressions. Today there are Buddhist Sunday schools as well as the YMBA (Young Men's Buddhist Association). There are Buddhist groups from Taiwan, Malaysia, and Singapore that focus on disaster relief and the self-development of peoples (e.g., Tzu Chi, founded 1966). There are Buddhist ambulance societies in Bangkok, Thailand, and Red Crescent Societies responding to human need in

2. The study of new religious movements began in the 1970s, coming mostly from the study of new religions that developed in Japan after World War II.

3. Vásquez and Marquardt, *Globalizing the Sacred*, 8.

4. See, e.g., one of the best examples of this literature: Cox, *Secular City*.

most Muslim countries today.[5] We can say that a religious vitality has been stimulated by the burgeoning interreligious and intercultural contacts. When non-Christian religions are revitalized by such adaptation of Christian forms and ideas, they resist Christian missions more strongly, in a sense inoculating themselves and becoming almost immune to the Jesus of Scripture.

The growth of Christian presence and international Christian participation in countries like Nigeria, Kenya, Malaysia, and Indonesia have revitalized Islam and Buddhism. Major religions have mutated in hundreds of ways; here we look at only a few of them.[6] In Latin America the extremes of poverty and wealth, along with growing Christian movements, have stimulated older, indigenous religions and catalyzed newer faiths. Numerous indigenous movements have been spawned or revived in Latin America and the Caribbean beginning at the end of the nineteenth century. In Brazil, for example, with its rich mix of African, Iberian, and indigenous cultures, many Afro-Christian and Afro-Brazilian religions have been spawned.

Umbanda probably originated in Brazil in the late nineteenth century, but in 1908 at a séance held in Rio de Janeiro a young man, just seventeen, was possessed by the spirits of an indigenous Brazilian and an African slave who was beaten to death. According to another telling of the story the young man was possessed by a deceased Catholic priest and was told to start a new religion. The spirit spoke to the unbelievers, telling them he was to be called Caboclo das Sete Encruzilhadas (Half-Indian Peasant of the Seven Crossroads) and that the young man was to found a new religion called Umbanda, a harmonizing and enduring religion.[7] A number of common features of Latin American indigenous religions are present here at the genesis of Umbanda. Such religions (1) strongly identify with indigenous cultures, which are often threatened by the European and African migrations as well as by the growth of Christianity and the decline of agrarian life; (2) are often enriched by African spirituality, including spirit possession and relation to the ancestors; and (3) offer a hope, or an eschatology, either for this world or for the next. In this case peace and harmony forever is prophesied for the end of time.

Another Afro-Brazilian religion, Candomblé, incorporates more elements of Catholicism. Candomblé originated among mostly Yoruba African slaves in Salvador, Bahia, centuries ago, but with the end of slavery and the rise of modern Brazil, this diverse religion grew, fragmented, and soon spread

5. Red Crescent societies are national humanitarian organizations that operate in Muslim nations. Most today are affiliated with the International Federation of Red Cross and Red Crescent Societies, the international umbrella network founded in 1919.

6. Because of the size and complexity of new religions in Asia, we look at NRMs in Asia later.

7. For a more thorough discussion of Umbanda see D. Brown, *Umbanda*.

throughout much of Latin America. The religion in many ways is typical of Yoruba religion of West Africa, but it has incorporated the use of crucifixes and statues of Christian saints. On saints' days, many Candomblé will attend mass to honor the same saints. These and many other Afro-Brazilian religions make up nearly 4 percent of the population of Brazil. The influence of these religions is not contained by the borders of Brazil, but, as with most religions today, has a global expression.

In the Caribbean the African influence is also very strong in many indigenous religions that, as in Latin America, combine elements of African practices and beliefs with Christian beliefs and practices. One of the most globally influential groups is the Rastafarians. Strongly Afrocentric, Rastas were influenced by Marcus Garvey (1887–1940) and his Pan-Africanism. His inspiration earned him the title of John the Baptist in the eyes of Rastas, who believed Ethiopian emperor Haile Selassie (1892–1975) was the coming savior. Rejecting modern Western culture ("Babylon"), they look to Africa, specifically Ethiopia, as Holy Zion. Haile Selassie, whose name in the Ge'ez language means "Holy Trinity," is recognized as the embodiment of the Trinity. Again, eschatology plays an important role in this new religion. In much of the music of the Rastafarians, for example from Bob Marley, the heavenly existence is pictured as in this world, specifically in Africa. Marley sang about resisting ongoing slavery (using Exodus motifs) with a call for universal love and redemption. In his song "One Love / People Get Ready," he describes basic Christian themes of love and worship ("Give thanks and praise to the Lord . . . One Love") in almost apocalyptic terms ("Let's get together to fight this Holy Armageddon"). The music has global appeal, but the message is infused with biblical themes and longings for the unity of humankind ("Let's get together and feel all right").

Rastafarian beliefs are very closely tied to the Bible (mostly the Old Testament), to the Christian Orthodox tradition of trinitarian faith looking through the lens of eschatology. Because of this interesting Christian dynamic, some have become more orthodox in their beliefs, while staying in the Rastafarian family.[8]

In the nineteenth century the "free-market" form of religion that developed in the United States was fertile ground for new religions. This pattern continued in the United States, but with the additional feature of adding "Eastern religious" dimensions. L. Ron Hubbard's *Scientology* (1952) and the Church of Scientology combine modern psychology, Eastern beliefs of reincarnation, modern self-help, Platonic views of dualism, and, of course, modern science. Almost a type of modern gnostic belief, Scientology has spread through certain

8. See Spencer, *Dread Jesus*.

sectors of Western society, most notably the wealthy, including among those in the entertainment industry.

The Universal Life Church (founded in 1977) is another example of a newer religious movement in the West. Based on only the most general beliefs in the unity of all humanity and the goal of rising to a higher and more enjoyable life, this church is shaped mostly by United States tax laws. Almost anyone can be ordained immediately by filling out forms and sending them to the church offices in Modesto, California. This is the most extreme example of independent religious development. The founder believed that each person will find his or her own religious path; each person's religion is completely individualistic, but all are held together by a single creed: "Do only that which is right."

Transcendental Meditation (TM), founded by Maharishi Mahesh Yogi in about 1957, is another NRM whose basic concern is good health and/or long life. Like Scientology, TM offers secret, or special, teachings that will help one live better and longer. TM, however, is based on the Vedantic tradition in Hinduism, and so Eastern thought is intrinsic to its basic teachings. During the founder's life the movement gained a large following in the West, especially among wealthy and influential people. By 2000 the organization held property worth close to $4 billion and had more than one thousand teaching centers. Many people have taken up TM as a form of relaxation therapy, more than as a religious commitment. TM, along with other newer North American religions, underscores the attraction people in the West have felt to movements of religion as therapy in the midst of rapid urbanization and the increased pace of Western life.

The New Age movement is a loosely affiliated collection of beliefs and practices that combine ancient beliefs (often from pre-Christian Europe) with modern beliefs and techniques. For the religious purist, the New Age movement often looks like a smorgasbord of religious choices. New Age devotees may be atheists, monotheists, or polytheists. Some follow ancient European practices; others find inspiration from Hinduism. New Age followers may use astrology, channeling spirits, meditation, diet, and music, as well as chanting, or even aromatherapy or massage therapy to help reach the fullest of human potential.

Neo-paganism, as expressed in various New Age beliefs, is most pronounced in the rise of Wicca. Wicca is more truly a worship honoring two main gods, Gaia (earth goddess) and the Horned God (representing the sun). The two are considered the main gods among a pantheon of gods, and they represent two basic forces of life in the universe. Wicca is a recovery of many ancient teachings from northern Europe and became recognized as a religion only in the 1960s. In this and many other NRMs in the West we can see the rejection of both secularization and Christendom and a rediscovery of the ancient paths. Now, however, these ancient paths are used in the service of personal fulfillment or to enhance one's own potential or experience in life. However, if we look closely, we can see that much of the attraction or appeal is a Western fascination with the East.

We can summarize this transformation that was taking place in religions by looking at the multiple causes. We have mentioned migrations (including the missionary movement as well as the movements related to empires and globalization). But other causes include urbanization and the loss of community and identity that are related to urbanization. Finally, modern Western culture, as it became more secular and more scientific in outlook, also became more intent on insulating itself from suffering and death. Science and technology took on some of the functions of religion by providing "answers" to suffering, if not death. Religions had always been a means to deal with suffering and to conquer death or to make the journey to the place of the dead (or to avoid the cycle of rebirths). Now, in a world where life was seen as only secular, religion began to function more as a way to avoid suffering. In the West, NRMs became means of therapy and happiness. Religions could lower blood pressure and take away anxiety and worry. It is true that for the whole century Christianity in the West was in constant decline, but religion—especially therapeutic religion—proved quite vital.[9]

Christianity and Asian Religions

In the twentieth century Western Christianity developed two minds regarding its relationship to other religious beliefs, especially in relation to Asian religions. Are these religions beautiful expressions of a search for God, or are they reflections of human resistance to God? One of the great themes of Christianity in the twentieth century is the development of theologies of religion related to Christian interaction with the great religions of Asia. We can mark the multifaceted influence of Asian religions on Christian theology and missionary practice in the twentieth century with a very important celebration in Chicago in 1893: the World's Columbian Exposition, also called the Great Chicago World's Fair. It was a remarkable event, marking the four-hundredth anniversary of the arrival of Christopher Columbus with great fanfare, buildings, the first Ferris wheel, and many parliaments to discuss issues such as anthropology, economics, trade, and religion. An important part of the Columbian Exposition was the World's Parliament of Religions. A seventeen-day

9. What Smith and Denton called "moralistic, therapeutic deism" in *Soul Searching*.

Figure 20. 1893 World's Parliament of Religions, Chicago

event involving about four thousand people marked a watershed in religious understanding. The World's Parliament was chaired by the eclectic pastor of First Presbyterian Church in Chicago, Rev. Dr. John Henry Barrows. Barrows was appointed by the chairman of the Exposition, Chicago lawyer and New Jerusalem Church[10] member Charles C. Bonney.

Interestingly enough, Bonney was fascinated by religions, but he himself was not a member of a mainline church. The New Jerusalem Church was a Swedenborg Church, and as such held to the teachings of its founder, Emanuel Swedenborg, who claimed to have had direct revelations from Jesus over a twenty-five-year period. Part of these revelations include the belief that Jesus was establishing a "new church," which would henceforth worship God only as Jesus Christ. Swedenborg also had visions of the final judgment and taught that believers must obey the Lord's commands. Thus the person who appointed a Presbyterian pastor to chair the conference was himself not an orthodox Christian.

This conference can be seen as an allegory of the two-minded nature of Christianity and its relationship to other religions in the twentieth century. First, there was great fascination and interest in the teachings of one of the central figures in the parliament, Swami Vivekananda of India. Vivekananda was a disciple of the famous Hindu reformer Ramakrishna, who emphasized that the divine is in all living things and therefore service and compassion for others was service to God. Vivekananda was a deeply spiritual man and great

10. Also called the Swedenborg Church, founded in 1787 by a group of people who followed the teachings of Emanuel Swedenborg. It holds on to a number of nontraditional doctrines such as a nontrinitarian theology and other beliefs that Swedenborg claimed came from years of special revelations from God to him. These are recorded in his *Arcana Coelestia* (Heavenly Secrets or Secrets of Heaven) (1749–56).

communicator. His presence at the Parliament of Religions had the effect
of showing the young nation the wisdom of the oldest religious traditions.
Vivekananda emphasized the open and welcoming nature of Hinduism. Part
of the openness of Hinduism was to show that all religions were found in the
universal search, which was pictured as various streams all coming to the same
ocean, all contributing their different gifts and different sources. The swami
was a national star. Years later, the great ecumenical leader and missionary
J. N. Farquhar wrote, "Vivekananda is undoubtedly the greatest figure in the
Parliament of Religions. After hearing him we feel how foolish it is to send
missionaries to this learned nation (India)."[11] This was the conclusion of many
in the West. What made this comment even more interesting is that Farquhar
had been a missionary to India beginning in 1891 for eleven years. Farquhar and
many in the West concluded that such a pure and open and reasonable religion
does not need missionaries. Theologies in the West began to support such a
generous spirit toward other religions, and we will look at this in a moment.

Second, others—like another future mission and ecumenical leader John R.
Mott—who attended the World's Fair and heard Swami Vivekananda, were mo-
tivated to take even more seriously the call to world evangelization.[12] Mott was
twenty-eight when he heard the swami, and the experience deeply impressed
him. At the time, he was serving as the national director of the Intercollegiate
YMCA and was one of the founders of the Student Volunteer Movement
(SVM) for Foreign Missions. In 1888 the SVM adopted as its watchword, "The
evangelization of the world in this generation," a slogan that was reaffirmed at
the first national SVM convention, held in Cleveland, Ohio, in 1891. Two years
later the young YMCA director heard the call from the Indian scholar. Mott
and many other "volunteers" were strengthened in their resolve to evangelize
the whole world, including the Hindu world of the swami's India. Thus the
combined influences of the modern missionary movement and globalization
helped to nurture this Christian two-mindedness about religions: embracing
all religions on one hand and new zeal for evangelization on the other hand.

Theological development in the West seemed to follow the warm interreligious encounters of the late nineteenth and early twentieth centuries.
Broadly speaking, theology in the twentieth century was largely a movement
to humanize and secularize the Christian tradition and the Christian scriptures. Commentaries on biblical books focused much of their attention on the
original sources of scriptural passages. In the case of the Gospels the focus
was on the earliest Christian communities that created the early biographies

11. Farquhar, *Religious Movements in India*, 202.
12. See Moore, "American Religion," 153.

of Jesus. Included in this search was the task to explain the types of editing or redaction that were involved as the final scriptures evolved into what we have today. Scripture was humanized even as Jesus was also critically reduced to more manageable proportions. A reduced Jesus and reduced corpus for preaching made Christianity much more like the other religions of the world. Western scholars studied religions in terms of the history of religions, that is, as human inventions that evolved over time to meet particular needs in various cultures. Religions were understood to be human strivings for meaning in a disenchanted universe. Now Christianity was becoming one of the many human efforts at making sense of an empty universe. The world of the first century was a mythical world that does not make sense to the modern scientific person. Therefore the magical and mythical must be revisioned or reinterpreted for the modern person. Doctrines like the incarnation, preexistence, and even the resurrection and ascension prevent modern persons from faith, so it was the job of theologians to demythologize the Bible with twentieth-century eyes.[13] Books appeared with titles like *The Myth of God Incarnate*, *Myth and Christianity: An Inquiry into the Possibility of Religion without Myth*, *The Myth of Christian Uniqueness: Toward a Pluralistic Theology of Religions*, and *God and the Universe of Faiths*, among many, many others.[14]

After biblical and systematic theologies evolved to include non-Christian religions, theologies of pluralism developed. Pluralism moved from a description (many religions existing together) to prescription (all religions are equal; there are many approaches to truth). Pluralistic theologies minimized conflict but also required lower Christologies. The pluralist answer was not an easy answer, and it retained many tensions. Paul F. Knitter, one of the leading theologians of pluralism, understood as well as any the complex issues related to pluralism in the modern world.

> And yet awareness of pluralism does not lead simply to a total celebration of diversity; nor is the pluralism without its problems. Many are troubled by the way relativity is easily equated with a relativism that has no room for discussing truth-claims and degrees of value. . . . Do not, many ask, the crises of our age constitute a call to the religions to cooperate in their solutions? Can the many religions legitimately live in lazy tolerance, or even worse, in a state of warfare?[15]

13. The study of comparative religion also developed in the twentieth century, taking off with many schools offering courses and majors after the middle of the twentieth century. Both history of religions and comparative religion were greatly aided by the translations of the Sacred Books of the East (1879–1910) under the editorship of Max Müller.

14. Hick, *Myth of God Incarnate*; Jaspers and Bultmann, *Myth and Christianity*; Knitter and Hick, *Myth of Christian Uniqueness*; Hick, *God and the Universe of Faiths*.

15. Knitter, *Introducing Theologies of Religions*, 8.

Figure 21. Peace councillors and trustees walk to the village of Acteal, in Mexico's Chiapas state, site of a dreadful massacre by paramilitary thugs on December 22, 1997. In November 1998 the International Interfaith Peace Council helped dedicate a memorial to the forty-five slain men, women, and childen. R-L: Paul Knitter (trustee); Samdech Preah Maha Ghosananda (peace councillor); Irfan Ahmad Khan (trustee). Maha Ghosananda (1929–2007) was the Buddhist patriarch of Cambodia; Dr. Irfan Khan is a widely influential Muslim scholar.

One of the great anomalies of religion in the twentieth century is that as Western scholars were explaining away the spiritual world in its secular de-mythologizing expressions, Western-trained missionaries were encountering a world more like the first than the twentieth century as they became embedded in African, Latin American, and Asian communities. Asians read the Bible and understood very well the need for healing and for spirits to be cast out. They understood the spiritual world of the Bible, and so conversion to Jesus, who had power over the spirits, was a reasonable, even helpful, response. Many, if not most of the conversions of Hindus, Muslims, and Buddhists in Asia involved an understanding or experience of the spiritual realm: healings, exorcisms, visions, or dreams. Thus the experiences of Asians in their encounters with Jesus were often at odds with Western scholars and their descriptions of Christianity and other faiths.

As Western theologians were developing a theology that could affirm the spiritual life of all religions, a more technical approach to religions developed: dialogue. Coming mostly out of encounters in India and the Middle East,

Western Christians developed both the theology and the practice of interreligious dialogue. As appreciation for other religions grew, the language evolved from dialogue with other *religions*, to dialogue with other *faiths*, to dialogue with other *living faiths*—greater sensitivity to people of other faiths was being expressed. Interreligious dialogue became an important element in the work of the World Council of Churches and of the Roman Catholic Church after Vatican II. For many of those in the dialogue movement, the motivation was reconciliation and peace among the religions. Much of the conflict of the twentieth century centered on religions, and so peacemaking was often approached by getting diverse religious leaders to talk together and then act together.

Theological, or, more exactly, missiological tension developed between the call to be peacemakers through dialogue and the call to be witnesses to all nations. A divide persisted through the end of the century between those who sought to bring about the conversion of people of other faiths and those who began to call missionary work "religious imperialism." This should help to explain the loss of Christian vitality in the West, the decline of missionary work among theological pluralists, and the divisions that persisted in the remnant of Western Christendom.

Newer Asian Religions

By the last decades of the twentieth century Christianity was having the greater impact in Asia, but its impact was not just conversion. It would be more accurately described as a threefold impact. New Christian communities began springing up in most countries of Asia. For the first time in history we can talk about the Christian movement in Nepal, Cambodia, South Korea, Malaysia, and other regions. This is the first influence. But also, as we saw in the nineteenth century, Christianity continued to be used by indigenous religious practitioners to enhance and spread new forms of Buddhism, Hinduism, and Islam. Finally, new religions developed in Asia, and some of these religions have been "inspired" or shaped by their encounter with Christianity. In 1960 a new religion (Divine Light Mission) was founded in northern India by Shri Hans Ji Maharaj. Later, his fourth son, Guru Maharaj Ji, extended the movement to the West, and after marrying an American woman, he intentionally "westernized" the Indian movement by wearing suits and changing the terminology, using more Western terms. In India the movement continued as a Hindu movement, with ashrams and teachers. Thus we can see most clearly here the movement out of Asian religions, the attraction of Eastern religions, and the transformation of Asian religions in Asia.

New religious movements in Vietnam were catalyzed in part by the long colonial experience under the French and the imperial support of the Catholic Church. The third-largest religion in Vietnam today, Cao Đài, was founded in 1926 by a civil servant named Ngo Van Chieu. We see many influences of Roman Catholicism in the Cao Đài faith. The religion is strongly monotheistic, and the founder claims to have had revelations from God (Duc Cao Đài). In organization it is hierarchical, even to the extent of having a supreme pontiff or pope, who is called Giáo-Tông. But like many NRMs, Caodaism borrows from many religions. Its ethical concerns sound more like Confucianism, its religious occult practices seem to be influenced by Taoism, and its view of karma is Buddhist. Strongly nationalistic, the religion has not had a cross-cultural following. Another newer religion in Vietnam, Hoa Hao, was founded in 1939 as a reforming sect of Buddhism. The reforms focus on the poor and peasant farmers and deemphasize typical Buddhist rituals. Of greater importance than temples and images are giving to the poor, building a more just community, and accepting an apocalyptic belief. Contact with the Christian West, the Communist insurgency, and migrations caused by urbanization all seem to be the context for this new religion.

In Japan, China, and South Korea, new religions have arisen in the twentieth century, and many of these have also been influenced by contact with Western thought and the rapid—even apocalyptic—changes that have taken place. In Japan, many of these new religions appear to be affirmations of certain elements of religious tradition, with new elements related to the modern world. Among these new religions are Soka Gakkai and AUM Shinrikyo. Soka Gakkai (The International Value-Creation Society, founded 1930) is a new form of Buddhism that shows evidence of contact with Christianity. In fact, without contact with Christianity many of these new religious movements would never have evolved. Soka Gakkai's engagement with society and its evangelistic zeal and call to conversion more closely mirror Christian missions than either Nichiren Buddhism or traditional Japanese Mahayana Buddhism. AUM Shinrikyo ("AUM supreme truth") grew very rapidly from its start in 1987, and by 1995 it claimed more than forty thousand members throughout the world.[16]

The most influential new religion in Korea, based much more directly on Christianity, is the Holy Spirit Association for the Unification of World Christianity (Unification Church) of Sun Myung Moon. The Unification Church was founded in 1954 and relies on the sacred book *Divine Principles* as well

---

16. In 1995 followers of AUM carried out sarin attacks on subway lines in Tokyo, causing the death of thirteen people and injuring many more. Today AUM is considered a terrorist organization by several countries. In 2007 a splinter group from AUM formed Hikari no Wa and AUM renamed itself Aleph.

as the speeches of Rev. Moon for the final authority. The Christian Bible is interpreted through Moon and *Divine Principles*. The Unification Church has developed into a large international religious, political, and business enterprise, focusing its outreach in three of the wealthier countries of the world: South Korea, Japan, and the United States. In 1992 Moon silenced all speculation when he declared himself to be the promised Messiah who will bring about the restoration promised in the Bible. As with other religions we have looked at, Moon has had a very large following in the West, and his religion promises something of great concern to the modern world: peace and unity.

In China, religion was severely persecuted during the Maoist period, but once economic reforms began to take place, new religious vitality and creativity became evident. Buddhism began to recover, and Christianity did more than recover, for it had never been a significant religion on the national scene. Both Buddhism and Christianity are closely monitored by the Chinese government, but today religions are not seen as being evil and expedient, but as useful and inevitable. Many Christian-influenced sects developed in China, often around some apocalyptic theme or urgent concern. As in the nineteenth century in the West, the rapid change in society, a more free-market economy, movement of people, and the resulting threat to identity led to the formation of new religions with eschatological concerns (or answers).

One of the most influential and closely watched Christian-influenced religions in China is the Eastern Lightning. Eastern Lightning was founded by Zhao Weishan in Heilongjiang province in 1989. Zhao started as a member of a Christian group called the Shouters, but then, with a few followers, he left and started the Church of the Everlasting Foundation. He called himself "The Powerful One," and another leader, a woman named Deng, was soon called "The Almighty God." She was seen as the return of Christ in the flesh, a female Christ figure. They took the name "Eastern Lightning" from Matthew 24:27. By the end of the century the religion had hundreds of thousands, if not millions, of followers, mostly coming from new Christian households. Now called the Church of the Almighty God, it has become more of a doomsday cult involved in violence and murder. Its followers see themselves as living at the edge of the end of the world. They have become an enemy of the Chinese government and a thorn in the side of the Chinese church. The Chinese government is aware of many religious groups in the past who have sought to control the country. This includes Buddhist sects and indigenous Taoist and Christian sects as well. We should remember that the largest civil war in world history, with the greatest loss of life, was the Taiping Rebellion (1850–64), led by a Christian-influenced apocalyptic prophet: Hong Xiuquan. More than twenty million people died in this religious rebellion.

Newer religions in Asia reveal the vitality of religious life brought about by globalization (including the opening of trade), the modern missionary movement, and migration. The newer Asian religions are a sign of this religious vitality, but they are also a sign of the anxiety of societies in the midst of rapid social change. We can say that some religious developments are defensive, religious reform as a way of adapting to the modern realities. Other religions are offensive mutations, aggressively constructing new realities. Christianity has been a cause, or at least a seed idea, for many of these new developments. Often, as with Caodaism and the Church of the Almighty God, the new religions become major communities of resistance to Christian development.

Religious Conflict and Search for Shalom

From the beginning of the twentieth century, religious conflict marked the spread, repression, and development of Christianity. The restructuring of global Christianity we have been talking about occurred both in spite of and because of some of these major conflicts. Religious conflicts erupted in the Middle East, Europe, Africa, and Asia. In the Middle East the major cause of religious conflict was the establishment of the state of Israel (1948) and the migration of Jewish people from Russia, Europe, and North America. The migration to Israel, the economic and military support of Israel from the West, and the displacement of Palestinians (both Muslim and Christian) set up religious conflicts for half a century, even up to the present day. In this conflict, as with others we will mention, new approaches to peace or shalom developed over time. Peace studies in the late twentieth century began to take religion seriously as a key element in bringing a lasting peace.

Additional conflicts in the Middle East centered on religion. The Armenian genocide in the declining Ottoman Empire was noted in an earlier chapter. We would have to add the rising conflicts within Islam such as the Iran-Iraq War (1980–88), which was fueled by the Iranian Revolution and the fear of Iraq that Shi'as in Iraq might side with Iran. Another religious war in the Middle East was the long civil war in Lebanon (1975–90), which involved a Maronite Christian majority with both Sunni and Shi'a minority communities and an influx of Palestinian Muslims displaced through the formation of Israel. The conflict facilitated the migration of hundreds of thousands of refugees, mostly Christian. Thus the war increased Muslim tensions (especially those of Sunnis and Shi'as) and contributed to the decline of Christianity in the Middle East.

In Africa, conflict often, but not always, had religious dimensions. The century started with conflict in South Africa—the Second Boer War. This war pitted the British and their allies against the South African Boers. Religion played a role in this important conflict in that the Boers developed a religious identity as chosen people arriving in the promised land of the Transvaal. Their relentless pursuit of independence and control of South Africa was related to their theology as being a chosen (and superior) people of God. Later in the twentieth century, such theology was an important element of apartheid. Religion played a significant role in the long, drawn-out tension and violence in South Africa, but it also played an important role in the resolution of the same conflict. The dismantling of apartheid and slow rebuilding of a civil society was possible because of Christian religious beliefs that called for reconciliation and a refusal to seek retribution. Although South Africa is not officially a Christian country, it was these beliefs that helped to bring a degree of healing for people of all religions in the country.

Another war in Africa that was more clearly religious was the internal conflict in Uganda during the reign of Idi Amin, a Muslim who ruled a predominantly Christian nation (about 85 percent Christian). Called the Uganda Genocide (1971–79), it was fully an expression of the will of Amin, a leader whose only experience before his coup was in the military. Amin quickly put friends from his Kakwa tribe, a group that converted from Catholicism to Islam in 1910, in places of power. More than 80 percent of the military rulers were Muslim in a country that was only 5 percent Muslim at the time. Amin's genocide was both tribal and religious, like much of the religious violence of the twentieth century. During his reign Amin reversed earlier foreign policies and established relations with Libya, the Soviet Union, and Saudi Arabia. Islam was supported and Christianity was persecuted to the extent that Christian activities were all but prohibited by 1978. Priests were murdered for protesting, and churches were burned.

By the end of the twentieth century a number of Islamic groups began to form in opposition to Christian growth and in opposition to Western secularization. Most of the newer Muslim groups were not formed specifically to resist Christianity; they evolved out of the mixed cauldron of modern beliefs and practices in Muslim societies. Purification of the religion was the main concern. In fact, Islam has built into its very fabric the need for "purity."[17] From the founding of the prophetic faith under Muhammad in the seventh century, the main concern has been for a pure religion, unpolluted by local worship, idols, images, or immoral activity. Groups like the Taliban, Muslim Brotherhood, Wahhabism, Jamaat-e-Islami, and Boko Haram seek both a pure

---

17. *Jihad* is the term for "struggle" in Islam, which includes the personal struggle for purity and the social struggle for the purity of the religion. Throughout Islamic history jihads have been waged against nominal Islam and non-Muslim groups.

Islam and a pure Islamic state. Both the internal purity, with no infiltration of modern culture, and the extension of the Islamic land (Dar al Islam) are driving concerns that have created great tension within Islam (precipitating great migrations of Muslims) and tension between Islam and the West.

Muslim modernists, Christians, and Jews all become the enemy in the fight for Islamic purity. This type of religious violence flared up after decolonization. Without the heavy hand of European empires—including the Soviet Union—local Islamic alliances formed around tribal and religious identity. The century ended with conflicts and religious tensions between Muslims and Christians in West Africa, but also within Islam in sub-Saharan Africa, North Africa, and West Asia. The resources for increased violence were culled from obscure teachings, often mixed with ethnic loyalty. The resources for peace and reconciliation were also found, but less often used, within the Muslim and Christian books and traditions.

This type of religious violence has devastated the Christian presence in many communities where the church had existed for nearly two millennia. Places like Lebanon, Syria, Egypt, Iraq, and Iran have witnessed major emigrations of Orthodox (and some Protestant) Christians. However, the violence and subsequent forced migration of Christians and Muslims has also had a very different result. At the same time, and for the same reasons, many Muslims who have been exiled by Islamic violence have been more open to the teachings of Jesus than ever before. Afghans in the West are more responsive to the gospel than they were in their home country. Similarly, Syrians, Iranians, Egyptians, and others who have fled violence are developing Christian communities elsewhere. Violence from within Muslim communities is having complex results, both in Asia and in the new homelands of refugees.

Many other places have been troubled by religious conflict in the twentieth century, but perhaps what would be more valuable than listing these conflicts is to generalize about what these conflicts have meant for Christianity. First, religious violence has been complex, seldom purely about religion. Ethnic identity, involving ethnocentrism and racism, has been closely linked with religious violence. Tribal conflicts are only exacerbated by religious identity issues. Economics, especially unemployment of young men and of educated young people, also increases religious violence. Second, modernity and its worship of the secular and sensual have increased religious violence. Most religions do not easily abide gambling and the highly sexualized and violent culture of the modern world. The 9/11 attack on the World Trade Center in New York City targeted Western materialism and trade. Third, religious violence has led many to leave their religion and turn to the secular alternative, a more secularized form of their own religion, or to a search for a religion of peace. Thus Muslims moving to the West have become far more secularized than in their home countries, and some are open to learning from the Injil (New Testament). Churches of immigrant Muslims are forming in the West as never before.

Shifting Beliefs and Relationships

I want to emphasize that Western Christianity in the twentieth century lost its confidence. In retrospect we can say that it lost its misplaced confidence. Rather than trusting in the work of God through Jesus Christ as its power, Christendom leaders trusted in their institutions, their empires, and the cultural forms of faith. These cultural forms proved inadequate for villages in Africa or the cities of Asia. Jesus was obscured by Western cultural forms that were intermixed with the teachings of the humble Savior. Misplaced confidence and loss of confidence in the Christian message eroded Christianity in North America and Europe. Let's look at this transformation from another angle.

Before the nineteenth century, and especially before the publication of the Sacred Books of the East Series (fifty volumes between 1879 and 1910) under the editorship of Max Müller, Christian perspectives on other religions centered on an assumption that Christianity was the religion for all people. All people would eventually hear the gospel, and (probably) most would follow Jesus Christ. Christians in the West believed in a progressive growth of the faith. With the publication of these sacred books of the religions of Asia, the arrival of many Asian scholars in the West, and the World's Parliament of Religions in 1893, other religions looked more appealing. Jesus, who had been *the* way for Christians, was increasingly understood to be *a* way, one of many beautiful ways to God. Many scholars began comparing religious beliefs, practices, and ethics and found the similarities noteworthy. The modern study of religions was fueled more by missionaries than by isolated scholars at their desks in Europe. Missionaries, primarily working in India, China, and Japan, were pioneers in the study of religions. Their reason for studying Buddhist belief and practice was to better communicate Christianity, but the door was open and a new field of comparative religions was born. At first the study of comparative religions, housed in universities, and later the history of religions developed as other ways to "objectively" study religions of the world. However, by the early decades of the twentieth century, seminaries and divinity schools were beginning to adopt the same approach to the study of religions, Christianity now being one of the religions among many. The great

divide between Christianity as a religion revealed by God and the human institutions of the world known as "religions" was narrowed. Christian mission
seemed less relevant, the sacrifice less appropriate.

The assumed similarity of religions meant there was little reason to leave
one religion for another, or to convert a person to another religion that was so
similar. Theologians in many traditional seminaries began to focus on common ethical and ritual practices, downplaying any unique features or claims of
Christianity. Other religions are often built around "myths," and so the story
of Jesus was often understood as a "myth," whether historically accurate or
not. The importance of religions is not their history, but the story they tell.
Theologians like Rudolf Bultmann and Paul Tillich were little concerned about
historicity and, as when studying other religions, focused on the teachings or
myths contained in the religions. Later, John Hick wrote and edited books like
The Myth of God Incarnate, which questions whether a belief such as that
God became a human is really helpful or necessary. Hick's essay in the book
is on Jesus and world religions. In a similar book, Hick states,

> The conception of a religious myth as a story which is not literally true, or an
> identifying concept or image which does not literally apply, but which may be
> "true" in virtue of its power to evoke an appropriate attitude enables us to see
> the mythological character not only of the christian concept of the incarnation,
> but also of the corresponding concepts of other religions.[18]

Hick's theological pilgrimage mirrored in his ninety years (d. 2012) what Western culture went through in four hundred years. He was converted to a fairly
orthodox form of evangelical Christianity and slowly moved to a pluralist
understanding of religions, with Christianity (often spelled with a small *c*) as
one of many. Such an anemic form of Christianity appealed little to Western
people by the end of the century. Christianity in the West, in an age of great
comfort and affluence, slowly dissipated as it became its own worst enemy,
dying by suicide, or at least by growing irrelevance.

All of these ideas were not really new, but the "scientific" and scholarly approach was new, and the fact that an increasing number of Christian professors
were promoting these ideas was also new. In reality most of these ideas were
common features of the Enlightenment. In 1779 Gotthold Ephraim Lessing
wrote a play called *Nathan the Wise* that shows the equality of all religions.
In the play, which was not performed until after Lessing's death, Nathan is
asked by Saladin which of the religions is true. In answer to this query, Nathan
tells a story of a man who had a special heirloom, a ring that, if worn, made

---

18. Hick, *God and the Universe of Faiths*, 175.

the owner pleasing and acceptable to God. However, the man had three sons, and so he had two replica rings made and gave them to his sons upon death. How would they know which was the true ring? A wise judge said, "Live as if you have the true ring, and its powers will prove true for you." All religions are a matter of living into a truth one cannot know. The tale takes place in Jerusalem, and the three religions are Christianity, Islam, and Judaism. Not much has changed since the eighteenth century.

In the twentieth century Christians in the West became more pluralistic and less concerned for missionary work among people of other faiths. Ironically, in Asia, where many of the ideas of pluralism resonated—especially in India—Christians were actively proclaiming and spreading Christian faith. Asian Christian convictions about the centrality of Christ first came from missionary teaching. By the end of the century Asians appropriated their own understanding of Jesus, and Jesus became an Asian Christ calling all to see their cultures fulfilled in his kingdom. Thus we can say that a major cause of the great reversal of the twentieth century was a matter of ideas. Ideas matter.

Religions Growing and Declining

During the twentieth century religious allegiance in the world changed dramatically. While the West developed in two directions, or in two minds, regarding its understanding about non-Christian religions, the non-Christian religions were going through revivals, civil strife (especially Islam), and decline. Western Christians continued to witness the conversion of Buddhists, Hindus, and others, but Western academics began to develop more tolerant philosophies and theologies of religions. The modern globalized world, which was the fertile ground for pluralism, also included purely secular ideologies such as Communism. These modern secular ideologies had as much of a negative effect on religions like Buddhism, Islam, Hinduism, and Sikhism as did Christian missions. And the modern world and materialist ideas eroded Christianity in the West as well as these other religions. It is not possible to give statistics on all the religions of the world in the twentieth century, but it will help to fill out the picture if we compare some statistics on the major intercultural faiths with statistics on the development of Christianity.

The best statistics on world religions in the twentieth century come from Todd M. Johnson and Kenneth Ross's *Atlas of Global Christianity* and the Pew Research Center Religion and Public Life Project. Even though these are two of the best places to look for statistics on religions, counting religious noses is a very inexact science. One example will suffice. In East Asia, Chinese culture has developed with a Confucianist core surrounded with other religious beliefs: Buddhism, ancestor worship, polytheism, and various beliefs related to astrology and feng shui. In some places a person who lives according to this mixture of beliefs is called simply a "Chinese religionist" or an adherent of Chinese folk religions. In a single family some members may visit a Confucian temple where the ancestral tablets are kept, while others might visit a Buddhist temple where there is a section of the temple dedicated to Guanyin (Kwan Yin). When one is counting religious adherents, would such a family be considered Buddhist? When the family converts to Christianity, have the number of Buddhists and the number of Chinese folk religionists both gone down? It is not clear. The numbers of adherents in various forms of folk Islam, both in Asia and in Africa, are similarly ambiguous.

Let's start with these Chinese folk religionists in the twentieth century. According to Johnson and Ross, in 1910 about 22.3 percent of the world's population were Chinese folk religionists. This statistic includes almost all the Chinese in China. By 2010 the percentage, thanks mostly to Mao and the Communist revolution, was reduced to 6.5 percent. This is the largest decline of any religion in the twentieth century. Many Chinese in China are returning to forms of Buddhism, but the folk-religious aspect of Chinese religious life is not returning. Buddhism, which is mostly found in South and East Asia, declined from 7.8 to 6.8 percent of the world's population between 1910 and 2010.

Hinduism remained a strong religion limited almost solely to India and to Indians who have migrated around the world. In 1910 Hindus represented 12.7 percent of the world's population, and in 2010 they represented 13.7 percent. Although Hinduism is found throughout the world, it is being spread by migration, not conversion. Hindu temples are being built in major Western cities to serve Indian immigrants.

A category that has gone through many redefinitions in the past decades is that of (non-Chinese) folk, ethnic, or traditional religions. These religions are mostly practiced by a particular ethnic group with particular cultural (often geographic) symbols and significance. Modernity, migration, and communications have tended to erode traditional folk-religious practices. In the twentieth century the percent of folk religionists declined from 7.7 percent of the world's population to 3.8 percent, for a decrease of more than 50 percent.[19] In countries like Myanmar and Thailand and in much of sub-Saharan Africa, traditional religions have bowed to the influences of Islam and Christianity. In

19. Pew Research Center Religion and Public Life Project estimates 6 percent, but Pew includes Chinese folk religions in this statistic. See the Pew-Templeton Global Religious Futures Project: http://www.globalreligiousfutures.org/religions/folk-religionists.

Figure 22. The Islamic Center of America, the largest mosque in the United States, located in Dearborn, Michigan

general, monotheism, with its integrated ethical system (everything is under one God) overwhelms folk or traditional religions. Christianity has grown particularly robustly among these religions in the twentieth century.

The greatest growth in a religion in the twentieth century was that of Islam, which grew from 12.6 percent to 22.4 percent of the world's population (1.6 billion). Islam spread mostly by migration, with Muslims migrating to Australia, Europe, and North America. Islam, like Christianity, also grew in Africa, but in different regions, provoking religious divisions and conflicts that we witness today.

Toward the end of the twentieth century a countermovement began to arise in response to the rapid growth of Islam. Muslims in Southeast Asia, South Asia, and Africa began to come to faith in Isa (Jesus). In some places fully Christian worshiping communities developed within Islamic contexts, but in others, the members could more accurately be called Muslim followers of Jesus. In some villages imams who came to faith in Jesus continued the call to prayer and began to teach more about Jesus than from the Qur'an. Another movement that was just beginning to be studied was that of the many Muslims who began to come to faith because of dreams or visions. These unconventional movements within Islam seemed to have begun in the 1980s and mark the first time such a large movement, spread over all of the

Islamic world from West Africa to the South China Sea, has developed. Islamic violence in places like Iran, Iraq, Syria, and Palestine has not quelled such movements.

The Middle East has been a region of conflict for centuries (even millennia), and the ongoing conflict today is both between different forms of Islam vying for leadership in the region and between non-Israelis with opposing opinions as to how to coexist with Israel. It is interesting that so much of the conflict we have discussed is around the formation of the state of Israel even though the Jewish population in the world decreased in the past century. From 1910 to 2010 the Jewish population went from 0.7 to 0.2 percent of the world's population (14.6 million). Approximately two-thirds (6 million) of European Jews were killed in the Holocaust, the single largest percentage of a race or nationality killed in the century.[20]

Two categories that were hardly visible in 1900 or 1910 but that are now quite significant are agnostics[21] and new religionists. We have mentioned some of the new religions that developed in the twentieth century, but it continues to be a fertile field of human culture. New religionists grew from 0.4 percent to close to 1 percent of the world's population (64.5 million). Agnostics (mostly in the West and in China and Russia) grew from 0.2 percent to more than 11 percent of the population. In percentage terms this is the largest growth of any religion (or nonreligion), a 5,500 percent increase in one century. Thus even while some religions are growing, while new religions are forming, and while religious pluralism is on the rise, more and more people are opting out of religious belief and practices completely.

Finally, the percentage of the world population that was Christian stayed almost the same in the twentieth century, declining slightly from 34.8 to 33.2 percent. But the basic concern of this volume is not that Christianity stayed about the same in terms of global representation, or that it did not grow, but that it was so transformed from within. In 1910 the 612 million Christians in the world lived mostly in the West: 495 million, or about 81 percent. In 2010 the 2.292 billion Christians lived mostly outside the West. Only about 38 percent of the Christians lived in the West. Thus although Christianity has been fairly stable worldwide, it has been in the midst of a dynamic change internally. If Christianity were personified, we would describe how it changed during the century in the following way: it now has a darker complexion and speaks more

20. About 25 percent of the Roma, or gypsies, were killed by the Germans during the same period. The *Holocaust Encyclopedia*, a service of the US Holocaust Memorial Museum, is an excellent resource for these statistics (http://www.ushmm.org).

21. Often the two categories of agnostic and atheist are combined, making comparison inexact.

languages and dialects than any other religion in the world. The twentieth century was a Christian century in that Christianity finally completed the movement out of Western Europe to become a truly global faith—a process that began in the fifteenth century. It was also a Christian century in that Christianity finally began to see its purpose fulfilled, the purpose set forth by Jesus as recorded in Matthew 28:19, that Jesus's followers were to "make disciples of all nations," or as recorded in Acts 1:8, that the disciples were to "be . . . witnesses in Jerusalem, and in all Judea and Samaria, and to the ends of the earth" (NRSV). Finally, it was a Christian century in that the vision of John in Revelation was closer than ever to being fulfilled:

> After this I looked, and there was a great multitude that no one could count, from every nation, from all tribes and peoples and languages, standing before the throne and before the Lamb, robed in white, with palm branches in their hands. (Revelation 7:9 NRSV)

Epilogue

Future Hope and the Presence of the Past

Never again will they hunger; never again will they thirst. The sun will not beat on them, nor any scorching heat. For the Lamb at the center of the throne will be their shepherd; he will lead them to springs of living water. And God will wipe away every tear from their eyes.

Revelation 7:16–17 (NIV)

Where the Twentieth-Century "Great Reversal" Has Brought Us

What can we say about these remarkable changes that took place in global Christianity in the twentieth century? Few scholars, politicians, or church leaders were aware of what was going on, or why. Consider the following assessment of the course of Christianity by someone who was more attentive than most.

It is even suggested sometimes that probably we are now passing through the "Great Divide," through the greatest change in the history of our civilization, which is much greater and more radical than the change from Antiquity to the Middle Ages, or from the Middle Ages to the modern times. If it is true at all, as it was contended by Hegel, that "history is judgment" (*Die Weltgeschichte ist Weltgericht*), there are some fateful epochs, when history not only judges, but as it were, sentences itself to doom. We are persistently reminded by experts and prophets that civilizations rise and decay, and there is no special reason to expect that our own civilization should escape this common fate. If there is any historical future at all, it may well happen that this future is reserved for another civilization, and probably for one which will be quite different from ours.

It is quite usual in our days, and indeed quite fashionable, to say that we are already dwelling in a "Post-Christian world"—whatever the exact meaning of

Figure 23. The church in Brazil reflected in Christian graffiti ("Jesus Christ, Son of God") and a rural church plant. Brazil is ranked seventy-ninth in terms of GDP.

this pretentious phrase may actually be—in a world which, subconsciously or deliberately, "retreated" or seceded from Christianity. "We live in the ruins of civilizations, hopes, systems and souls."

This is, of course, the view of someone in the West who is looking on the decline of Christianity and the cultural influence of Christianity on the West. We might imagine that Western Christianity is ready to sentence itself to doom. Many have used the term "post-Christian," or at least "post-Christendom," to describe the decline of Christianity in the West. However, this passage above was not written recently, and not by a Western European or American. This was written over half a century ago, in 1955, by the Russian historian and theologian Georges Florovsky.[1] Exiled with his family from his native Odessa in 1920, Florovsky taught in Paris, New York (at St. Vladimir's and Union Theological seminaries), at Harvard University, and at Princeton University. He saw the decline of Christianity under the Soviets, the decline of Christian influence in France, and then the loss of Christian culture in the United States. After World War II, he was convinced that Christianity, at least in the West, had little hope. However, he was broad-minded enough to realize that "if there is any historical future at all, it may well happen that this future is reserved for another civilization, and probably for one which will be quite different from ours." This odd expression, "historical future," is what we have discovered in the unexpected twentieth century. There is a vitality, hope, and life to Christianity, and this hope is now a historical reality among the poor and minority groups. The great global powers and civilizations have turned their backs on the Christian story, and now the historical future is among powerless Christian minorities in Asia and among the poor in Africa and in Latin America. The Christian hope has settled in surprising places like China, Nigeria, Mongolia, and Brazil.

Writing in 1907, just before his death after forty-four years of missionary work in China, Calvin Wilson Mateer remarked:

> The dark and discouraging days are over and the future is bright with promise. As I look back over the first 25 years of my missionary life, it seems like a troubled dream. The last fifteen years have wrought wonders in China. Old customs and prejudices are giving way. . . . The most conservative and immovable people in the world, persistently wedding to the old ways, are getting used to new things. . . . I often wish I were young again. . . . In a large sense the future of the church and of the world lies wrapped up in this great people. Why in the providence of God the gospel of salvation has not long ere reached this oldest and greatest nation is an unexplained mystery.[2]

Many would argue that Mateer was right, but he was just a century early with his prediction. We prefer to hold on to his last sentence. Although we can and must learn much about Christianity in the past, there is always much mystery that evades our wisdom to control this Christian movement. It was a mystery a century ago just as it is today why China resisted three early introductions of Christianity. With all of our sophisticated analysis, it is still a mystery why Christianity is so much at home today in China, or

---

1. Florovsky, "Faith and Culture," 29–30.
2. Quoted in Hyatt, *Our Ordered Lives Confess*, 230.

Ghana, or South Korea. Mateer's optimism and hopefulness were in part an expression of his age; he lived at the tail end of the age of progress. His reflections, however, are more than just expressions of his culture. Mateer was also expressing Christian hope ("bright with promise") in the midst of human failure and disappointment ("prejudices . . . old customs . . . immovable people"). As we have traced these nearly two thousand years of Christian history, particularly in our focus on the last one hundred years, we have seen how confidence in the Christian hope moves Christianity forward, even as the old prejudices and customs seem to resist that same movement. And now we see that there may even be Christian hope in one of the most ancient and immovable civilizations, China. But China, as an ancient civilization, and Christianity in China today are both as diverse as Christianity has ever been. The great diversity still expresses the incarnational principle of Christianity. That Christians recognize themselves across such cultural and social divides shows the centeredness of Christianity in the person of Jesus Christ.

On October 18, 2008, Patriarch Bartholomew I of Constantinople delivered an address on the Word of God to the Twelfth Ordinary Synod of Roman Catholic Bishops in Rome. The Orthodox patriarch, a Turkish citizen, was invited by Pope Benedict XVI, and for the first time in history, an Orthodox patriarch stood before a global representation of Roman Catholic bishops, this time in the Sistine Chapel in Vatican City. The significance of the address and its meaning for worldwide Christianity cannot be overstated. The title of the talk gives the Christian hope: "The Day Will Come When Our Two Churches Will Fully Converge."[3] The talk was significant in how the patriarch identified what is common to all Christians and what must be at the center of Christian development in the future. After our meanderings through the great diversity of Christian witness in the twentieth century, it is important to finish with some understanding of what holds Christianity together in the midst of this great diversity of languages, liturgies, theologies, and practices. The synod focused on the Word of God, and the patriarch accepted that subject for his address, expanding on how the Word of God must keep Christians united. Then he explained three ways that the Word of God is expressed and can unite: "*hearing and speaking* the Word of God through the Holy Scriptures; *seeing* God's Word in nature and above all in the beauty of the icons; and finally on *touching and sharing* God's Word in the communion of saints and the sacramental life of the Church."[4]

3. Bartholomew I of Constantinople, *Speaking the Truth in Love*, 276.
4. Ibid., 277 (emphasis added).

Lipsiong Chen

Figure 24. Chongyi Church in Hangzhou, Zhejiang Province. One of the largest churches in China, this building can accommodate about five thousand worshipers.

This outline of the patriarch's presentation is a reminder that Christians are united around the Word of God, revealed in the Bible, revealed in creation, and incarnate in the communion of his followers. Christians will not all agree on the role of icons, but in the twenty-first century, ecological concerns (role of nature) unite Christians of all families and cultures. The centrality of the Word of God, as we have seen in our story, unites all Christians and, it must be said, divides them from others. The patriarch also explains what he means by the Word of God.

> Mission and evangelization remain a permanent duty of the Church at all times and places; indeed they form part of the Church's nature, since she is called "Apostolic" both in the sense of her faithfulness to the original teaching of the Apostles and in that of proclaiming the Word of God in every cultural context every time. The Church needs, therefore, to rediscover the Word of God in every generation and make it heard with a renewed vigour and persuasion also in our contemporary world, which deep in its heart thirsts for God's message of peace, hope and charity.[5]

5. *The Day Will Come When Our Two Churches Will Fully Converge*, Bartholomew I Ecumenical Patriarch of Constantinople to the Synod of Bishops of the Catholic Church, October 18, 2008. Available at http://www.focolare.org/repository/PDF/081018_InterventoBartolomeoI_en.pdf.

This is, in part, what we described. Christian history is the story of Christians, as witnesses of Jesus Christ, engaged in mission, "at all times and places" living and proclaiming the Word of God "in every cultural context." In doing so, Christians rediscover the Word of God in every generation, and it enters into every "nation, tribe, people and language" (NIV). This engagement of Word in particular contexts reveals the one who himself is the love, justice, reconciliation, peace, and hope for all of creation.

The Orthodox patriarch's hopeful vision, delivered at a moment of "hope" before the Synod of Catholic Bishops in Rome, is a well-informed and thoughtful ecumenical statement that was richly theological and daringly hopeful. Not all statements of hope for the future are so well informed or realistic. Many are hopeful but fanciful. Others are realistic, but not hopeful.

Caught up in the early period of Christian cooperation (ecumenical movement) when the Age of Progress was in full bloom, John R. Mott[6] was ever the optimist about the future. His was a very different kind of hope than that expressed above. Now that we have traced the surprising lines of Christian development in the twentieth century, Mott's vision underscores how mistaken the Christian West was about its early twentieth-century hope. Although we could go to many places in Mott's writings, one very popular book will reveal the Christian hope of many Christian leaders of his time. The book is titled *The Decisive Hour of Christian Missions*. My personal copy that I am looking at now is from 1915, so I assume the book was still being printed five years after the original printing.[7] It is a book of challenge and hope immediately following the 1910 World Missionary Conference. "In the history of Christianity there has never been such a remarkable conjunction of opportunities and crises on all the principal mission fields and of favoring circumstances and possibilities on the home field."[8] The book does not shy away from tensions and problems, but with every problem the opportunities and possibilities are much greater. The pictures in the book tell the whole story. It is not that the gospel has been spread so carefully and faithfully, but more than anything else, Mott sees technology and commerce as the great hope.

The book contains seventeen photographs showing the advances in physical culture and commerce as compared to the backward ways of traditional Asian cultures. The first picture shows a "Railway penetrating the old wall of

6. Mott is a very important figure since he was one of three or four early ecumenical leaders who helped to guide the Western church toward what would become the World Council of Churches (1948). Mott expressed in bold relief the hope of Western Christians at the beginning of the century. It was a hope as much technological as it was theological.
7. This very popular book was translated into Dutch, French, and German. You can still buy it now either as an ebook or a reprint.
8. Mott, *Decisive Hour*, v.

Peking." It seems self-explanatory, showing that even the old walls of China cannot keep out the gospel, or at least modern communications. It is interesting that all of Mott's pictures are of Asia (mostly China) and the United States (New York and Connecticut). There is not one picture of Africa or of Latin America. The West has always been fascinated by East Asia and India, and Mott's volume illustrates this preoccupation. Mott's illustrations show technological progress (coal mines in China) and the advance of Western political ideals (the first Parliament in Turkey) vis-à-vis the old ways of the Chinese examination system and Hindu festivals. The illustration that caps it off is the five-section foldout map at the end of the book. What does the map illustrate? Not church growth, or even newer mission stations. The map is titled "Commercial Expansion: Existing and Projected Railways and Leading Steamship Routes." The reason for Christian hope was technology, Western governments, and commercial expansion. It was all of a single unholy fabric for Christians in the first decade of the twentieth century. Today it is embarrassing to see how Christian leaders—who should have been very clear about human pride and sin—could identify scientific progress or commercial success with "success" in mission. Whatever our blind spots are today—and speaking as a historian I am sure we have our own blind spots—they are not that we are collapsing sociology or science into Christianity.

What the Twentieth-Century "Great Reversal" Has Taught Us

It is a little early to draw conclusions as to what we have learned from the remarkable development of Christianity in the twentieth century; there is still much discussion about what happened in the nineteenth century. However, facts cry out for interpretation, stories for endings. A few tentative lessons, not about history but about the nature of Christianity, present themselves to us after this brief survey through five lenses.

First, as we hinted at the beginning, the Jesus movement has always been about clay vessels and the glory and power within. More directly, the transformative power of Christianity is not in worldly power, as Mott and other Western leaders seemed to assume. Most Christians have always known this, but it is very hard to live that way when you have so much political or economic power to use for the Lord's work. A person can talk theoretically about how indigenous churches should be self-supporting, but when one can write a quick check to pay for a building or to support local salaries for years, it is hard to watch local people "suffer" under lack of resources. The West has had (indeed still has) a difficult time not just writing checks to solve spiritual problems. But what we have seen in the previous chapters is that the power of Christianity has come from the weak, from the margins, and (most often) from the oppressed. "Christendom," where political and religious realms are woven together, has been in decline for centuries. We just saw it most dramatically in the past century.

Second, the Jesus movement thrives on borderlands, where cultures overlap and encounter one another. Another way of putting this is that Christianity is nurtured in cultural encounters, and it then develops and nurtures cultures. Although missionaries quite often bring a culturally inhibiting or erasing gospel, with Gothic churches and Western hymns, Christian development thrives on epochs of cultural engagement. In turn, local cultures thrive when Jesus is translated into local cultures. In the past, social scientists and historians have seen Christianity as a religion overwhelming or smothering local cultures; this was the stated goal of missionaries in the period of progressivism. Social Darwinism was a quietly assumed mandate: white man's burden. But this ideology has been proved both oppressive and theologically bent. It is not Christianity—in the sense of forms of enculturated faith—that is to be spread, but the pleasing aroma of Christ that is to penetrate each culture. It was when Chinese people took in and nurtured Jesus in Confucian ways that Jesus became Chinese enough to be understood, and to stand up in China enhancing all things Chinese. American architects designing Chinese-looking buildings on the campuses of Christian universities in Beijing are such a small part of contextualization. What is vital and necessary is letting go of the gospel to let it be fully alive and nurtured by Chinese believers. When these cultures overlap—through missionary engagement as well as migration—Christianity is most at home.

Third, we have learned again that the apostolic nature of Christianity is part of its essence. Another way of stating this is that Christianity atrophies without missionary expression. A faith that is expressed as an institution in a culture rather than as an outpost reaching other cultures is not fully Christian. When the faith is crossing boundaries—geographically, linguistically, economically, culturally—it is most alive. When it is not doing so, or when it is not at least seeking to do so, it is in decline. I remember moving from a Christian campus ministry in a state university in my midtwenties to a Christian seminary. Both the student ministry and the seminary were evangelical institutions, but when I moved from an environment where I was crossing boundaries of faith every week in evangelistic conversations, to where I was with Christians all day every day, I found my understanding of Christian faith changed. Conversations became more inward looking and less significant to the world around me. Ultimate questions faded, and parsing theological minutiae took center stage. In the twentieth century Christian vitality has blossomed when the church has expressed its apostolic nature.

Finally, it should be remembered that the unexpected Christian century is a paradox, the type of paradox that is at the root of Christianity. Jesus talked in parables about the need for a seed to die for it to bring fruit, the yeast that must be lost in the lump of dough, and the mustard seed, that tiniest of all seeds, which brings forth a great tree. He also said, more directly, that unless people lose their life, they will not find it. Suffering and death are essential to the DNA of Christianity. This paradoxical century of Christian reversals can best be understood as the planting of Christian seeds throughout the globe during the "Great Century."[9] As the seeds were being planted through the great missionary movement, the base of that missionary movement in the West was slowly dying. The Western form of Christianity that had so interwoven the religious institutions with political structures was slowly dissipating all the time. Both the unhealthy alliance with power, and the challenges to Christian assumptions that came in the form of modernity, slowly scraped the veneer of Christianity off of many and proved the loyalty of a few. The missionary movement made the miraculous growth in Africa and in parts of Asia possible. The hidden seed in China took root and spread almost imperceptibly for decades while the outside world did not even know the seed had survived. Many of the older Christians who carried and spread the faith during China's Cultural Revolution remembered the mission societies and the names of the missionaries. The miracle of Christian growth in China is directly related to missionary activity in earlier decades and even centuries. This is an abridged explanation, but it is an important part of the explanation. The appropriation of that gospel message was the work of local people, but the message that was delivered was given in a form that could be understood and then be reshaped to make sense to local farmers and traders.

Ethiopians remember the lifelong devotion to East Africa of W. Don McClure, and so they tend his grave and honored the appearance of McClure's grandson when he came to visit.[10] In Seoul the graveyard of missionaries is a place honored by Korean Christians as they come to visit and remember the sacrifice of both North Americans and Europeans. In the 1990s I attended a remarkable sesquicentennial celebration of the arrival of Adoniram Judson

---

9. So called by Kenneth Scott Latourette (to whom I am greatly indebted) because of the great missionary movement out of Europe and the great accomplishments in mission in the long nineteenth century: 1792 to 1910. See Latourette, *Expansion of Christianity*, 7 vols. The subtitles for volumes 3–6 each begin with "The Great Century" followed by the particular geographic region to be covered during the nineteenth-century period.

10. In a newsletter the story was told of Jonathan McClure visiting the site of his grandfather's grave (in about 2002) and being treated royally, thirty years after his grandfather's death.

Fred Foy Strang

Figure 25. A Masai Christian youth takes advantage of evangelistic and discipleship camp opportunities led by a consortium of African churches during school breaks.

to Myanmar (Burma). The celebration was delayed for political reasons, but when it was held, it was grandiose. As a foreign guest, I was invited to sit in the front row to listen to all the choirs who traveled from around the country to be part of the celebration. Chins, Kachins, Karen, Burmese, Chinese, all came representing their churches. The centerpiece of the celebration was a half-hour drama of the life and experience of Judson in Myanmar. Many people knew the story of his suffering, loss of wives and children, imprisonment, and small victories. But many did not understand the sacrifice clearly until that night. Judson is remembered, as are thousands of other missionaries who made the unexpected Christian century possible. Now those apostolic types are mostly Asian.

It is not common today to honor missionaries for their work, but it would be inaccurate if we did not point out that the development of Christianity in the twentieth century resulted from the synergy of Western missions and non-Western appropriation. Both were needed, and this is where we end with hope. Much of the missionary work was done with inadequate understanding of local languages and cultures. Much missionary work was simplistic or filled with more zeal than wisdom. And yet missionary work, with great sacrifice and suffering, established some small, local Christian presence. Then, in each of the many contexts, local people adopted the teachings of Jesus and made them their own. Often they suffered the loss of family or of life to remain loyal to Jesus, who spoke to their hearts in their heart language. What this century should tell us is that the message of the gospel is more powerful than human motives and more gentle than human powers. Today most missionary work is being done by Koreans, Chinese, Brazilians, Nigerians, Indians, Ghanaians, and even Egyptians, Lebanese, and Costa Ricans. They move across cultural, language, and faith barriers in ways not that different from the Europeans and Americans in the past, but with little of the worldly power. They are inadequate, often improperly trained, and they often go with mixed or unclear motives. This unexpected history of Christianity in the twentieth century should give us some hope. A gentle and suffering Savior will be Lord of all these efforts in the future, as in the past.

Appendix 1

African Independence and Colonizers

Country	Date of Independence	From
Liberia	July 26, 1847	United States
Egypt	February 28, 1922	United Kingdom
Libya	December 24, 1951	Italy
Sudan	January 1, 1956	United Kingdom/Egypt
Morocco	March 2, 1956	France
Tunisia	March 20, 1956	France
Ghana	March 6, 1957	United Kingdom
Guinea	October 2, 1958	France
Cameroon	January 1, 1960	France (UN Trusteeship)
Senegal	April 4, 1960	France
Togo	April 27, 1960	France (UN Trusteeship)
Madagascar	June 26, 1960	France
Congo (Dem. Rep. of)	June 30, 1960	Belgium
Benin Republic	August 1, 1960	France
Burkina Faso	August 5, 1960	France
Cote d'Ivoire	August 7, 1960	France
Chad	August 11, 1960	France
Central African Republic	August 13, 1960	France
Congo	August 15, 1960	France
Gabon	August 17, 1960	France
Mali	September 22, 1960	France

Country	Date of Independence	From
Nigeria	October 1, 1960	United Kingdom
Mauritania	November 28, 1960	France
Niger	December 18, 1960	France
Sierra Leone	April 27, 1961	United Kingdom
Burundi	July 1, 1962	Belgium (UN Trusteeship)
Rwanda	July 1, 1962	Belgium (UN Trusteeship)
Algeria	July 5, 1962	France
Uganda	October 9, 1962	United Kingdom
Kenya	December 12, 1963	United Kingdom
Tanzania	April 26, 1964	(Union) United Kingdom (UN Trusteeship)
Zambia	October 24, 1964	United Kingdom
Gambia	February 18, 1965	United Kingdom
Malawi	July 6, 1966	United Kingdom
Botswana	September 30, 1966	United Kingdom
Lesotho	October 4, 1966	United Kingdom
Mauritius	March 12, 1968	United Kingdom
Swaziland	September 6, 1968	United Kingdom
Equatorial Guinea	October 12, 1968	Spain
Somalia	October 21, 1969	United Kingdom/Italy
Guinea-Bissau	September 24, 1973	Portugal
Mozambique	June 25, 1975	Portugal
Cape Verde	July 5, 1975	Portugal
Comoros Islands	July 6, 1975	France
São Tomé and Principe	July 12, 1975	Portugal
Angola	November 11, 1975	Portugal
Seychelles	June 29, 1976	United Kingdom
Djibouti	June 27, 1977	France
Zimbabwe	April 18, 1980	United Kingdom
Namibia	March 21, 1990	South Africa
Eritrea	May 24, 1993	Ethiopia
South Africa	April 27, 1994	United Kingdom/Apartheid regime ends
Ethiopia		(never colonized)
Mayotte, French territory		France
Réunion Island, overseas region of France		France
Sahrawi Arab Dem. Rep. / Western Sahara		Morocco

Appendix 2

Asian Independence and Colonizers

Country	Date of Independence	From
Afghanistan	August 19, 1919	United Kingdom
Mongolia	July 11, 1921	China (to Soviet oversight)
Iraq	October 3, 1932	United Kingdom
Lebanon	November 22, 1943	France (after Ottomans)
Korea	August 15, 1945	but two occupied zones, then permanent division
Vietnam	September 2, 1945	France
Syria	April 17, 1946	France
Jordan	May 25, 1946	United Kingdom
Philippines	July 4, 1946	United States
Pakistan	August 14, 1947	British India
India	August 15, 1947	United Kingdom
Burma/ Myanmar	January 4, 1948	United Kingdom
Sri Lanka	February 4, 1948	United Kingdom
Israel	May 14, 1948	United Kingdom
Laos	July 19, 1949	France
Indonesia	December 27, 1949	(declared in 1945, won by 1949) Netherlands
Cambodia	November 9, 1953	France
Malaysia	August 31, 1957	United Kingdom (became modern Malaysia in 1963; lost Singapore in 1965)
Kuwait	June 19, 1961	United Kingdom

Country	Date of Independence	From
Maldives	July 26, 1965	United Kingdom
Singapore	August 9, 1965	Malaysia
Yemen	October 30, 1918; November 30, 1967; and May 22, 1990	N. Yemen from Ottoman Empire; Aden (S. Yemen) was given back by United Kingdom; finally N. and S. Yemen officially reunited
Bangladesh	March 26, 1971	Pakistan
Bahrain	August 15, 1971	United Kingdom
Qatar	September 3, 1971	United Kingdom
East Timor	April 1974 (July 1976)	Portugal (but soon taken over by Indonesia)
Brunei	January 1, 1984	United Kingdom
Georgia	April 9, 1991	Russia
Kyrgyzstan	August 21, 1991	Russia
Azerbaijan	August 30, 1991	Russia
Uzbekistan	September 1, 1991	Russia
Tajikistan	September 9, 1991	Russia
Armenia	September 21, 1991	Russia
Turkmenistan	October 27, 1991	Russia
Kazakhstan	December 16, 1991	Russia
Hong Kong	July 1, 1997	Independent from United Kingdom, but returned to China
Macao	December 20, 1999	Independent from Portugal, but returned to China
East Timor	May 20, 2002	Indonesia

Never Colonized

Iran (but land was reduced by Russian wars and British colonialism)

Bhutan (although a treaty was signed with the British to guide Bhutan's foreign affairs)

Japan (was a colonizing power in Asia)

Nepal (though parts were taken over for a while by the British)

Saudi Arabia

Thailand (buffer state between British and French colonial lands)

Unique

Republic of China or Taiwan

Turkey (October 29, 1923, when it became a sovereign state after the collapse of the Ottoman Empire)

Bibliography

Adogame, Afe. "Contesting the Ambivalences of Modernity in a Global Context: The Redeemed Christian Church of God, North America." *Studies in World Christianity* 10, no. 1 (2005): 29.

Anderson, Allan. *African Reformation: African Initiated Christianity in the Twentieth Century.* Trenton, NJ: Africa World Press, 2001.

———. *Spreading Fires: The Missionary Nature of Early Pentecostalism.* Maryknoll, NY: Orbis, 2007.

———. *To the Ends of the Earth: Pentecostalism and the Transformation of World Christianity.* Oxford: Oxford University Press, 2013.

Asamoah-Gyadu, J. Kwabena. *Contemporary Pentecostal Christianity: Interpretations from an African Context.* Eugene, OR: Wipf and Stock, 2013.

Ashe, Kaye. *The Feminization of the Church?* Kansas City, MO: Sheed & Ward, 1997.

Atkin, Nicholas, and Frank Tallett. *Priests, Prelates and People: A History of European Catholicism since 1750.* Oxford: Oxford University Press, 2003.

Azariah, V. S. "The Problem of Co-operation between Foreign and Native Workers." In vol. 9 of *World Missionary Conference, Edinburgh, 1910: History and Records of the Conference*, 306–15. New York: Revell, 1910.

The Balfour Project. *Britain's Betrayal of the Sacred Trust in Palestine, Prof John Dugard.* http://www.balfourproject.org/britains-betrayal-of-the-sacred-trust -in-palestine/.

Barrett, David B., George T. Kurian, and Todd M. Johnson. *World Christian Encyclopedia: A Comparative Survey of Churches and Religions in the Modern World.* 2nd ed. 2 vols. Oxford: Oxford University Press, 2001.

Bartholomew I of Constantinople. *Speaking the Truth in Love: Theological and Spiritual Exortations of Ecumenical Patriarch Bartholomew.* New York: Fordham University Press, 2011.

Bartleman, Frank. *Azusa Street: An Eyewitness Account.* Centennial ed. Gainesville, FL: Bridge-Logos, 2006.

Bassham, Rodger C. *Mission Theology, 1848–1975: Years of Worldwide Creative Tension; Ecumenical, Evangelical and Roman Catholic.* Pasadena, CA: William Carey Library, 1979.

Bays, Daniel H. *A New History of Christianity in China.* Oxford: Wiley-Blackwell, 2012.

Bell, G. K. A., ed. *The Stockholm Conference 1925: The Office Report of the Universal Christian Conference on Life and Work Held in Stockholm, 19–30 August 1925.* London: Oxford University Press, 1926.

Berdyaev, Nikolai. *The Meaning of History.* New Brunswick, NJ: Transaction Publishers, 2006.

Best, Wallace D. *Passionately Human, No Less Divine: Religion and Culture in Black Chicago, 1915–1952.* Princeton: Princeton University Press, 2005.

Bhide, Nivedita Raghunath. *Swami Vivekananda in America.* Electronic book. Chennai, India: Vivekananda Kendara Prakashan Trust, 2002.

Blumhofer, Edith L. *Aimee Semple McPherson: Everybody's Sister.* Grand Rapids: Eerdmans, 1993.

Böhning, W. R. "International Migration and the Western World: Past, Present, Future." *International Migration* 16, no. 1 (1978): 11–22.

Briggs, John, Mercy Amba Oduyoye, and Georges Tsetsis, eds. *A History of the Ecumenical Movement.* Vol. 3, *1968–2000.* Geneva: WCC Publications, 2004.

Brockman, James R. *Romero: A Life.* Maryknoll, NY: Orbis, 1989.

Brown, Callum G. *The Death of Christian Britain: Understanding Secularisation, 1800–2000.* London: Routledge, 2001.

Brown, Diana DeGroat. *Umbanda: Religion and Politics in Urban Brazil.* New York: Columbia University Press, 1994. First published in 1986 by UMI Research Press, Ann Arbor, MI.

Brown, G. Thompson. *How Koreans Are Reconverting the West.* Bloomington, IN: Xlibris, 2008.

Bundy, David. "Keswick Higher Life Movement." In *The New International Dictionary of Pentecostal and Charismatic Movements,* edited by Stanley M. Burgess, 820–21. Grand Rapids: Zondervan, 2002.

Burgess, Stanley M., ed. *The New International Dictionary of Pentecostal and Charismatic Movements*. Grand Rapids: Zondervan, 2002.

Bush, R. A. *Religion in Communist China*. Nashville: Abingdon, 1970.

Butler, Anthea D. *Women in the Church of God in Christ: Making a Sanctified World*. Chapel Hill: University of North Carolina Press, 2007.

Carson, Clayborne. "Martin Luther King, Jr. and the African American Social Gospel." In *African-American Christianity*, edited by Paul E. Johnson, 159–77. Berkeley: University of California Press, 1994.

Carson, Clayborne, Ralph Luker, Penny Russell, and Peter Holloran, eds. *The Papers of Martin Luther King, Jr.*, vol. 2. Berkeley: University of California Press, 1994.

Casiday, Augustine. "Georges Vasilievich Florovsky." In vol. 2 of *The Blackwell Companion to the Theologians*. Edited by Ian S. Markham, 46–65. Oxford: Blackwell Publishing, 2009.

Central Intelligence Agency of the United States of America. *The World Factbook*. Central Intelligence Agency of the United States of America. https://www.cia.gov/library/publications/the-world-factbook/.

Cochrane, Arthur C. *The Church's Confession under Hitler*. Philadelphia: Westminster Press, 1962.

Coffman, Elesha J. *The Christian Century and the Rise of the Protestant Mainline*. New York: Oxford University Press, 2013.

Constitution of Egypt. 1971. http://www.constitutionnet.org/files/Egypt%20Constitution.pdf.

Cornwall, John. *Hitler's Pope: The Secret History of Pius XII*. New York: Penguin Group, 2000.

Cox, Harvey. *The Secular City*. New York: MacMillan, 1965.

Daughrity, Dyron B. *The Changing World of Christianity*. New York: Peter Lang, 2010.

Davies, Noel, and Martin Conway. *World Christianity in the 20th Century*. London: SCM, 2008.

Day, Dorothy. *The Long Loneliness: An Autobiography*. New York: Harper and Row, 1952.

———. "Our Country Passes from Undeclared War to Declared War; We Continue Our Christian Pacifist Stand." *The Catholic Worker* 1, no. 4, 1942. Dorothy Day Collection: http://dorothyday.catholicworker.org/articles/868.html.

Denney, James. "The Demands Made on the Church by the Present Missionary Opportunity." In vol. 9 of *World Missionary Conference, Edinburgh, 1910: History and Records of the Conference*, 322–29. New York: Revell, 1910.

Dorsett, Lyle W. *The Essential C. S. Lewis*. New York: Colliers/Macmillan, 1988.

du Plessis, David. *Simple and Profound*. Orleans, MA: Paraclete, 1986.

Ecumenical Conference on Foreign Missions. *Ecumenical Missionary Conference, New York, 1900: Report of the Ecumenical Conference on Foreign Missions*. New York: American Tract Society, 1900.

Ellsberg, Robert, ed. "An Address to Missionaries." In *Gandhi on Christianity*, 33–37. Maryknoll, NY: Orbis, 1991.

Faith and Martyrdom: The Eastern Churches in Twentieth Century Europe. Proceedings of the meeting on contemporary church history, Vatican City, October 22–24, 1998. Vatican City: Vatican Library, 2008.

Farhadian, Charles, ed. *Christian Worship Worldwide: Expanding Horizons, Deepening Practices*. Grand Rapids: Eerdmans, 2007.

Farquhar, J. N. *Modern Religious Movements in India*. London: Macmillan, 1915.

Federation of Asian Bishops' Conferences. http://www.fabc.org/about.html.

Fey, Harold E., ed. *A History of the Ecumenical Movement, 1948–1968*. Vol. 2. London: SPCK, 1970.

Florovsky, Georges. *Bible, Church, Tradition: An Eastern Orthodox View*, vol. 1. Belmont, MA: Nordland Publishing, 1972.

———. "Faith and Culture." *St. Vladimir's Quarterly* 4, nos. 1–2 (1955): 29–44.

———. *The Universal Church in God's Design*, vol. 1. London: SCM Press, 1948.

Fouilloux, Etienne. "Friar Yves, Cardinal Congar, Dominican: Itinerary of a Theologian." *US Catholic Historian* 17, no. 2 (1999): 63–90.

Geertz, Clifford. *The Interpretation of Cultures*. New York: Basic Books, 1973.

Gilbert, Martin. *History of the Twentieth Century*. Concise ed. New York: William Morrow, 2001.

González, Ondina E., and Justo L. González. *Christianity in Latin America: A History*. Cambridge: Cambridge University Press, 2008.

Goodall, Norman, ed. *The Uppsala Report 1968: Official Report of the Fourth Assembly of the World Council of Churches, Uppsala July 4–20, 1968*. Geneva: World Council of Churches, 1968.

Gornik, Mark R. *Word Made Global: Stories of African Christianity in New York City*. Grand Rapids: Eerdmans, 2011.

Graham, Billy. *Billy Graham Evangelistic Association*. http://billygraham.org/about/biographies/.

Granberg-Michaelson, Wesley. *From Times Square to Timbuktu: The Post-Christian West Meets the Non-Western Church*. Grand Rapids: Eerdmans, 2013.

Gutiérrez, Gustavo. *The Power of the Poor in History: Selected Writings*. Maryknoll, NY: Orbis, 1983.

Hanciles, Jehu J. *Beyond Christendom: Globalization, African Migration, and the Transformation of the West*. Maryknoll, NY: Orbis, 2008.

Hartch, Todd. *The Rebirth of Latin American Christianity*. New York: Oxford University Press, 2014.

Harvey, Thomas. *Acquainted with Grief: Wang Mingdao's Stand for the Persecuted Church in China*. Grand Rapids: Brazos, 2002.

Hick, John. *God and the Universe of Faiths: Essays in the Philosophy of Religion*. Oxford: One World, 1993.

———. *The Myth of God Incarnate*. Philadelphia: Westminster, 1977.

Hochschild, Adam. *King Leopold's Ghost: A Story of Greed, Terror, and Heroism in Colonial Africa*. New York: Houghton and Mifflin, 1998.

Hocking, William Ernest. "Psychological Conditions for the Growth of Faith." In vol. 8 of *Report of the Jerusalem Meeting of the International Missionary Council, March 24–April 8, 1928*, 138–61. New York: International Missionary Council, 1928.

———. *Re-Thinking Missions: A Laymen's Inquiry after One Hundred Years*. New York: Harper and Brothers, 1932.

Hoge, Dean R. "Facts and Figures: The State of the Priesthood." In *The Boston College Magazine*, Summer, 2005. http://bcm.bc.edu/issues/summer_2005/c21_hoge.html.

Hooft, Visser't, and J. H. Oldham. *The Church and Its Function in Society*. London: George Allen and Unwin, 1937.

Hutchinson, Mark, and John Wolffe. *A Short History of Global Evangelicalism*. New York: Cambridge University Press, 2012.

Hyatt, Irwin T., Jr. *Our Ordered Lives Confess: Three Nineteenth-Century American Missionaries in Shantung*. Cambridge, MA: Harvard University Press, 1976.

Irvin, Dale T., and Scott W. Sunquist. *History of the World Christian Movement*. Vols. 1 and 2. Maryknoll, NY: Orbis, 2001/2012.

Jacobsen, Douglas. *The World's Christians: Who They Are, Where They Are, and How They Got There*. Oxford: Wiley-Blackwell, 2011.

Jaspers, Karl, and Rudolf Bultmann. *Myth and Christianity: An Inquiry into the Possibility of Religion without Myth*. New York: Noonday, 1958.

Jenkins, Philip. *The New Faces of Christianity: Believing the Bible in the Global South*. Oxford: Oxford University Press, 2006.

———. *The Next Christendom: The Coming of Global Christianity*. Oxford: Oxford University Press, 2002.

Johnson, Todd M., and Kenneth R. Ross. *Atlas of Global Christianity*. Edinburgh: Edinburgh University Press, 2009.

Kagawa Toyohiko. *The Religion of Jesus*. Translated by Helen F. Topping. Philadelphia: John C. Winston Co., 1931.

Kalu, Ogbu. "Africa, Christianity in." In *Christianity: The Complete Guide*, edited by John Bowden, 2–12. New York: Continuum Press, 2006.

———, ed. *Interpreting Contemporary Christianity: Global Processes and Local Identities*. Grand Rapids: Eerdmans, 2008.

Kerr, Fergus. *Twentieth-Century Catholic Theologians*. Oxford: Blackwell, 2007.

King, Martin Luther, Jr. *The Papers of Martin Luther King, Jr.*, vol. 2. Edited by Clayborne Carson, R. Luker, P. Russell, and Peter Holloran. Berkeley, CA: University of California Press, 1994.

King, Russell, ed. *People on the Move: An Atlas of Migration*. Berkeley: University of California Press, 2010.

Kinnamon, Michael, and Brian E. Cope, eds. *The Ecumenical Movement: An Anthology of Key Texts and Voices*. Geneva: WCC Publications, 1997.

Kinnear, Angus I. *Against the Tide: The Story of Watchman Nee*. Fort Washington, PA: Christian Literature Crusade, 1973.

Knitter, Paul. *Introducing Theologies of Religions*. Maryknoll, NY: Orbis, 2002.

Knitter, Paul, and John Hick. *The Myth of Christian Uniqueness: Toward a Pluralistic Theology of Religions*. Maryknoll, NY: Orbis, 1987.

Kolodiejchuk, Brian. *Mother Teresa, Come Be My Light: The Private Writings of the "Saint of Calcutta."* New York: Doubleday, 2007.

Koschorke, Klaus, Ludwig Frieder, and Mariano Delgado, eds. *A History of Christianity in Asia, Africa and Latin America, 1450–1990*. Grand Rapids: Eerdmans, 2007.

Kraemer, Hendrick. *The Christian Message in a Non-Christian World*. Edinburgh: Edinburgh House Press, 1938. Reprint, 1969.

Latourette, Kenneth Scott. *A History of the Expansion of Christianity*. 7 vols. New York: Harper and Brothers, 1937–45.

Laurent, Bob. *Watchman Nee: Sufferer for China*. Uhrichsville, OH: Barbour Publishing, 1988.

Leith, John H. *The Church: A Believing Fellowship*. Atlanta: John Knox, 1965.

"Letter from Chicherin to Sun Yat-Sen." Marxists Internet Archive. http://www.marxists.org/history/ussr/government/foreign-relations/1918/August/1a.htm.

Lewis, C. S. *Surprised by Joy*. Orlando: Harcourt, Inc., 1955.

Lewis, Donald M. *Christianity Reborn: The Global Expansion of Evangelicalism in the Twentieth Century*. Grand Rapids: Eerdmans, 2004.

Lewis, Harold T. *A Church for the Future: South Africa as the Crucible for Anglicanism for a New Century*. New York: Church Publishing, 2007.

Maffly-Kipp, Laurie F., Leigh E. Schmidt, and Mark Valeri, eds. *Practicing Protestants: Histories of Christian Life in America, 1630–1965*. Baltimore: Johns Hopkins University Press, 2007.

Mandryk, Jason. *Operation World: The Definitive Prayer Guide to Every Nation*. Downers Grove, IL: InterVarsity, 2010.

Manning, William Thomas. *The Call to Unity: The Bedell Lectures for 1919 at Kenyon College*. New York: The Macmillan Company, 1919.

Martin, Marie-Louise. *Kimbangu: An African Prophet and His Church*. Grand Rapids: Eerdmans, 1976.

Marx, Karl, and Friedrich Engles. "Zur Judenfrage." In vol. 1, *Werke*. Berlin, Germany: Dietz Verlag, 1976.

McClung, L. Grant, Jr. *Azusa Street and Beyond: Pentecostal Missions and Church Growth in the Twentieth Century*. South Plainfield, NJ: Bridge Publications, 1986.

McGee, Gary B. *Miracles, Missions, and American Pentecostalism*. Maryknoll, NY: Orbis, 2010.

McGuckin, John. *The Orthodox Church: An Introduction to Its History, Doctrine and Spiritual Culture*. Oxford: Blackwell, 2008.

McKay, John. *Ecumenics: The Science of the Church Universal*. New York: Prentice Hall, 1964.

McLellan, David. *Karl Marx: Selected Writings*. Oxford: Oxford University Press, 1977.

McLeod, Hugh, and Werner Ustorf, eds. *The Decline of Christendom in Western Europe, 1750–2000*. Cambridge: Cambridge University Press, 2003.

Menzies, Robert, and Wonsuk Ma. *The Spirit and Spirituality*. Vol. 4, *Essays in Honor of Russell Spittler*. Journal of Pentecostal Theology Supplement, Book 24. London: T&T Clark, 2004.

Moore, R. Laurence. "American Religion as Cultural Imperialism." In *The American Century in Europe*, edited by Laurence R. Moore and Maurizio Vaudagna, 151–70. Ithaca, NY: Cornell University Press, 2003.

Mosley, Brooke J. *Christians in the Technical and Social Revolutions of Our Time: World Conference on Church and Society*. Geneva: World Council of Churches, 1966.

Mott, John R. *The Decisive Hour in Christian Missions*. New York: Student Volunteer Movement for Foreign Missions, 1910. Reprint, 1915.

Move Europe. http://www.artiszelmenis.lv/moveeurope/.

Mwaura, Philomena N. "Women in African Instituted Churches in Kenya," *African Christian Studies* 18, no. 3 (2002): 57–72.

Newbigin, Lesslie. *The Household of God*. New York: Friendship Press, 1954.

Niles, D. T. *The Preacher's Task and the Stone of Stumbling*. New York: Harper and Row, 1958.

Oduyoye, Mercy Amba. *The Wesleyan Presence in Nigeria, 1842–1962: An Exploration of Power, Control, and Partnership in Mission*. Ibadan, Nigeria: Sefer, 1992.

Pew Research Religion and Public Life Project. *Asian Americans: A Mosaic of Faiths*. Washington, DC: Pew Research Center, 2012. http://www.pewforum.org/2012/07/19/asian-americans-a-mosaic-of-faiths-religious-affiliation/.

———. *The Future of the Global Muslim Population*. Washington, DC: Pew Research Center, 2011. http://www.pewforum.org/2011/01/27/future-of-the-global-muslim-population-regional-europe/.

———. *The Religious Affiliation of U.S. Immigrants: Majority Christian, Rising Share of Other Faiths*. Washington, DC: Pew Research Center, 2013. http://www.pewforum.org/2013/05/17/the-religious-affiliation-of-us-immigrants/#overview.

————. *In Spirit and Power—A 10-Country Survey of Pentecostals*. Washington, DC: Pew Research Center, 2006. http://www.pewforum.org/2006/10/05/overview-pentecostalism-in-asia/.

Pew-Templeton Global Religious Futures Project. *Folk Religionists.* Washington, DC: Pew Research Center, 2010. http://www.globalreligiousfutures.org/religions/folk-religionists.

"The Problem of Co-operation between Foreign and Native Workers." In *World Missionary Conference, Edinburgh, 1910: History and Records of the Conference*, 306–15. New York: Revell, 1910.

Robeck, Cecil M., Jr., and Amos Yong, eds. *The Cambridge Companion to Pentecostalism*. New York: Cambridge University Press, 2014.

Robert, Dana. *Christian Mission: How Christianity Became a World Religion*. Oxford: Wiley-Blackwell, 2009.

————. *Gospel Bearers, Gender Barriers: Missionary Women in the Twentieth Century.* Twentieth Century. Maryknoll, NY: Orbis, 2002.

Rosell, Garth M. *The Surprising Work of God: Harold John Ockenga, Billy Graham, and the Rebirth of Evangelicalism*. Grand Rapids: Baker Academic, 2008.

Rouse, Ruth, and Stephen Charles Neill, eds. *A History of the Ecumenical Movement, 1517–1948*. London: SPCK, 1954.

Ruddy, Christopher. *The Local Church: Tillard and the Future of Catholic Ecclesiology*. New York: Crossroad, 2006.

Russell, Letty M. "Encountering the 'Other' in a World of Difference and Danger." *The Harvard Theological Review* 99, no. 4 (2006): 457–68.

Saich, Tony. *The Origins of the First United Front in China*. Leiden: Brill, 1991.

Sanneh, Lamin. "Christian Missions and the Western Guilt Complex." *Christian Century*, April 8, 1987, 330–34.

————. *Whose Religion Is Christianity? The Gospel beyond the West*. Grand Rapids: Eerdmans, 2003.

Sanneh, Lamin, and Joel A. Carpenter, eds. *The Changing Face of Christianity: Africa, the West and the World*. Oxford: Oxford University Press, 2005.

Schall, Richard. "Revolutionary Challenge to Church and Theology." *Princeton Seminary Bulletin* 60, no. 1 (1966): 25–34.

Scott, Jean, and Bertrice Y. Wood, eds. *We Listened Long, Before We Spoke*. A report of the Consultation of Women Theological Students, Cartigny, Switzerland, July 1978. Geneva: WCC Publications, 1979.

Smith, Christian, and Melinda Lundquist Denton. *Soul Searching: The Religious and Spiritual Lives of American Teenagers*. New York: Oxford University Press, 2009.

Spencer, William David. *Dread Jesus*. London: SPCK, 1998.

Stackhouse, Max L., and Diane B. Obenchain. *God and Globalization*. Vol. 3, *Christ and the Dominions of Civilization*. Harrisburg, PA: Trinity Press International, 2002.

Stanley, Brian. "The Outlook for Christianity in 1914." In vol. 8 of *The Cambridge History of World Christianities, c. 1815–1914*, 593–600. Cambridge: Cambridge University Press, 2006.

Sullivan, Maureen, OP. *The Road to Vatican II: Key Changes in Theology*. New York: Paulist Press, 2007.

Sung, John. *Journal Once Lost: Extracts from the Diary of John Sung*. Compiled and edited by Levi Sung. Singapore: Genesis Books, 2008.

Sunquist, Scott W., ed. *Dictionary of Asian Christianity*. Grand Rapids: Eerdmans, 2001.

Swedenborg, Emanuel. *Arcana Coelestia, or Heavenly Secrets Which Are in the Sacred Scriptures*. Translated by John Merchant. England, 1750.

Tabar, Paul. "Lebanon: A Country of Emigration and Immigration." Beirut: LAU Press / Institute for Migration Studies, 2010. http://www.aucegypt.edu/gapp/cmrs/reports/documents/tabar080711.pdf.

Thorud, Espen, ed. "International Migration, 2009–2010: SOPEMI Report for Norway." December 2010. http://www.regjeringen.no/upload/BLD/IMA/Report_oecd_2010_final.pdf.

Tutu, Desmond. "Foreword by Archbishop Desmond Tutu." In vol. 6 of *Truth and Reconciliation Commission of South Africa Report*. Kenwyn, Cape Town: Juta & Co., 2003. http://www.justice.gov.za/trc/report/finalreport/vol6.pdf.

Twain, Mark, and Charles Dudley Warner. *The Gilded Age: A Tale of Today*. Hartford: American Publishing Company, 1873.

United Nations Refugee Agency. http://www.refworld.org/docid/3dee03944.html.

United States Holocaust Memorial Museum. *Holocaust Encyclopedia*. http://www.ushmm.org/.

Ustorf, Werner. "Franz Michael Zahn." *International Bulletin of Missionary Research* 21, no. 13 (1997): 124–27.

Vásquez, Manuel A., and Marie Friedmann Marquardt. *Globalizing the Sacred: Religion across the Americas*. New Brunswick, NJ: Rutgers University Press, 2003.

Vereb, Jerome-Michael. *Because He Was a German! Cardinal Bea and the Origins of Roman Catholic Engagement in the Ecumenical Movement*. Grand Rapids: Eerdmans, 2006.

Visser 't Hooft, W. A. "Reports of Sections: Unity." In *The New Delhi Report of the Third Assembly of the World Council of Churches 1961*, edited by W. A. Visser 't Hooft, 116–22. London: SCM, 1962.

Wacker, Grant. *Heaven Below: Early Pentecostals and American Culture*. Cambridge, MA: Harvard University Press, 2001.

Walls, Andrew, and Cathy Ross. *Mission in the 21st Century: Exploring the Five Marks of Global Mission*. Maryknoll, NY: Orbis, 2008.

Wickeri, Phillip. *Reconstructing Christianity in China: K. H. Ting and the Chinese Church*. Maryknoll, NY: Orbis, 2007.

Wild-Wood, Emma. *Migration and Christian Identity in Congo (DRC)*. Leiden: Brill, 2008.

Wilson, John. *Introduction to Modern Theology, Trajectories in the German Tradition*. Louisville: Westminster John Knox, 2007.

Winter, Ralph. *The 25 Unbelievable Years, 1945–1969*. South Pasadena, CA: William Carey Library, 1970.

World Council of Churches. "The Basis of the WCC." World Council of Churches, 2014. http://www.oikoumene.org/en/about-us/self-understanding-vision/basis.

World Missionary Conference, Edinburgh, 1910. *History and Records of the Conference*. 9 vols. New York: Revell, 1910.

———. *Report of Commission I: Carrying the Gospel to All the Non-Christian World*. New York: Revell, 1910.

Index